THE AMERICAN FOREIGN POLICY LIBRARY

SUMNER WELLES, EDITOR

DONALD C. MCKAY, ASSOCIATE EDITOR

The United States and Britain

LONDON : GEOFFREY CUMBERLEGE

OXFORD UNIVERSITY PRESS

THE
UNITED STATES
AND

Britain

By

Crane Brinton

HARVARD UNIVERSITY PRESS
Cambridge, Massachusetts
1948

MAPS PREPARED UNDER THE CARTOGRAPHIC
DIRECTION OF ARTHUR H. ROBINSON

PRINTED AND BOUND BY NORWOOD PRESS
J. S. CUSHING CO.; BERWICK AND SMITH CO.;
C. B. FLEMING & CO.
NORWOOD, MASSACHUSETTS, U.S.A.

CONTENTS

PART I

The Background: A Survey of Modern Britain

PART II

The British Isles in the War

PART III

Anglo-American Relations in the Past

PART IV

Problems of the Present and the Future

vi *Contents*

MAPS

INTRODUCTION

During the war it has become more and more apparent to the people of the United States that the ability of the major powers to coöperate during the years to come is an indispensable prerequisite to the establishment of any peaceful and prosperous world of the future. It is today already recognized as axiomatic that the United Nations Organization will not be able to function successfully unless it is founded upon such collaboration between the United Kingdom, the Soviet Union, and the United States.

In these latter years it has far too often been assumed by public opinion in the United States that a harmonious relationship between the United Kingdom and the United States may be taken for granted. There can be no question that it should be much easier for the peoples of Great Britain and the United States to get along together than for the majority of the peoples of the world. The same language, the similarity in their customs and habits of thought, their common devotion to representative self-government, all tend to make it easier. But many of us too often overlook the fact that there do exist material grounds for friction between the leading Anglo-Saxon peoples. The surest way of preventing these potential causes for trouble from becoming serious is for the peoples of both countries to analyze them objectively rather than emotionally, to recognize their true dimensions, and then to determine from the start that they can and must be equitably adjusted.

There is a tendency on the part of the Anglo-Saxon peoples, after they have taken part in a great war, to divorce themselves from their allies after the victory is won. There is an inclination on the part of all peoples after a major struggle to indulge in exaggerated nationalism. But if the decent and peaceful world which the Anglo-Saxon peoples wish to join in creating is to be successfully established, nothing is more essential than that the British and American peoples should resist these not unnatural tendencies. They will have among other things to make up their minds sedulously to beware of the obsession that their major partners in the great task of rebuilding international society are invariably trying to take undue advantage of them. They must decide to pursue parallel or complementary political and economic courses, rather than policies which are bound to end in head-on collisions.

Nothing would prove to be more fatally destructive of our present hopes for world peace than for the Anglo-Saxon powers to create an Anglo-Saxon bloc for the purpose of dominating or of "ganging up" on other nations. But a partnership between the United Kingdom and the United States for the purpose of making it possible for the World Organization to function successfully can greatly speed the attainment of that objective. It can help to build up a new world order established, not upon a balance of power, but upon a new foundation of international law, backed by force, and consented in by all states. The Anglo-Saxon powers, through their coöperation in such an endeavor, can afford a large measure of assurance to all peoples that world peace and world progress actually lie ahead.

The generations during which jealousy, suspicion, and traditional resentments colored relations between the United Kingdom and the United States are long since terminated. The problems which are now arising in their relations are economic, rather than political, and social, rather than strategic. It is essential that public opinion in the United States understand these problems, and grasp as well the methods by which they can be most fairly and most easily solved.

Mr. Brinton offers us that opportunity in the present volume. He has written a wise book. It is a book which is based upon a profound knowledge and understanding of British-

American relations, as well as of the underlying factors in the life of the British people today. His analysis is lucid. Although it is written in a friendly spirit, it never evades nor palliates the true issues as Mr. Brinton sees them.

A lasting understanding between the American and British peoples is vitally needed. It can be achieved notwithstanding the obstacles which may from time to time arise. For the two nations, with all of their individual idiosyncrasies or failings, possess that most solid of all foundations for mutual comprehension—a common belief in the right of every man to his individual freedom, faith that democracy is the best form of government so far devised, and the conviction that the standard by which peoples govern their dealings one with the other should be justice rather than force.

Sumner Welles

PREFACE

TO THE REVISED EDITION

In this revised edition I have tried as far as possible to look at the position of Great Britain afresh. The three years since this book was first published have been bad years for Western civilization, and especially bad years for Britain. But I am not convinced that the prospects of Britain and the Commonwealth and Empire are as bad as they are commonly painted nowadays by prophets of doom—including the professional economists. In the long run, the British Isles may decline in wealth and population, as so many areas of the world have declined in the past. But none of us live in the long run. In our day, I believe the prospects are for a revival of Britain—a revival of British production, an upswing in the charts the statisticians love to turn out. The precedents of both France and Germany in the 1920's would indicate that the necessity Britain now faces of rebuilding her shattered economy may well prove a stimulus to renewed national effort and to the construction of a superior national plant.

Nor can I convince myself that events of the last three years have wholly invalidated my final chapter. The development of what looks like a very old-fashioned balance-of-power alignment, with Russia in total opposition to America and Britain, has clearly made my "postulate of international anarchy" more plausible than my "postulate of international organization." But the long history of our modern system of nation-states gives no support to those who talk of a Russo-American war as *inevitable*. At any rate, the United Nations are still in being, and still the most hopeful element in actual international affairs. Some of the considerations brought out in my last chapter I have developed further in a little book called *From Many One* (Harvard University Press, 1948).

I should like to renew my thanks to my editors, and to Mr. Aaron Noland, who has made a thorough revision of Appendix I, which he had provided in the original edition; and I should like to thank Miss Elizabeth F. Hoxie for her careful preparation of the manuscript of this edition.

Crane Brinton

Cambridge, Massachusetts
April 9, 1948

PREFACE

Much of this book springs from my stay in Britain from December 1942 to August 1944 as a member of a war mission. A list of the individuals who helped me form my opinions of Britain at war and of the problems of Anglo-American relation would have to be a list of everyone I met, and I can do no more than thank them as groups: my own immediate colleagues, and our "opposite numbers" among the British and the exiled Europeans; my colleagues on the "Anglo-American Brains Trust" (how we disliked that pretentious name, not of our choosing), an informal discussion group which held discussions on Anglo-American problems with service groups in various parts of Great Britain and Northern Ireland; the educational authorities in both the British and the American forces; officers of the London School of Economics (at that time in Cambridge) and of the University of London, through whom I was able to hold discussions with British civilians; my friends of the Fire Guard at St. Paul's Cathedral; the shifting and always interesting group of Professor Harold Laski's Tuesday nights at home; and the good friends with whom on Sundays and holidays I walked over so many miles of the Home Counties. I am indebted to them all; but I must, in fairness to them, make the usual apology—I do not expect them all to approve what I have written in this book.

In the United States, I wish to thank my editors, Mr. Sumner Welles and Dr. Donald C. McKay, for giving me the opportunity to write this book, and for their editorial help; my

Harvard colleagues, Dr. David E. Owen, who has read the whole manuscript, and Dr. S. E. Harris, who has read Chapter VIII, both of whom have made helpful criticisms and suggestions; Dr. Conyers Read and Mr. Joseph E. Charles, who made their wide knowledge of contemporary Britain available to me; Captain Arthur H. Robinson, who has made the maps; and Mr. Aaron Noland, who has done the exacting work of Appendix I.

                                                Crane Brinton

Peacham, Vermont
September 4, 1945

The United States and Britain

PART I THE BACKGROUND:
MODERN BRITAIN

1. The Face of Britain

The complexity of things British begins right away, with naming. There are no simple names, like Sweden and Swedes, for the lands and peoples under George VI. We must start by getting a few geographical and political terms straight.

1. LANDS UNDER THE CROWN

The *geographic* term "British Isles" refers to the two big islands, Great Britain and Ireland, and a number of small and middle-sized islands grouped around them off the northwest coast of Europe. Since the establishment of a part of the island of Ireland in virtual independence under the old Celtic name of "Eire" in 1937, however, the British Isles are no longer a *political* unit. The historic kingdoms of England, Scotland, and Wales, together with six of the thirty-two counties of old Ireland, make up the *political* unit known officially by the long title of "United Kingdom of Great Britain and Northern Ireland," more familiarly as the "United Kingdom," or even, in these alphabetic days, as the "UK." The twenty-six remaining counties of Ireland form the republic of Eire, which is still commonly listed, at least by the world outside Eire, as a self-governing dominion and therefore as part of the "British Commonwealth of Nations." Its exact legal status is most ambiguous, and has been the subject of much fine word-spinning.

The "British Commonwealth of Nations," which includes in

general the self-governing dominions under the Crown, peopled, or at least ruled, by British or European stock, is the next step in the wider circle of things British. This does not correspond to any exact sovereign political organization. It includes the United Kingdom, Canada, Australia, New Zealand, South Africa, and perhaps Eire; and, as very recent additions, India, Pakistan, and Ceylon. Next comes a miscellaneous group of territories usually lumped together as the "Crown Colonies," "Dependent Territories," "Protectorates," and "Condominiums." These lands, varying in size from the tiny rock of Gibraltar to the African colony of Nigeria, which is almost as big as Texas and New Mexico together, vary greatly in political status. One of them, Newfoundland, is a temporarily demoted self-governing dominion which will probably attain its former status as soon as it overcomes the financial difficulties which caused it to lose its rights as a dominion in 1933. Most of these colonies and dependent territories enjoy at least some rights of self-government, such as a consultative assembly or council. Then there is the great subcontinent, India, divided in 1947 into two self-governing dominions, India (Hindustan) and Pakistan; but indeed the whole status of India is today so ambiguous and uncertain that even imperialist Britishers commonly list it in a category by itself. Finally, there are the "mandated" territories, former German colonies assigned to the British as trustees under the mandate system of the League of Nations. Some of these lands are under "British" mandate, that is, under the central government in London; others are mandated to the dominions of South Africa, Australia, or New Zealand.

The term "British Empire" is sometimes used rather loosely to include all lands in the great complex analyzed in the preceding paragraph. The dominions, however, dislike the inference that they are "colonies" and parts of an "empire," and all over the British world there is a rough agreement to distinguish among the United Kingdom, the Dominions and the "Empire" pure and simple, meaning the rest of the Empire. For the whole there really exists no satisfactory single term, though Mr.

Churchill pretty consistently refers to it as the "British Commonwealth and Empire."

We shall in this book be concerned mainly with the United Kingdom and with Eire, but we cannot, of course, understand the many problems of Anglo-American relations without constantly keeping in mind the fact that the United Kingdom is part of a vast, world-wide, and exceedingly complicated agglomeration of lands and peoples under the Crown.

And it is vast. Let us now, this time in descending order, look at a few magnitudes. In area, the 13 million square miles of this agglomeration is just about one-fourth of the land area of the globe; its 550 million people are also just about one-fourth of the total population of the globe. For the United States with all its territories and possessions, the comparable figures are 3¾ million square miles and 150 million people; for Russia, including Estonia, Latvia, Lithuania, Eastern Poland, and Bessarabia, the comparable figures are nearly 9 million square miles and nearly 200 million people. The "Big Three" are thus really the big three; together they have some 26 of the 51 million square miles of the earth's land and some 900 of the 2200 million of the earth's people. Add China, with Mongolia and Tibet, and you have over 4½ million square miles more, and over 450 million people more, so that the "Big Four" have roughly three-fifths of the land and three-fifths of the people of this world.

If from the whole British agglomeration you take out India— and it is a big amputation—you have left just over 11½ million of your original 13 million square miles, but only some 150 million of your original 550 million people. Take away further the "Crown Colonies" and other dependencies, or Empire in the narrow sense, and you have left in the British Commonwealth of Nations—the United Kingdom and the Dominions— just over 7 of your original 13 million square miles and just over 80 million of your original 550 million people. Much of the still considerable territory left is, of course, accounted for by the vast empty spaces of northern North America and central Australia. Take away the Dominions and you have left in

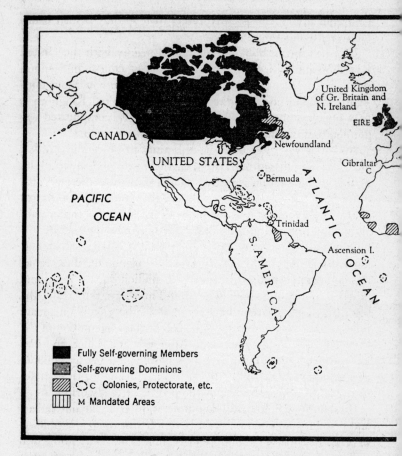

Fully Self-governing Members
Self-governing Dominions
◯ c Colonies, Protectorate, etc.
M Mandated Areas

the British Isles only 121 thousand of your original 13 million square miles, and 50 million of your original 550 million people. Amputated of empire, then, the British Isles are roughly of the magnitude of other important European states outside Russia. Their 120,000 square miles may be compared with the 212,000 of France, the 119,000 of Italy, the 225,000 of Greater Germany after annexation of Austria and Sudetenland. Their 50 million people may be compared with the 41 million of pre-war France,

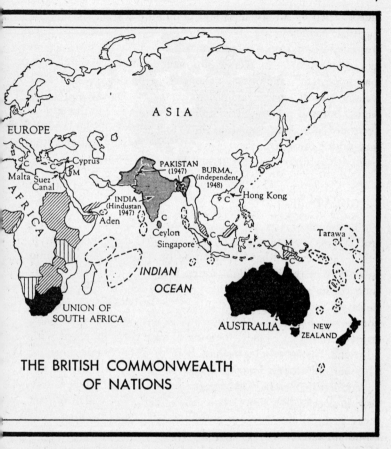

EUROPE

A S I A

Cyprus

Malta
Suez
Canal

PAKISTAN
(1947)

BURMA,
(independent
1948)

Hong Kong

A
F
R
I
C
A

INDIA
(Hindustan
1947)

Aden

Ceylon

Singapore

Tarawa

INDIAN
OCEAN

UNION OF
SOUTH AFRICA

AUSTRALIA

NEW
ZEALAND

THE BRITISH COMMONWEALTH
OF NATIONS

the 46 million of pre-war Italy, the 80 million of post-Munich
Germany.

These classic, simple measurements—area and population—are
in no sense complete measurements of "power," of the competitive strength of a society in a world where final decisions on the
life and death of a society are still made by warfare. Any such
index figure of "power" would have to take into account natural resources, economic and political organization, strategic

factors such as supply lines and communications, the host of spiritual elements for which the fashionable word is now "morale," leadership, perhaps even luck—so many variables, in fact, that any quantitative measurement is quite impossible. We may hope that some of these elements of British strength—and weakness—will emerge a little more clearly in the following pages. For the present, it is sufficient to note that the simple figures of area and population show that the whole agglomeration under the Crown is a great *World* Power, and that the United Kingdom itself is a great *European* Power.

2. GREAT BRITAIN

The island of Great Britain, comprising England, Scotland, and Wales, is about the size of New York state and Pennsylvania together, and has a population of about 47 million, some twice that of those populous states. It lies wholly north of latitude 50, in a position roughly corresponding to that of Labrador in North America. At its nearest point to the European continent, the Straits of Dover, it is only twenty-two miles from the coast of France. Its coast is frequently indented with "drowned" river valleys—Severn, Southampton Water, Thames, Humber, Tyne, the Scottish firths, Mersey—which provide excellent harbors and good access to the interior. Indeed, few British people live more than fifty miles from tidal waters. Very little of the island is absolutely flat, and its three main mountainous patches—Wales, the Lake Country, the Scottish Highlands—though rough and barren, are only three or four thousand feet high, by no means barrier-mountains. Britain is mostly a land of gentle hills and valleys, well tamed by two thousand years of cultivation, a land lacking in extremes. In such matters it is hard to separate fact from fancy; but many British people believe that the moderation of their landscape, its lack of limitless horizons and eternal snow-peaks, is in some way related to their national love of moderation and compromise.

The island may be divided, by a line running diagonally from the middle Severn to the lower Tyne, into a Northern highland region which is relatively poor farming country and a Southern lowland region which is relatively good farming country. There are, indeed, in the northern region some pockets of good land, such as the small plains of Lancashire and Cheshire and the admirable farmlands around Edinburgh in Scotland, but on the whole it is a land of mountains, hills, and moors, suited rather to grazing than to crops. The Southern region is almost wholly good plow-land. This contrast between North and South had important consequences in British history: it meant that the South, which is so near Europe, and has such good communications with the continent, would develop first; that all through the Middle Ages and early modern times the center of English civilization and wealth would be in the South, in easy and constant touch with European civilization. It meant that London, with its excellent location on the Thames, facing Europe, would early become the one great city of the island.

As long as Britain remained an agricultural society, with small-scale domestic industries and a foreign trade chiefly in wool with the cross-channel countries, the South—indeed the Southeast—remained the most important section of the island, with a minor center in Edinburgh, capital of an independent Scotland. With the great geographical discoveries of the fifteenth and sixteenth centuries, England began to turn toward the Atlantic. Her shipping now became one of her great assets; industry, though still small-scale, began to diversify; and though London was still the greatest of her ports, Bristol, Plymouth, and the smaller West Country ports began to grow. The Cabots, Drake, Hawkins—part naval leaders, part traders, indeed by modern standards part pirates—carried the English flag all over the world.

The historic concentration of wealth and population continued, however, to lie in the southern lowland region. It was the Industrial Revolution of the eighteenth and nineteenth centuries that first brought wealth and power to the region north of the Severn-Tyne diagonal, and effected one of the most rapid and extensive changes in economic geography any country has ever undergone. We in the United States often exaggerate the uniqueness of our own economic growth and pioneering. Great Britain in 1770 was not precisely an empty land, but in a century and a half it was to increase its 8 million people five and sixfold. The increase was, moreover, geographically uneven. Counties like Dorset or Oxfordshire, for instance, increased very little; Lancashire and Yorkshire grew at an American rate. In 1770 Liverpool was a small town of a few thousands; in a long lifetime thereafter it had become the center of a Merseyside metropolitan area of close to a million. The men who built Liverpool were in some ways as much "pioneers" as the men who built Chicago.

At the base of this extraordinary growth were those two main factors in the Industrial Revolution, coal and iron. Great Britain is rich in both, especially in coal, and the best deposits of both lie in the Northern and Western highland region or in the lowlands close to the Severn-Tyne diagonal. They are not in the old South. Moreover, a third factor, water power, was abundant in the damper North and West, with its dozens of small but dependable streams pouring down small valleys from the hills. Here, then, in Lancashire, Yorkshire, the Glasgow region, there grew up the great textile industries and their attendant machine and machine-tool industries on which British industrial greatness is based. The railways and the steamships came and heavy industries like ship building and locomotive manufacturing arose. Traditional industries like the cutlery of Sheffield in Yorkshire, the tools, small arms, and other metal industries of Birmingham in Warwickshire, were modernized. Coal, iron, and steel began to be exported, especially to Europe, where the Industrial Revolution had got under way a bit behind Britain. Free trade, achieved in 1846, enabled Britain to import food and raw materials, exchanging for them the products of her factories, and thereby supporting a population far in excess of her capacity to feed and clothe with home-grown materials. To make all this production by capitalist methods possible, there arose, chiefly in London, a great centralized banking system. By Victorian times Great Britain had become the richest country in the world, the first great modern industrial and capitalistic society.

Though the North and West had been the chief beneficiaries of this growth, metropolitan London had by no means lagged behind. It continued to be the greatest port; it continued to be the financial, political, and cultural center of the island; and it developed into a great manufacturing center, chiefly in lighter consumer goods. By Victorian times, London had become incomparably the greatest urban center of the world, not yet approached by New York, Tokyo, or Berlin.

The last seventy-five years have witnessed a relative—not an absolute—falling off in Britain's economic greatness. Britain is today by almost all statistical measurements richer than in 1870, but she is no longer without serious rivals. The United States, Germany, Japan, and indeed some of Britain's own daughter countries, now make for themselves many things they used to buy from Britain. In textiles, notably cotton, Britain has fallen markedly behind, and has seen some of her older textile centers fall to the status of "depressed areas." Even more conspicuously, her great coal-mining industry has been handicapped by poor organization, by exhaustion of easier-worked and richer seams, and by competition from petroleum (of which Britain has none, save for some at present uneconomic oil-bearing shales), so that until the recent war created a world shortage in coal, British coal-mining towns were often among the very worst of the depressed areas.

Yet Britain's industrial decline, it must be repeated, has been hitherto relative, not absolute. She has by no means failed to share in what has sometimes been called the Second Industrial Revolution, which was heralded by electricity, oil, the new alloy metals, the internal combustion engine, the assembly line, and automatic machinery. To a certain extent, this new industrial development in Britain has reversed the geographic trend of the last two centuries, and has brought industry once more towards the southern lowland region. The development of the internal combustion engine in the motor car and lately the airplane has tended to center in Birmingham, Coventry, London, and—of all places—Oxford. Electricity, which in the British Isles is almost wholly produced in coal-burning steam plants, is distributed by a very efficient national grid, so that plants need no longer be located near coal supplies. As a result, the period between the two wars has seen a great growth of new light industries in the area of London and the "Home Counties" (the seven counties adjacent to London—Kent, Surrey, Berkshire, Buckinghamshire, Hertfordshire, Middlesex, and Essex), in the Midlands, and in the Bristol area.

The last two centuries have brought great changes to the face of Britain. Coal, iron, and water power have brought smoking factories, slag-heaps, rows and rows of grimy jerry-built houses to a land once of farms, wild glens, and sheep runs. They have spread the "wen," as the sentimental lover of rural England, William Cobbett, called London as early as 1816, far out into the Home Counties. Electricity and the newest machine age have brought motor-factory suburbs to medieval Oxford, have lined the Thames valley from London to Reading with new factories of concrete and glass, have transformed old market towns like High Wycombe and Sevenoaks into suburban dormitories for London workers. Leisure obtained by these new productive capacities, and the Englishman's incurable addiction to the seaside for his holidays, have built up a good part of the island's coasts with villas and cottages, grown acres of red bricks, stucco, and tiled roofs in genteel seaside "wens" like Brighton and Bournemouth, less genteel ones like Blackpool. The First Industrial Revolution crisscrossed Britain with one of the densest railway nets in the world; the Second is now covering the island with a network of motor roads, which, in spite of the best effort of town planners and lovers of the countryside to prevent the process, are being lined with the sort of motor-fed semi-slum the British call "ribbon development." Urban and rural are thus not as sharply distinguished as they once were. Well over four out of five Britishers probably now live under essentially urban conditions.

Yet in spite of all this urbanization—which is not in fact more intense than that of our Atlantic seaboard between Baltimore and Boston—there is still a great deal of farming and grazing land in Great Britain. Britain's agriculture has now for the last century been unable to feed all her millions, but as the war has shown dramatically, it is far from dead. With the flood of cheap grains from overseas brought in by free trade British farmers could not compete, and much good arable land went into permanent grass. Competition from Australasian and North and South American sheep and cattle kept even grazing use of land to a minimum. Danish and Dutch farmers, well organized and efficient, competed successfully with British farmers in butter, cheese, and bacon in the British market. Yet somehow, even in the bad years just before 1939, the English countryside never looked run down, English farming land rarely went back, as so much New England and Virginia land has gone back, to weeds, brush, and scrubby forests. To an American traveler who had seen overgrazed lands in our West, the lush, under-grazed pastures of southern England were a puzzling sight. There seemed no animals to keep the weeds down, but there were very few weeds. Some of the neatness of English rural regions was, of course, the neatness of leisure; from the great estates of the rich, with parks of hundreds of acres, to the small country homes and gardens of retired professional and business men, Britain was dotted with land kept neat, if not very productive, by the owner's sense of propriety. In the war of 1914–1918, Britain's underused agricultural plant showed it could greatly expand; in the recent war, as we shall see, its expansion has been even more rapid and successful.

Even the hard facts of physical and economic geography are in some sense relative, if not subjective. So far in this brief outline, we have considered fairly hard and simple facts. The area,

the population, the Severn–Tyne diagonal dividing good farming lowlands from indifferent grazing highlands, the existence
of rich though now partly exhausted deposits of coal and iron,
the high degree of urbanization of Britain—all of these are plain
and unambiguous. So too is the fact that, save for coal and iron,
the island of Great Britain has almost none of the natural mineral resources necessary to the latest modern industry—no
copper, no bauxite, no wolfram, above all, no petroleum. Nor
has she, by Swiss, American, or Russian standards, great potential resources for hydroelectric development. She has far
outrun her supply of timber; notably, wood pulp for paper
and synthetic textiles must almost all be imported.

We are on less certain ground when we deal with British
weather. Most Americans think of the British Isles as pretty
constantly shrouded in fog and rain; most Britishers are aware
of that belief, and it rather annoys them. Most of them, except
perhaps those who suffer from sinus trouble, enjoy their climate, and are proud of it. The statistics are clear (see below).
London actually gets less rainfall in the course of a year than
New York. Yet the American belief that the British Isles are
damp is not wholly unfounded. Rainfall there tends to take the
form of drizzles; downpours are rare. Thus it takes a longer
time for a given amount of precipitation to fall. What really
counts is the total proportion of hours of sunlight, and here
the figures bear out to a certain extent American notions of
Britain as by no means a sunny land. It has been estimated that
on an average in Britain the sun shines clearly only one hour
out of three in the time it is above the horizon. This figure is,

Place	Mean annual precipitation (inches)	Mean temperature January (degrees)	July (degrees)
Lower Thames (London)	25	39	64
Lancashire (Liverpool)	40–60	38	59
New York City	41.6	32	74
Chicago	31.8	26	74
San Francisco	20.2	50	59

of course, that shocking unreality, an average. It is sunnier in summer than in winter; it is sunnier in the Southeast than in the Northwest. And at any time there may be "spells" of sunny weather as of cloudy weather. So too with temperature. The figures show that Great Britain enjoys cool summers and mild winters, the result of moderating breezes from the Gulf Stream, which, after it splits up in the North Atlantic, is now known as the North Atlantic Drift. But British standards of interior heating are to most Americans incredibly low, and therefore through large parts of the year the American visitor is likely to be uncomfortable when he is indoors in the islands; and outdoors the dampness and lack of penetrating sunshine are likely to make him feel much colder than in the same temperature at home. Conversely, the Britisher in the United States, unless he is unusually tactful, is likely to give offense by complaining about the unhealthy warmth of our offices and homes, the searing heat of our summers, or the discomforts of blizzards and below-zero temperatures in winter.

On the whole, however, the differences between American and British climates probably give rise to more humorous clichés than to expressions of bad temper. It seems clear that the British climate, which like the British landscape is essentially a moderate one, is a good climate for modern industrial and intellectual activity, neither too stimulating nor too relaxing. Indeed, the American Professor Ellsworth Huntington, who has worked out elaborate statistical indices to correlate climate and "civilization," rates the British climate very high in these respects.

Size, too, is relative. Englishmen, and less often Scotchmen, are fond of referring to their "tight little isle"; but they are not altogether pleased when an American wisecracks to the effect that it's hardly worth owning an automobile in Britain, since in all directions you're likely to run overboard into the sea when you've hardly got started. If we measure space by the speed of a jet plane, it is true that you can go from Cornwall to the Shetlands in little over an hour; but by the same standard you can also go from New York to San Francisco in a little over four hours. By such standards, the whole world has shrunk to the size of a county in the horse-and-buggy days, and all nations are pretty small. At the other end of the scale, which is what a man can see about him at a given time, the British Isles, if not precisely Texas-wide, are by no means a claustrophobe's nightmare. What you see about you in the urbanized areas in Britain, apart from architectural differences and the fact that in normal times British urban areas are rather neater than ours, is pretty much what you see about you in American urban areas. And it is no harder to escape into the country from London than from New York or Chicago. What you see about you in British farming country is not totally unlike what you see about you in the country immediately west of Philadelphia, green, well-cultivated farmlands with plenty of trees, but no shaggy, endless forests. It is even possible in the British Isles to find wide open spaces, with no sign of human habitation—Dartmoor, the Lake Country, the Pennines between Lancashire and Yorkshire. Parts of northern Scotland—Sutherland, for instance—are as lonely as the most romantic could desire. British intellectuals and upper-class people generally are rather worried about the preservation of their open spaces and have organized various societies and pressure-groups to protect them. It is true that if the population of Lancashire were suddenly to invade the near-by Lake Country *en masse* the land of Wordsworth would be quite transformed; but so far most of Lancashire seems to prefer Blackpool, which is their Coney Island.

There is, indeed, a not too paradoxical sense in which the tight little island is subjectively less crowded than much of these United States. The British upper and middle classes, at least, are much less gregarious than such people in our country. They seem to many Americans to be almost pettily insistent on domestic privacy. Every Britisher who possibly can surrounds his house, even if it is only a semi-detached suburban house in a long row of identical houses, with a wall, fence, or good solid hedge. Here he can retire to his garden and have tea on the lawn, with no one overlooking him. One of the things that most strikes the British visitor to America is our—to him—almost communal way of living, our trim suburban houses where each lawn and garden melts into another with no walls or fences between.

In spite of its comparatively small area, Great Britain presents great local and regional variety. Centuries of living on the land in days before the unifying effect of rapid transport have impressed all sorts of differences on the human geography of the island. The Cotswolds are a sheep-country of fairly large fields enclosed with stone walls, of little stone-built villages in valleys folded into the hills, of clear brooks filled with trout (so they say) and water cress. A few miles east, and the fields of the South Midlands are smaller and enclosed with hedges, the soil is heavier, woods and copses more abundant, and the villages mostly built of brick. A few miles further east, and the big, often unenclosed wheatfields of Norfolk begin, and the countryside takes on a broader, almost continental sweep. There are variations in speech, which as between a Highland Scot and a Dorsetshire farmer go so far that one cannot understand the other. There are variations in drink—cider in Herefordshire, beer in Derbyshire, and, as everyone knows, whiskey in Aberdeenshire. Many British people prize these picturesque local variations very much, and are worried for fear schools, radio, newspapers and rapid transport will eliminate them and make everyone as alike as peas. That same fear was expressed one hundred and fifty years ago by Sir Walter Scott, and so far has not been wholly realized. It is possible that there is a tendency for human beings to build up local variations which resist the contrary tendency to cultural uniformity. In our own "young" nation such differences exist, though the regions are on a larger scale than the British. No one would mistake Arizona for Connecticut, nor, in spite of their physical juxtaposition, would anyone who really knows them mistake Vermont for New Hampshire. In our time, certainly, the human geography of Britain will not be flattened out into a dull sameness.

3. IRELAND

The island of Ireland, which is about the size of the state of Maine and has a population of about four million, a little less than that of Massachusetts, lies about fifty miles west, on an average, of the central part of the island of Great Britain. It is divided politically into two parts: Northern Ireland, which, though it has a local legislature, is legally a part of the United Kingdom, and the more or less independent republic of Eire. Northern Ireland is about the size of Connecticut, and has a population of 1,279,000—about half a million less than that of Connecticut. Eire is about the size of West Virginia, and has a population of almost three million, a bit over that of Alabama.

Ireland is not physiographically very different from her sister island. The low but sharp and impressive Irish mountains rise in a discontinuous rim around her coast, leaving in the center a large and relatively flat basin, the best part of which is drained by the river Shannon. Ireland, too, has admirable natural harbors—Cobh (formerly Queenstown), Belfast, Londonderry. Her climate is wetter than that of all but some of the western parts of Great Britain, since she is even nearer the North Atlantic Drift. Like Britain's, hers is an even climate of cool summers and mild winters. The greenness of the Emerald Isle is by no means a figment of exiled Irishmen's imagination. The American traveler who sees Ireland at any time of year is bound to confess that for once the tourist folder is right. Though there are many bogs and moors, the soil of Ireland is on the whole good; it is not by nature a poor country in the sense that Greece is by nature a poor country. But it is a little too far north, and much too damp, for the classic grains such as wheat. It is much better suited for stock raising and for intensive agriculture of the Danish sort. Political difficulties have kept Ireland's peasantry poor and for years she relied too much on the potato.

Nor has Eire, in particular, as yet achieved much industrialization. One reason is obvious: unlike Great Britain, Ireland has

practically no good coal and iron. The natural basis for industrial growth in the nineteenth century simply was not there.
Yet in Northern Ireland, or Ulster, the dour Scotch-Irish (as
we call them in America; at home they are known as Ulster
Scots) have built up in the Belfast area a great linen industry
and a great ship-building industry. The dour Calvinists of Massachusetts, too, industrialized their state without having their
own coal and iron. It would seem that the failure of Eire to
get beyond an agricultural economy must be sought for in its
most distressful history, in the long struggle to get rid of the
English landowner and the rest of the English "garrison." Eire
does possess in the Shannon a river from which hydraulic
power can be obtained, and much progress has already been
made in electrification there; but even so, Eire's resources are
not such as to make intensive industrial development very
likely.

The "look of the land" in Ireland is not wholly different from
that in Great Britain, and indeed suggests regional and local
variations in the British scene rather than a different order of
human geography. The language remains English—with a
brogue, perhaps, but still English: you can travel a long way
in Eire without hearing a word of Gaelic. The green is even
greener than in England; the fields are usually smaller, sometimes incredibly small, the trees fewer—Ireland has been largely
deforested—the coast-line more rugged. The whitewashed cot-
tage is everywhere in Ireland, and the villages look quite different from English villages. The countryside is not quite as
spick-and-span as in England, but it is far neater than the average American countryside. The slums of Belfast and Dublin are
unlovely, but they are no worse to look at than the slums of
Liverpool or Glasgow. By American middle-class standards of
living the Irish, both North and South, are not well off; in
comparison with current English standards, the Irish are less
well furnished with the amenities of the machine age. But there
should be no exaggeration: Ireland is not the Balkans or Sicily,
and even in Eire, its people have come a long way from the
famine days of the 1840's.

4. STRATEGIC GEOGRAPHY OF BRITAIN AND THE EMPIRE

The islands of Great Britain and Ireland are a part of Europe. This simple geographical truth has now become, even to the remnants of the British isolationists, an unavoidable strategic truth. Once more the English Channel, thanks to the R.A.F. and the Navy, has kept a continental army from British soil. But the Channel itself, for nearly a thousand years an effective strategic protection, was in this war little more than a very superior tank ditch. The airplane, the robot plane, the giant rocket, had no trouble crossing the Channel. Given the normal progress of science, already evident in the atomic bomb, it is possible that in another generation a well-equipped foreign army, under a barrage of such weapons, could cross the ribbon of water which has held off Napoleon, William II, and Hitler.

The Commonwealth and Empire, finally, is so far-flung that, unless its separate constituents are well-armed, unless its naval bases are fully maintained, and unless its central authority possesses a very strong navy and air force—and some cast-iron friendships outside Europe—it is strategically weak. The potential strength in war of the agglomeration under the British Crown is very great indeed, but it is a *dispersed* strength which can easily become in fact weakness. The fate of Singapore made this crystal clear to the most easy-going Britisher, and it is safe to say that an awareness of this fact dominates the thinking of responsible people all over the Commonwealth and Empire.

Strategically, then, the British Isles are almost as much a part of Europe as the Iberian peninsula. Our habit of making maps with the North to the top here plays a trick on our senses. Most maps show vast expanses of water to the North and West of the British Isles, and thus lead us unconsciously to think of them as off by themselves in splendid isolation. If, however, you construct a map with its top to the East, its bottom just off the Atlantic coast of Ireland, then the strategic facts of Britain's geography strike you at once, and the North Sea and the Baltic are seen to be what they really are—a Northern Mediterranean, a Northern Black Sea. (See map p. 219.)

If the British Isles are thus in modern times open to invasion from Europe, the converse is of course also true; Britain in the recent war has been the jumping-off place for an invasion of the continent. The "unsinkable aircraft carrier" has proved in this war, in spite of the fears of some theorists, big enough to shelter a huge air force and a huge army of invasion. And most of Ireland was not this time available to us as a base. There are, also, plenty of generous harbors to serve as naval bases, and the best of these bases are off the north and northeast coasts of Great Britain and the north and south coasts of Ireland— that is, in places relatively difficult for a continental enemy to get at. The coasts nearer the continent contain harbors ample for the shelter of the smaller craft necessary for an army to invade the continent.

A second major strategic factor in the situation of Great Britain is her vital need to keep open her sea lanes, if not to Europe, then at least to the rest of the world. Britain could, by a most intensive use of her agricultural possibilities, maintain her present population for quite a while on a semi-starvation diet, even though she were shut out from imports; but—and this is the real limiting factor—she has, save for coal, salt, and slender margins in iron, none of the complex mineral resources without which the maintenance of modern land, air, and sea forces is quite impossible. It is, therefore, the stark fact that Britain *must* keep her maritime and air communications open, or give up. There seems little likelihood that within the next generation or so—if ever—air communications alone would be enough to supply the islands with what they need. Sea power, properly supplemented by air power is, then, an absolute necessity for the British.

Just how much of the overseas lands under the Crown are

essential to Britain's status as a great power—or, in the currently fashionable term, as a "super-power" along with the U.S.A. and the U.S.S.R.—is hard to measure. The great population of India swells the manpower statistics of the present Empire, though per capita wealth and productive power in India are very low. Moreover, Britain can hardly count very securely on India's forming in the near future a loyal part of the Empire. Even without India, however, Britain can probably remain a great power if she can rely on the loyalty and coöperation of the present dominions, if she can retain her valuable African possessions, and at least Malaya in Asia, and if she can maintain certain key bases essential to her fleet and her air force. Another war and even more miraculous weapons may, of course, make even this core or shield of empire indefensible, at least in part. Malta all but proved indefensible in the present war. But, on the basis of current experience, a minimum would seem to be Gibraltar, Malta, the Suez Canal, Aden, a base in India or Ceylon, and Singapore, Britain's lifeline to the East. Add to these the facilities Canada, Australia, New Zealand, South Africa, and Eire can offer, and a few bases in her African possessions, and Britain can remain a great power. British Tories would certainly add Hong Kong to the list, but there is no reason to believe that that island, which is, of course, Chinese, is strategically a "must" for Britain. Nor is the island of Cyprus absolutely essential. Britain's possessions in the Caribbean basin are no longer part of the shield of Empire; they depend for defense on the United States.

Even at its minimum, Britain's strategic task of defense is enormous. Indeed, in view of the probable future of air power, it is perhaps an impossible task unless Britain can count on the firm friendship of a great and industrially developed continental power somewhere on earth—or on a world peace so secure and well organized that all calculations of military potential are unnecessary.

2. Government and Politics

Those who attempt to interpret Great Britain to Americans are confronted at the start with a major difficulty: they must insist that Britain is a democracy, and they must admit that Britain has a King. But to ordinary Americans this is a contradiction, and ordinary Americans are too good children of the Age of Reason to take such contradictions in their stride. You may explain very carefully that the King has no real power, that he "reigns but does not rule," but, as anyone who dealt with American soldiers in Britain during the recent war knows well, you will not remove the deeply rooted American feeling that kings and democracies do not mix. It is well to recognize that such feelings do not change, or change but slowly. This American attitude towards the British monarchy need no more be an obstacle to good relations with the British than the American attitude towards the British climate, or the American belief that the Englishman is very slow to understand a joke. And Americans who write about Britain for Americans must take good care that, in explaining the role of the British Crown, they do not explain it away altogether. After all, the King exists, and is important.

He is not very important in the making of political decisions. He is important, even politically, in that for the great majority of the British people his person is a focus for the sentiments that bind men together in the Commonwealth. He is not the sole such focus; British people, like ourselves and indeed all peoples, are bound together by many things—by their flag, by their

national songs, by their attachment to Magna Charta, the Bill
of Rights, and the rest of their partly written, partly unwritten,
constitution, by all the complex web their history has woven
for them. We Americans may feel that with all this to hold
them together the British do not need a King. The British do
not feel that way; few, even of their Labour Party, wish to do
away with the Crown. The pomp and ceremony of royalty,
the British feel, is part of the necessary ritual of patriotism.
Their publicists almost always add a further argument for
the Crown; they say that, even though the United Kingdom might hold together as a republic, the scattered, diverse
territories that make up the British Commonwealth and Empire cannot do without the living symbol of the Crown,
above party and above geography. The Crown, they say,
is the essential cement of Empire. Here again there is no
use arguing: we are dealing with a belief, and though beliefs may change in time, they are at any given moment
among the hardest of facts, harder than logic, harder even
than statistics.

Moreover, you cannot really describe a government as you
might describe a machine. You can, after all, with patience
and diagram, make fairly clear to the well-intentioned inquirer
just what a carburetor does in a gasoline engine. You cannot
similarly make clear just how the House of Commons works,
or just what the Crown does. At any rate, by the empirical
test afforded by the reception of books and articles trying to
do this, no one ever has described the workings of the British
government to the satisfaction of all concerned. Notably, no
one could *describe* the place of the Crown in Britain to the
equal satisfaction of a Tory, a Liberal, and a Labour man, let
alone attempt a critical and philosophical analysis of the function of the British Crown. No one not a lawyer or at least a
legal historian could satisfy the ardent lovers of the British Constitution. Indeed, the notion that that Constitution is inde-
scribable, ineffable, a mystery in the religious sense of the term,
is widespread in Britain, and is an important factor in British

political stability. We shall have to rush in where angels have long since occupied the ground.

1. THE MACHINERY OF GOVERNMENT

The classic framework of executive, legislative, and judicial functions, when proper qualifications are made, will do for a rapid analysis of the government of the United Kingdom. But it must be clearly understood that neither in fact nor in theory is the present-day government of Britain a government of separation of powers, of "checks and balances," like our own. Indeed, as far as the central organs of government are concerned, the British government is so directly concentrated in the cabinet and House of Commons relationship that, were there no obstacles in tradition, habit, and public opinion, it could be turned into a totalitarian dictatorship without a formal institutional and political revolution. Let it be firmly noted, however, that those obstacles are at present quite insurmountable.

The King is not in fact part of the executive. Statutes are issued in his name, and, indeed, he signs them. They must, however, also be signed by a minister. The King may not refuse to sign—that is, he has no power of veto. There is no written constitutional law to say that he must sign; the compulsion he is under is a stock example of what is called the unwritten law of the constitution. This should not be hard for Americans to understand, since we have a number of such unwritten constitutional laws; for instance, it is doubtful if there is any way to compel a duly elected presidential elector to vote in the electoral college for the party candidate to whom he is "pledged." No elector has ever refused to so vote. Such a refusal, we commonly say, is "unthinkable." So, too, would be a refusal by a British monarch to sign an act of parliament.

The real executive in Britain is the Prime Minister, working with his cabinet and the host of administrators who make up the civil service. The popular instinct which assumed that

Mr. Churchill was the "opposite number" of Mr. Roosevelt was dead right. The Prime Minister in modern Britain is essentially the president of the United Kingdom; he is in fact, though not in form and not directly, chosen for this position by the votes of the British people.

The process by which he is chosen is not "direct." Neither Mr. Churchill nor Mr. Attlee ever "stood" (the British word) for Prime Minister in exactly the way Mr. Roosevelt "ran" (the American word) for President. What happens in Britain is roughly this: There are two main parties, the Conservatives and the Labour Party, and, at present, a third and relatively minor party, the Liberals. For the present, it will be enough to say that these are national parties not basically unlike our national parties in their functions. Each party has a leader. The leader is not chosen by a formal national party convention, like our presidential candidates. He is chosen as a result of the give-and-take of political life in parliament, of which he has usually long been a member. He has usually held important cabinet office before he attains the leadership of his party, is indeed often a former Prime Minister. Our own defeated candidates for the presidency are usually out for good, but think of Cleveland and Bryan and you will get a good idea of the British practice. Note that, just as in the United States a presidential candidate may not be the most striking personality in his party, so in Britain a party leader may come to the top as a compromise between stronger, or at least more forceful, leaders. Some commentators believe Mr. Attlee owes his position to rivalry between Mr. Bevin and Mr. Morrison, just as in our country certain Whig presidents owed theirs to the rivalry between Clay and Webster.

In normal times there is a national parliamentary "General Election" every five years. Since no written constitutional provision makes such elections a rigid requirement, a parliament can in an emergency prolong its life from year to year, as the war parliament, elected in 1935, did; but this is in no sense a normal proceeding, and so impatient did the public become with its ten-year-old parliament that Mr. Churchill had to promise a general election after the defeat of Germany, even though the war with Japan was still unfinished. This promise was duly carried out in July, 1945. At a general election, then, each party presents candidates in each constituency (district) of the House of Commons, hoping to secure a majority of its 640 seats. There are indeed a few incurably one-party constituencies where the opposing parties may not bother to present candidates, which is a little as though the Democrats should not even try to elect a congressman from Vermont, but in general each party presents a full national slate. The Prime Minister and his cabinet members also stand for some constituency, usually as "safe" a one as they can decently choose, since they must be members of parliament. The election may return a majority for the party in power before the election. In that case the Prime Minister continues to be Prime Minister; he has been "reëlected" by a popular consultation in fact as direct as ours. For though he is chosen by a majority vote of the 640 members of the House of Commons, and though close elections in some constituencies and sweeps in others may mean that a party can get a majority in the House without having a majority of the popular vote, we should not forget that, because of the mechanics of the electoral college, precisely this result can be obtained in the United States. Indeed, Hayes in 1876 and Harrison in 1888 did not even obtain a popular plurality. Sometimes death or retirement of a Prime Minister may lead to the appointment of a leader next in line as Prime Minister, as the Vice-President may succeed in the United States. The late Neville Chamberlain was such a "Vice-President"; he was never popularly elected as Prime Minister. If, however, a party other than that in power wins a majority of seats in the House of Commons, the King, usually on the recommendation of the outgoing Prime Minister, appoints the leader of that party to the prime ministership. This is what happened in the appointment of Mr. Attlee. On rare occasions a leader is passed over as in 1924 Lord Curzon was passed over in favor of Mr. Baldwin. But the King did so then only on the strong advice of prominent men in both parties.

When, as today, there are more than two national parties, a general election may give a majority to none. Then there is nothing for it but a coalition government, headed by the strongest leader, usually from the party with at least a plurality in the Commons. Or a national emergency as in the war or as in the gold-standard crisis of 1931 may make a coalition government necessary. But the British do not like government by coalition; there is still a strong national feeling that the two-party system is essential to effective democratic government. It is indeed probable that in 1945 a good many British moderates, by no means "socialists," voted Labour rather than Liberal for this, among other reasons: they did not believe a Liberal majority possible, and they did not want so strong a Liberal group in the Commons that a Liberal-Labour or a Liberal-Conservative coalition government would be forced on the country. They voted, in a sense, for the traditional British two-party system.

The Prime Minister, through the form of the Crown, exercises the normal powers of the executive in a modern democracy. He chooses, in effect, his colleagues in the cabinet, who head ministries—War, Labour, Foreign Office and so on—essentially like our departments headed by Secretaries. Note that these do not need to be "confirmed" by the legislative, as similar appointments by the American President must be confirmed by the Senate, and that in so unified and so relatively small a country, the Prime Minister does not need to worry much about the sectional distribution of his appointees—though a cabinet without a Scot is unthinkable. On the other hand, his colleagues in the cabinet must all have seats in parliament, or must get one in a by-election if they have none. The very democratic principle is followed that no member of the Government can accept a new office unless his appointment is ratified by the voters. In other words, the executive, far from being separated from the legislative, is in a sense a committee of that legislative. The analogy with a committee is imperfect, however, since the cabinet has an authority over parliament, and a prestige in the country, not ordinarily associated with a derivative body like a committee.

What happens if parliament passes a measure the cabinet does not want passed, or refuses to pass one it does want passed? No more than the King does the Prime Minister possess the veto power. In case of a quarrel between executive and legislative there are two possibilities; first, the Prime Minister and his cabinet can resign, and the political leaders can try to put together a new cabinet acceptable to the House of Commons; second, the Prime Minister, acting formally through the Crown, can dissolve parliament, even though it has not run its full five-year course, and order a new general election in the hope that the country will give a clear verdict for or against him. The first *can* happen, did indeed happen in 1931, but it is not a procedure the British people like. Certainly the politically educated among them—and they are numerous—realize that the manipulation of cabinets during the lifetime of a given legislature has proved in practice a major evil in countries like the France of the Third Republic, that it is associated with the multi-party system, that it is a threat to governmental efficiency. The second course, dissolution and an appeal to the country, is therefore their constitutional preference. As a matter of fact, there is a certain tendency to hope, at least, that executive and legislative will be able to get along together for the normal five-year period, and if things go well with Britain, this five-year interval may get as well established as our own constitutionally provided four-year presidential term.

Britain is, of course, a great modern state, and it has a great deal of government—at least as much as we have. The bulk of this day-to-day detail of governing, executive work in a sense, is done by nonpolitical appointees, the famous civil service. The top permanent officials are by no means mere clerks; they often make very important decisions on what are really matters of policy. But for any given department there is always some elective official responsible, and he can be called to task by parliament—and by the electors. The multiple needs of modern government in Britain, as in the United States, have called into existence many more departments than existed in Victorian days. British practice differs from ours in that the British do not seem to mind creating new "ministries," while we do not often create new "departments." Thus, for example, in the recent war the British organ for propaganda was frankly called the "Ministry of Information," but ours was called the "Office of War Information," and was an agency, not a department. This is a minor difference and can be explained by the fact that a new American department would have to have a Secretary with a seat in the cabinet, whereas a new British ministry need not necessarily carry with it a seat in the cabinet. The cabinet is thus a smaller body within the larger group called the ministry. The size of the cabinet is not fixed; it depends on whom the Prime Minister calls to it. In wartime the cabinet is deliberately kept down to seven or so and many modern students of parliamentary government, such as Mr. Leopold Amery, anxious to preserve the real leaders of the country from deadening routine and departmental red tape, have urged that the small cabinet be permanently adapted for peacetime use.

Again, when a new need in administration arises, or seems to arise, the British often make use of a device we do not have: they create an "executive," which is in effect an agency governed by a committee of the collaborating ministries interested in the particular job. Finally, the English make much use of the "public corporation" at the day-to-day level of administration. This is a chartered, nonprofit corporation with many of the normal self-governing powers of any corporation, but with a board of directors appointed by the government, or at least directly responsible to the government. We too have the public corporation, such as the Reconstruction Finance Corporation. The public monopoly in radio broadcasting, the BBC (British Broadcasting Corporation), is an excellent example of the British use of the public corporation. How independent of the government the BBC is in normal times is debatable; it probably is a bit freer, has a bit more life of its own, than a regular department. To judge from the first experiments made by the Labour government, nationalization in Britain will take a form rather nearer that of the public corporation than that of the regular department.

Whether the British system of ministries, executives, public corporations, and other administrative groups or the American system of departments, agencies, boards, commissions, public corporations, and the like is more efficient is also a debatable matter. It must be admitted that British administrators seem often to have an extraordinary gift for good committee work. Nevertheless, jurisdictional disputes, which are the major curse of all modern governmental bodies, have by no means been few or unimportant in the British war effort. The ordinary citizen in both countries is likely to sigh about "bureaucracy" and let it go at that.

The legislative power in Great Britain is in the House of Commons. Of its 640 members, 628 are chosen in single-member constituencies (districts) by universal male and female suffrage, and are eligible for reëlection. Owners of business property may vote in both business and residential constituencies when these are not identical. Graduates of British universities elect twelve members representing their respective universities, and may also vote in their residential constituencies. No one may vote thrice, and only a very insignificant proportion of the electorate vote twice. There is not in Britain, as there is in the United States, an unwritten law by which a member must be a legal resident of the constituency which he represents, and writers on government have often made much of that fact, maintaining that the British system emphasizes national over petty local politics, eliminates the "pork barrel," and secures a higher average of ability in the House, since the whole reservoir of national political talent can be tapped without regard for local limitations. But British M.P.'s can by no means afford to neglect the local affairs of their constituents; "nursing a constituency" has been a necessity of British politics for a long time. There is over the last fifty years an increasing tendency for members to live in their own constituencies. Nor is the caliber of the average M.P. as much higher than that of the average congressman as it was the fashion, during the debunking period of American intellectual history, to maintain. Of recent years, both the Conservatives and Labour have tended to reward an undue proportion of party hacks with good safe seats.

The main job of the House of Commons is to "make" laws. The initiative for all important laws comes from the cabinet, and the technical work of drafting these government bills is done by experts in the civil service. The House can and does amend bills—to the extent the cabinet, or to use the British term, the "Government" with a capital G, will accept such amendment; and of course its debates, which are still well reported in the press, give important problems a good public airing. But the old concept of the House as somehow producing legislation out of its bosom is no longer true. The House is certainly more than a rubber stamp, though British lovers of the good old days like to complain that it is getting to be more and more of a mere registry for laws the Government and the bureaucracy want.

Procedure in the House is very different from that of our House of Representatives. It sits, not in a sort of amphitheater, but in a rectangular room which gets incredibly crowded if all the members are present at once. The Speaker's chair is in the middle of one of the short sides of the rectangle; on one of the long sides sit in parallel rows of benches the Government, on the other the Opposition, separated by a broad aisle. The front row of the Government benches is occupied by the ministers, the leaders of the party in power; the front row of the Opposition benches is occupied by the leaders of the Opposition. The two parties thus confront each other in dramatic physical separation. The system serves also to mark off the leaders from the "back benchers," the private members who vote, speak occasionally, but very rarely initiate any legislation. Indeed, procedure distinguishes sharply between a "Government" bill and a "private member's bill"; the latter are increasingly rare and unimportant. On the fate of the former, of course, the Government must stand or fall. If a Government bill is defeated, or amended in a way the Government cannot accept, the Government—not just the Prime Minister, but the whole ministry—must either resign or call a new election. When, as in 1945, a coalition Government breaks up before an election, then the whole ministry resigns and a one-party ministry is put together to fight the election. Debate in the Commons is more informal and less oratorical than in the House of Representatives, and the committee work on the whole less important than in our national legislature. The House of Commons is still often called one of the best clubs on earth, and certainly it possesses a corporate spirit which has converted some of the members of the Labour Party to a rather surprising identification of themselves with the ways of the "ruling classes."

The back bencher comes into his own in the "question period," which is one of the most useful of parliamentary procedures. A portion of a given session is set off for questions on any phase of the Government's activities. These may be addressed by any member to any minister, in writing or, as matters are explored, orally. The minister replies as best he may, explaining why a British Fascist has been released from detention, why His Majesty's consul in Tangier was unable to protect a British subject there from a lawsuit, what steps the Government are taking to fight the spread of the Colorado potato beetle—all the incredibly varied details of the life of a great state. Mostly, perhaps, the questions are petty, but sometimes they come close to high policy. Note, however, that unlike the procedure in similar question periods in continental parliamentary democracies, the question period in Britain does not lead to a vote, and hence cannot in itself produce the fall of a cabinet. The questions and answers are well reported by press and radio. The question period is a good device for keeping the ministers aware of their responsibilities to the House and to the public, it is good for the egos of the back benchers, and it is to a certain extent a check on the bureaucracy.

Legislative and executive, Commons and cabinet, then are really one, not two as with us. If they should quarrel the people would decide at once between them; the spectacle of an executive of one party and a legislative of another, which with us occurred in Wilson's administration in 1918–1920 and in Truman's in 1946–1948, cannot be found in Britain. But the two great systems of democratic government, the parliamentary and the congressional, are not today as far apart as they were when classic writers like Bryce described them in the last century. The links between Capitol Hill and the White House are far closer than they used to be. We may not talk of "Government bills" but we do talk of "Administration bills." The President may not in theory initiate legislation, but in fact leaders in the American House and Senate are known as administration men, and before an important measure comes into the legislative mill there has been a lot of conferring with cabinet members, agency heads, and the rest of the complicated Washington administration. If cabinet members should be allowed to appear before House and Senate, though without a vote, as has been proposed, we should get a very close approximation to the British question period.

The perceptive reader may have noted that so far we have not mentioned the House of Lords. The Lords, perhaps even more than the Crown, are a puzzle to the ordinary American. He feels that socially the existence of "His Lordship" is not consistent with real democracy; politically, he thinks it clearly undemocratic that the Upper House, which he feels must be in some sense the equivalent of our Senate, should be a privileged, hereditary, nonelective body. We may waive the social question for the moment. Politically, the ordinary American, to judge from experience with the G.I. in Britain in this war, misunderstands the position of the House of Lords. It is in no sense the equivalent of our Senate. It is indeed no longer a real legislative body at all, since in 1911, by what we should call a constitutional amendment, it was deprived of the power of preventing a bill passed by the House of Commons from becoming a law. It can delay a bill for a maximum of two years, but in practice it has taken little advantage of this vestige of power. Mr. Attlee's government now proposes to reduce this time limit to one year. There was noise of protest, but by no means deafening noise. The Lords do not really excite the British. Some few dozens of its hundreds of eligible members come to the sessions of the House of Lords, and its debates sometimes provide checks in details of legislation, but it is no longer what it was even in the days of Gilbert and Sullivan, when it did nothing in particular and did it very well. It is nowadays generally agreed, for instance, that the Prime Minister could not possibly be a member of the House of Lords, though there is no written law to prevent it.

The complete elimination of the House of Lords, leaving Britain in form what it is in practice, a land with a unicameral legislative, is by no means impossible. The Labour Party has at least talked of such a step. There is also some talk, at least among the Conservatives, of reforming the Upper House to bring it to a position of real power, presumably by making it elective. But it must be reported that the whole question stirs very little interest in Great Britain. There is certainly not towards the Lords the same widespread feeling of loyalty that there is towards the Crown. Few Britishers apparently feel that the Lords are a necessity; but not very many feel that they are a nuisance. Here, as so often, the ordinary Englishman seems to agree with the aphorism of an eighteenth-century back bencher, "Single-speech" Hamilton: "When it is not necessary to change, it is necessary not to change."

On the judicial side, there is no British institution corresponding to our Supreme Court, with its famous power of judicial review. When parliament has duly passed a bill, it becomes a law no matter how many previous laws and customs it contradicts. Politically, we must repeat, Britain is a most "direct" democracy, with none of our famous institutional checks and balances in the way of carrying out what a popularly elected Commons-and-cabinet want to do. In one sense, however, the British judicial system does display the separation of powers. Its judges, though appointed by the Crown—that is, by the Government—hold office for life during "good behavior"; they cannot be removed save by due process of law, by a procedure essentially like that we call impeachment. Its courts are organized in a series of lower and upper courts, with a process of appeal. At the top of the hierarchy, corresponding with our Supreme Court only in this sense, that it is the highest court of appeal, is the House of Lords. But, again by rigid custom, this is not the whole house, but only a special committee of "law lords," who are appointed, not hereditary. These law lords, headed by the Lord Chancellor, are, of course, distinguished lawyers by profession.

British courts judge according to the same system of judge-made Common Law which is the common inheritance of all Anglo-Saxon peoples. This Common Law has, of course, come to vary somewhat between the United Kingdom and the United States, and in both it is perhaps today overshadowed by the vast mass of accumulated and constantly increasing statutory law, the laws made by legislative bodies. In both countries there is a growing body of what is really administrative law—that is, rules and regulations made in the administrative interpretation of their functions by the dozens of government bodies that make up the bureaucracy. And in both countries many lawyers are worried by the growth of this sort of administrative regulation and are desirous of protecting the Common Law from too much encroachment by the bureaucrats. The British make a distinction we do not make between the barrister, who pleads cases in the courts, and the solicitor, who does the more drudging work with legal documents. On the other hand, the British do not have our term "corporation lawyer," though they certainly have the thing.

In local government, the British do not have any state governments as links between the central government and the basic local administrative areas. Those areas—counties, cities, towns, rural and urban districts—have much the same machinery of government we have: elected councils, aldermen, mayors, appointive boards for special functions, municipal employees protected by civil-service tenure, and so on. The British have not felt it necessary to experiment, as we have, with city managers and commission government. They have not had in their cities to deal with large numbers of foreigners, and their municipal politics are on the whole "cleaner" than ours. They have certainly not incurred the same troubles with spectacular gangster politics. But their local government is not quite as idyllic as some Americans think it. They have not altogether avoided scandals over contracts and other forms of petty graft, and on occasion have provided some good ripe corruption for newspaper airing. Nor have they avoided a condition which is the real root of weaknesses in local government in both countries; in Britain as in America altogether too many voters fail to take part in local elections, fail to take a direct personal interest in the politics which are after all closest to them and which they might directly influence. Public-spirited citizens in Britain still put in much admirable work in local politics, and it would be an exaggeration to say that this sound base for self-government no longer exists. But it is at least menaced by the abstention of the great majority of ordinary citizens, and those who have observed the temper of young Britons in the armed forces are not too optimistic about the possibilities of spurring them to more active participation in local government.

2. THE PARTY SYSTEM

British politics, like ours, are party politics. They are, at least in ideal, two-party politics, which in our time seem to have proved to be the best protection against totalitarian one-party politics. Now the politics of one country are almost always puzzling to citizens of another country, and parties, which are the living flesh on the institutional skeleton of the body politic, are most difficult for the outsider to understand. One of the most frequent questions Britishers put to Americans about this country is "Just what is the difference between a Republican and a Democrat?" That is a difficult question to answer briefly, and it is no easier to analyze briefly the differences between a Conservative and a Labour Party man.

To take the simpler matters of organization first, British parties are voluntary groups organized locally, regionally, and finally nationally, supported by the contributions of the faithful—in the case of the Conservatives, by fairly large contributions from the rich as well as by smaller sums from the rank and file, in the case of the Labour Party chiefly by workers' dues canalized through the Trades Unions—and devoted to the usual party activities, propaganda in press and public meetings, nomination of candidates, and getting them elected. The British have no system of primaries, and therefore their parties do their work by what is essentially the party-caucus system. Since they have no direct elections for national executive office, the key task is the nomination and election in each constituency of members of the House of Commons. This task, in keeping with the British method of emphasizing national rather than local issues in parliamentary elections, is carried out by the national party headquarters—but always in consultation with the local party organization. Patronage in Britain in modern times has not been the evil it has been in America, largely because of the earlier and more complete development of the civil service. But what might be called honorific patronage has certainly played an important part in British politics; after all, party workers need some reward, and there are not enough seats in parliament to go around. At the top level, peerages, knighthoods, and decorations have proved a useful form of such patronage. The Labour Party are supposed to disdain these medieval trappings, but there are Labour knights, and even Labour peers.

The real problem of parties is what holds them together,

what they want, what they "stand for." Britain has no great regions with diverging economic interests like America, and above all she has nothing like our Solid South, though when Ireland sent members to parliament in London, she had something even harder to handle. No British party has a problem quite like that of reconciling Mr. Carter Glass, Mr. Henry Wallace, Mr. Sidney Hillman, and Mr. James Michael Curley. But it would be a great mistake to assume that the British have no problems of party unity—that the Conservatives are all agreed, for instance, on a minimum of state interference in business, that the Labour Party are all agreed on the maximum of such interference. Broadly speaking, the Conservatives do stand in public for private property and private initiative in industry, and the Labour Party for some form of socialism—as a matter of fact, so far at least, a pretty attenuated form of socialism. Even today, the party is more often called "socialist" by its opponents than by its own members. Its Right and Center, though they are perhaps not exactly afraid of the word "socialist," obviously prefer the old title "Labour Party." There are all sorts of qualifications to be made in this simple opposition of principles. The Tories—this, by the way, is their opponents' smear word for the Conservatives—have Young Tories like Mr. Quintin Hogg, who would go very far towards collectivism; on the other hand some of the old-time trades-unionists in the Labour Party are no more—well, very little more—socialists than is Mr. Green of our A. F. of L.

So too with other issues. The Conservatives are traditionally nationalist and imperialist, believers in a strong Navy and as strong an Army as possible, and the Labour Party are traditionally internationalist, anti-imperialist, and pacifist. Only a few years ago the Conservatives were protectionists and the Liberals, predecessors of the Labour Party, were free-traders. What seems to have happened in recent times, however, is a sort of melting together of these great issues, so that neither Conservatives nor Labour really present clear-cut differences in platform. Both insist they want social security, British participation in an international organization to preserve peace, British collaboration with other countries in the restoration of international trade. This sort of "agreement" is, of course, not unknown in American party platforms.

In spite of the campaign oratory of 1945, with each party accusing the other of extremism—socialism or individualism— the current opposition of Conservatives and Labour Party is not very different from the old opposition of Conservatives and Liberals. Nor is it very different *fundamentally* from that between Republicans and Democrats in the United States. In both countries, whatever the party politicians *say*, their actions show they agree on more things than they disagree on. That is, both countries are as democracies going concerns, and their opposing parties are not wholly representative of mutually exclusive interests, economic, political, or social. A defeated party accepts defeat, and works for victory next time, knowing well that its victorious opponent is not really going to change things a great deal. This state of affairs *may* be changing in Britain. The opposition between Conservatives and Labour may really be a genuine opposition between social and economic classes. Yet in spite of nationalization of banking, coal, and railways, the Labour Party after three years of power still looks Fabian-reformist rather than Marxist-revolutionary. Typical is its action in voting a generous $200,000 annual allowance to Princess Elizabeth and Prince Philip. Only seventeen votes, two of them Communist, were cast against this measure in February, 1948.

With all due allowances for the real differences between British and American politics, it is still safer to consider the sweeping Labour victory at the polls in July, 1945, as more like the sweeping victory of the Democrats in the United States in 1932 than like a prelude to revolution, let alone revolution itself. Labour polled about twelve million votes, and the Conservatives nearly ten million, which means that His Majesty's Opposition is still strong and well-rooted in the country. Government measures will have to be hammered out in the usual way on the anvil of opposition, which means that they will be shaped in part by opposition in the democratic way of compromise. And do not be misled by the term "nationalization." As we shall see in a later chapter on what the war has done to Britain, the economy of Britain had under Mr. Churchill's government been in fact thoroughly nationalized as a war measure. The Attlee government has expropriated no capitalist; it has compensated owners of nationalized industries with interest-bearing bonds. Indeed, from a strictly Marxist point of view, it has helped perpetuate a *rentier* class. Nor is Labour committed to the wholesale transformation of the British economic system into anything like collectivism on the Russian model, and the Conservatives are not committed to a wholesale return to nineteenth-century laissez-faire individualism. The two parties differ on the *degree* of government intervention in economic matters, not on the root-and-branch question of government intervention in itself. It is precisely under such conditions of party difference in degree rather than in kind that democracy can exist. The election of 1945 is a confirmation of British political democracy.

There are other parties in Britain. The Liberals, once the great alternative to the Conservatives, have lost ground steadily since before the war of 1914–1918, as most of their members have drifted into the Labour Party. The Liberals look to an outsider like a survival of nineteenth-century literal believers in individual liberty, in "old-fashioned individualism," hostile alike to the state and to great corporations and destined to ultimate extinction. But their surviving remnant contains men of ability and distinction, and they may be able to gain enough strength in the future to keep the Conservatives or Labour from attaining a majority in the House, and may thus be able to force coalition government. The war saw the rise of the Commonwealth Party, a group of predominately middle-class idealists with overtones of Christian socialism, which was able to take advantage of its exemption from the war-time party truce to elect a few M.P.'s at by-elections. The odds are against

Commonwealth's becoming a major party in peacetime Britain. It made a poor showing in the election of 1945, electing but one member, but it may gain enough strength to complicate still further the delicate balance of the two-party system if things go badly for the Labour government. Finally, there is a Communist Party, with one member in the Commons of 1935–1945, from a radical working-class constituency in Scotland, and with two members in the new House. But it is really no more than a splinter party. Its 100,000 total vote in 1945 was only about one-half of one per cent of the total vote cast. Few British people believe it will gain enough adherents in the immediate future to count in British politics.

3. ECONOMIC FACTORS IN POLITICS

Most of us, even though we should deny indignantly that we are Marxists, are nowadays used to thinking of politics in terms of the economic interests we feel sure are at the bottom of them. Britain is a mature industrial economy, and its politics are not worlds apart from ours, which are increasingly those of a mature industrial economy. But Britain matured sooner than the United States, and it has a much less important agricultural interest than we; both these facts have had their effect on the structure of British politics.

It is not quite true to say that British farmers have no place in British politics. There are still a few largely rural constituencies in parliament; many urban Britishers have a sentimental interest in preserving the countryside; and the two world wars have made everyone aware of the need of maintaining British agriculture at the highest efficiency possible. But it is doubtful if these motives are strong enough to afford British farmers much protection in peacetime against competition from the outside world. Certainly there does not exist anything in the British Isles comparable to the farm blocs which play such an important part in American politics.

British industry is well organized, and much of it is Big Busi-

ness even by American standards. British manufacturers have
in their Federation of British Industries (the initials F.B.I. thus
have in Britain quite different connotations from the ones they
have with us) a powerful organization similar to our National
Association of Manufacturers. Their giant chemical combine,
the Imperial Chemical Industries (I.C.I.), is in a class with our
own DuPont organization, with whom, as we all know now, it
has close relations in world commerce. Unilever is a huge vertical combination which sends out its own whalers, grows its
own vegetable oils in the tropics, makes its own soaps and
other products in the model town of Port Sunlight near Liverpool—and has an important daughter-concern in the United
States. The list could be continued for a long time. Banking,
insurance, and stock market are correspondingly developed
into a huge interlocking network with its center in London.
The "City"—the square mile of financial and business firms in
the historic center from which London has grown into Greater
London—is in fact as in common parlance the opposite number
of our "Wall Street." Again, three years of Labour have not
destroyed the "City." On the whole, the British business community has tended to give the Labour Government a sporting
chance. Even in Pall Mall clubs, Mr. Attlee is not sneered at
as "that man in Downing Street."

The whole structure of the Conservative Party is shored up
by this business and financial world. It is a rare Tory M.P. who
is not a director of one, and usually of several, corporations.
Big Business is by no means without opposition in modern
Britain. The Labour Party is of course against it, though there
are many who say that Labour is not against Bigness itself in
industry, but merely against those who now control Bigness,
and that what Labour really wants is to have a state dominated
by Labour take over industry and run it. But there is also opposition from little and middling business, from old-fashioned
"individualists," from those who fear the dangers of monopoly
in the hands of either the state or private corporations.

Just how strong this opposition is in Britain it is impossible to say. The traveler must notice how many thousands of small retail shops, small business concerns, small factories, there are. The fact is that in Britain as in the United States this "middle" middle class is numerically very strong. But in Britain even more than in the United States it has no very effective political means of expression. Its members must choose between the Conservatives, whose leadership is dominated by Big Business, and the Labour Party, whose leaders are essentially trades-unionists used to thinking in terms of mass organization. These middling Britishers feel very much ground between the upper and the nether millstone, as you can find by talking with them, but they seem unable to do much about it. They might rally to the Liberals or build a party for themselves, but so far they show few signs of doing so.

The truth is that, in spite of occasional outbursts from the "Society of Individualists" and such groups, the British seem pretty well reconciled to large-scale organization in economic life, reconciled even to "planning," "regimentation," or whatever name, good or bad, you choose to give it; that, indeed, is what we mean when we say that Britain has a "mature" modern economy. General practitioners among British physicians did indeed vote 86 per cent in 1948 against the Labour government's scheme for "socialized medicine"; but that is only one more bit of evidence that generally in the Western World the medical profession is politically conservative. In Britain, the profession will probably gradually adjust itself to a tempered socialism. It is interesting that this highly organized profession has proved a greater stumbling block for the present government than any "business" group so far. "Big Business" seems to get along better with "Big Government" than does an organization like the British Medical Association, individualistic and quasi-corporative in an almost medieval sense. It is by no means unimportant that Britain has never had a Sherman antitrust act, has never found the term "trust"—or any synonym—a very exciting fighting word. Historically, it is perhaps true that nineteenth-century free-trade Britain had no need of trust busting, that the law of the land as interpreted in the courts was sufficient to protect her from monopolistic abuses. But today Britain certainly has trusts—and seems not to fear them greatly. Indeed, all sorts of Britishers, including many economists and civil servants, are quite willing to accept trusts —and their equivalent in international trade, cartels—as part of the inescapable facts of life. This, as we shall see, may give rise to one of the most acute problems of Anglo-American relations.

The completeness of labor-union control in Britain is perhaps the most striking difference between the politico-economic structures of the United States and Britain. There is, for instance, no real issue over the existence of labor unions in Britain; employers, and indeed even the government as employer, everywhere accept the unions, if not joyfully at least without question. Nor is the British Labour split in anything like the A. F. of L.–C.I.O. antagonism. The Trades Union Congress (T.U.C.), if it is not without internal struggles, does at least group all British labor in a single organization. Furthermore, the trades-unionists have their own political party, the Labour Party, which is nation-wide in scope. Employers and employees do of course differ over wages and conditions of work, and there are strikes; there has even been a strike of coal miners against their new employers—the government Coal Board. But these quarrels are conducted in an atmosphere of customary arbitration, and both sides are so used to one another, so used to the rules of the game, that the bitterness of American labor disputes is lacking. Indeed, to the militant socialists in Britain the British labor movement seems to have been too successful, to have got half the prize too easily, and to be content with something much less than the whole prize of a workers' state. It is true that as the T.U.C. has become very much a going concern it has developed certain conservative characteristics—caution, dislike for novelty, regard for form and habit, an attitude of safety first, of peace at any reasonable price. You will hear bright young radicals in Britain

railing at the "trades-union bureaucrats" with even more bitterness than at the Tories.

There is, then, a certain hardening of the structure of British
politics and economics into a maturity which may seem the
opposite of what Anglo-Saxons on both sides of the Atlantic
regard as their birthright—individual initiative, economic expansion, a free, adventurous, hopeful life where something
good—something even better, and certainly more romantic,
than prosperity—is always just around the corner. Prophets of
doom are not lacking, even in Britain, who foresee in the near
future a tired, but perhaps not unhappy Britain, shorn of Empire and reconciled to a sort of respectably totalitarian society.
But such prophets have been crying "finis Britanniae" ever since
the days of Queen Elizabeth, and they may be wrong again.
Certainly a rapid review of religion, education, culture, and
society in contemporary Great Britain, which we shall undertake in the following chapters, suggests that Britain may yet
preserve her great place in the world.

3. Religion and Education in Britain

What struck Voltaire two hundred years ago as most strange in England has always been to Americans one of the most homelike things in that country—the variety of churches. An American strolling through an English or Welsh town of any size would note church buildings of all sorts, and would see familiar names like Methodist, Baptist, Congregational, Presbyterian, Unitarian; he might note that certain churches well filled of a Sunday morning bore no labels on the outside, and turned out on investigation to be Roman Catholic. He would feel quite at home. But if he were at all a noticing sort, he would begin to notice differences. He would note that most of the churches labeled Baptist, Congregational, Methodist and the like, as well as most of the Roman Catholic churches, were usually small and not very old; were he sensitive to architecture, he would note that they were mostly ugly, or at best plain. He would discover that the lovely village churches and the great medieval cathedrals bore no identifying labels, and on inquiring would find that they belonged to the Church of England, which we call the Protestant Episcopal Church in America. He would finally discover that the little Baptist, Congregational, and Methodist churches were not even called churches, but only chapels. He would begin to realize that there are differences as well as similarities in the religious life of the two countries.

In England, there are three groups of churches, the Established Church, the Free Churches, and the Roman Catholic.

All, it need hardly be said, enjoy complete freedom of worship. In Scotland, the Established Church is the Presbyterian, but Establishment in Scotland now has little more than a sentimental meaning. In Wales the Church of England was disestablished in 1914, thereby leaving the Episcopalians in that country in the same position towards the state as the numerically dominant Free Churchmen.

1. THE ESTABLISHED CHURCH

Economically, the Establishment in England still rests on survivals of the medieval tithe, but these have been incorporated in land values so that they no longer burden those outside the Church of England. Politically, Establishment means that the King is the supreme head of the Church, that high ecclesiastical offices are filled by Crown—that is, by ministerial—appointment, and that parliament has the final word in important legislation concerning the Church. Actually the Anglican Church is through its Convocation very largely a self-governing body, and if the Prime Minister has a certain latitude in choosing say an Archbishop of Canterbury, he has not in modern times used that latitude to foist upon the Church anyone unwelcome to it. Yet if the government has of recent years always shown itself most considerate of the spiritual independence of the Church, the fact remains that the Church is legally under the government. Therefore the Establishment is under fire, and not only from nonconformists, freethinkers, and others who hold that reason and modern democracy demand complete separation of Church and State; it is also under fire from some of its own High Churchmen, who hold that God does not want his Church ruled, even in theory, by a parliament in which are to be found all sorts of unbelievers. Many within the Church of England itself are therefore anxious to give up the fleshpots of Establishment.

Most of the English upper classes are members of the Church of England—the aristocracy, the country gentlemen, many of those enriched by trade and industry. The greater part of the professional classes are also Anglicans, and though Oxford and Cambridge have since 1870 opened their doors to noncomformists and Roman Catholics, they remain Anglican in temper. The great majority of farming villagers, though not of mining villagers, are Anglicans, and the Established Church has considerable strength in the urban middle and lower classes, especially in the South. The Church of England is, in fact, the strongest single church in Great Britain.

But is it a *single* church? It has always been hard for foreigners, and especially for continental Europeans, to understand how so many forms of doctrine, ritual, and behavior could be gathered together in the Church of England. This brief report is also by an outsider, and must miss many of the subtler things that make men good Anglicans. But from the outside there seem to be at one extreme High Churchmen who think of themselves as Catholics, better Catholics than the Romanists, and who preserve practically everything of Roman Catholic liturgy, ritual, and dogmas, save for the use of Latin and the supremacy of the Pope. At the other extreme are Low Churchmen who are not very far from the edges of Unitarianism. In between are various shadings, and a fairly large central group of Broad Churchmen who have hit a happy English compromise between ritualism and evangelicalism, between Rome and Geneva, between this world and the next. At one parish church you may find the Host reserved in the Lady Chapel, at another you may find no Lady Chapel at all. One Anglican clergyman will be indignant if you call him a priest, another will be indignant if you do not. Some Anglican clergymen hold very firmly indeed to belief in the celibacy of the clergy; others marry and multiply. Somehow or other the Church of England manages to hold all these differing people together. There has been no considerable formal schism in the Church since the Methodists, most reluctantly for the most part, split off at the end of the eighteenth century.

The customary comment is that all this is a perfect example

of the happy or unhappy ability of the English not to be disturbed by logic, of their gift for endless compromise. It is unwise to quarrel with so obvious a commonplace. But it may be suggested that the Church of England holds together partly by a process close to natural selection. The logical have left it in years past for the Roman Catholic and the nonconformist churches, and those who remain have not for a long time had a really clear-cut choice before them. To abandon the Anglican communion now would be to lose the great prize of Englishness, their share in something reassuringly national, unique. The English will always insist that they are quite logically illogical.

2. THE FREE CHURCHMEN

The Church of England was separated from Rome in the sixteenth century by the action of that most English monarch, Henry VIII, Defender of the Faith; it was never a revolutionary movement, politically or theologically. The dissenting churches (Congregational, Presbyterian, Baptist, and others) split off from the Church of England in the seventeenth century in the course of a real social revolution more violent than most Englishmen today like to remember it as being. The triumphant Puritan revolutionists cut off the head of Charles I quite as completely as the Jacobins in France cut off the head of Louis XVI, and for a time England was a republic. The Puritan revolution, after the manner of most successful revolutions, was followed by a reaction, and the monarchy was restored. But such reactions never wipe the slate clean; the nonconformists remained, and have never ceased to play an important part in English life. In Scotland and in Northern Ireland the less radical wing of the Puritans, the Presbyterians, were able to maintain themselves as the dominant group even after the Stuarts were restored.

Persecuted at first in England after the Restoration of 1660, the Puritan sects gradually acquired in the eighteenth century complete freedom of worship, and in the nineteenth complete freedom to vote, to hold office, and finally in 1870, to matriculate at Oxford and Cambridge. Their history is neatly summed up in the names by which they were commonly called; from "dissenters," which suggests something unpleasant, they became by Victorian times "nonconformists," which suggests something reasonably pleasant, or at least acceptable; and nowadays they are known as "Free Churchmen," which is a most agreeable term. The original Puritans, though by no means unrepresented among the gentry, had their core in the middle classes of the towns and the yeomen farmers of East Anglia. This is not the place to debate the question of the relation between Calvinism and modern capitalism. The fact remains that during the Industrial Revolution a number of nonconformists made a lot of money, and many more attained good solid middle-class ease. Under pressure of great wealth, the children of many a Baptist or Congregational millionaire went over to the Church of England; the rank and file of the nonconformists were still in modest circumstances. Nevertheless, by Victorian times the nonconformists as a whole were no longer the repressed and struggling underdogs they had been a century earlier. They could feel that they were the backbone of England. They were the guardians of that "nonconformist conscience" under which the British Empire was doing such a good job among less conscientious people. They had put their stamp on a large part of the Church of England itself which, save for a few who were being lured to Rome, was in Victorian times really protestant and puritan.

Many even among Free Churchmen think that the Free Churches today have lost ground. They have on the whole been less successful than the Anglicans in combating religious indifference. They have been much less willing than some Anglicans to explore the possibilities of the latest form of radicalism, socialism, or communism. They have little new, little exciting, to offer the young. They have lapsed into a sort of Establishment of their own, a nonpolitical and financially inadequate Establishment. They are, as organized churches, poor, often desperately poor. As in America, they talk about federation of the sects, but they do not federate.

Yet, again as in America, it will not do to assert that sectarian protestantism is dead. Movements like the Salvation Army and the Boy Scouts owe much to the Free Churches. The famous nonconformist conscience wakens at times to vigorous life, sometimes in unlikely places, as among the trades-union leaders of the Labour Party during the crisis over the marriage of Edward VIII. For, though the objections to Mrs. Simpson came from many different sources, it seems clear that one of the strongest came from the thoroughly respectable rank and file of the working classes, who would have no truck with divorce in high life. The British nonconformists have indeed become essentially conformists; but they are thus all the more firmly rooted in British life.

3. THE ROMAN CATHOLICS

Like the Free Churchmen, the Roman Catholics have since the sixteenth century passed through stages of persecution and partial toleration to complete political and religious freedom. They are recruited from three main sources: the nucleus of old Catholics who withstood the persecutions; the great migrations of Southern Irish, especially to the regions of Liverpool and Glasgow in the last century; and converts from all classes, seeking in the old faith a certainty not for them to be found elsewhere in the conflicts of modern ideas. This last group, of whom Cardinal Newman remains in the public mind as the great example, has had a level of distinction high above the average, and Roman Catholicism has played a greater part in the intellectual history of modern Britain than the numbers of its communicants would indicate. But, though the Roman Catholic Church has grown considerably since Newman's conversion a hundred years ago, it is still very much in a minority outside Eire, and to judge from its past rate of growth will continue in the measurable future to be a minority. It has in contemporary Britain nothing like the importance it has in the United States. Active, open hostility to the Roman Catholic Church is no longer important in Great Britain, though in Northern Ireland such hostility, at almost seventeenth-century intensity, is never far beneath the surface. There remains in Great Britain itself among the Protestant majority, and especially among the Low Churchmen and the Free Churchmen, an inherited distrust of the Papacy which is not altogether without influence on British foreign policy.

Great Britain, then, is like the United States, and in spite of the existence of established churches in England and in Scotland, a modern land of complete religious freedom. The cynic might say that she has therefore become a land of complete religious indifference, but the cynic would be no more right than he usually is in his dealings with us poor human beings. The fires of religion—and this is no mere metaphor—no longer burn in Britain save in a few individual breasts, among a few consecrated groups. But Britain, like America, is a conventionally Christian land. From either, or both, countries there may spring an unconventional group of Christians, as in both countries there arose in the midst of the prose and reason of the eighteenth century the evangelical movement of the Methodists. Religion is one thing we have pretty much in common with the British.

4. BRITISH EDUCATION

We have, too, popular education in common with the British. There are many and notable differences in the educational systems of Britain and the United States, but the differences have been greatly exaggerated. We shall return later to the "public school," which nearly every American knows is in American terms a private school. For the present, we shall consider the system of tax-supported public education which is that under which the great majority of the British people have been trained.

It is not a neat, simple system, for it has been growing up since the Middle Ages, in what the British like to think is a typical British unsystematic way. But ever since shortly after the great Education Act of 1870 primary education became free, universal, and compulsory, it has been increasingly well tied together under the authority of a national Ministry of Education. There remain a certain number of "Church schools" which receive public funds and are subject to some public inspection and control. Since teaching appointments in these schools are controlled by the ecclesiastical authorities, Anglican or Catholic, they are to a certain extent centers of friction, and their status in the postwar world is now very much a subject of debate. Most primary and secondary state-supported schools, however, are wholly run by local authorities. These authorities are now the 328 councils which supplanted early in this century the 2,527 local school boards of the original education act. These councils (County Councils, County Borough Councils, certain Borough and Urban District Councils) are the Local Education Authorities, in good bureaucratic usage the L.E.A.'s.

At the primary level, the British child who goes through the council schools receives a training not greatly unlike that of the American child. His school building is likely to be much less elaborate, less well equipped with gymnasia, swimming pools, theaters, and batteries of electric stoves than the latest product of prosperous American suburbs. His curriculum is likely to be more limited to the old "three R's" than it would be in America. He is more likely to have a man teacher, even when he is in the lower grades. If he is a country child, he is not likely to have the advantage of a big central district school and a free daily bus ride. But what conservative Britishers call the "Americanization" of Britain is proceeding apace in the field of education. British "educationists" have their eyes on what American "educators" are doing; they too want white blackboards, indirect lighting, education for modern life, and better salaries. British educational authorities have been, in comparison with American, rather niggardly in such matters, or perhaps merely rather conservative.

Yet the great Education Act of 1944, passed in the midst of a war, provides for an educational system as complete and as democratic as Americans could wish. The school-leaving age is raised to sixteen; and County Colleges will be set up to provide for some compulsory part-time education up to eighteen. Secondary education in one form or other will thus be available on as universal a scale as prevails in the wealthier American states. Private secondary education is, of course, available to those who can afford it. Bright boys and girls of the lower and lower middle classes go usually with scholarship aid obtained after competitive examinations to public-supported high schools, though many of them may obtain scholarships at some of the private secondary schools. The poor boy or girl, then, if good enough in studies, may go to the equivalent of our high school, thence to a university. The competition is keen, but not quite as devastatingly bookish as it used to be in the French *lycées*. Working one's way through the higher schools by getting part-time jobs in the outside world has not yet become a part of British education. Publicly supported secondary schools in Britain are not the social whirls they often are in this country; they have sports and clubs, but they are almost always non-coeducational, and they stick pretty closely to books, laboratories, and the other staples of old-fashioned education. The British teen-age boy or girl gets no such early introduction to adult life and courtship as do American children and as a result the average boy or girl is much less precociously worldly-wise than in this country.

There is a further winnowing out at the level of higher education. In proportion to the populations of the two countries, roughly ten times as many Americans as Britishers attend a college or university. It must be admitted, however, that

American definition of what constitutes a college or university is somewhat generous. The British universities are all institutions of the highest academic standing. Oxford and Cambridge in England and the four Scottish universities are old foundations. The University of London and the provincial universities, Manchester, Liverpool, Bristol and the rest, are all modern foundations. None of them are equivalents of our great state universities, since they depend on endowments and students' fees for a large part of their income; but none are, from this point of view, exact equivalents of Harvard or Yale, since even Oxford and Cambridge today receive considerable direct subsidies from the national government. They all offer a classical "liberal" education, but they also all offer a modern scientific education. Oxford has long had a reputation as a determined opponent of things modern, the last refuge of an obstinate classicism; actually Oxford is today a very good place to study science, and in particular the medical sciences.

The rule that used to apply to secondary education still applies to higher education: for young people whose parents can afford it, higher education is open to all save the manifestly unfit; young people whose parents cannot afford it may, if they are ambitious and bright, win competitive scholarships supported from state grants or from endowments, scholarships big enough to enable them to get along without washing dishes, waiting on table, or watching babies while the parents are at the movies. It should be pointed out that at this stage many of the well-to-do turn to Sandhurst and other military or naval schools to prepare for careers as officers, or, contenting themselves with their "public-school education," go directly into business or—and this is getting rare in Britain—to living on their income. Many of the scholarships, of course, are won by children of clergymen, teachers, and others of the genteel poor; but some are won by children of working men. There is, then, in Britain a "career open to talents" kept open to the very top of the educational ladder; but, in contrast to the American system, the talents are almost purely intellectual, not predominately social, and certainly not athletic. There are no athletic scholarships in Britain. The poor boy is often unhappy, because, as we shall see, his successful ascent of the ladder by no means signifies that he is fully assimilated socially to the "ruling classes." Even at Oxford and Cambridge there are more of these lads without benefit of Eton, Harrow, or any "public school" than Americans always realize; about half the scholarship holders at older universities come from schools not commonly listed as "public schools."

There are also the special higher schools. In teacher training, Britain has not yet come to requiring the bachelor's degree of all teachers. Elementary-school teachers are trained separately at the level we used to call that of the Normal School; the secondary-school teachers have university training. Teachers have much the same economic and social status they have in America. There are also special schools for scientific, engineering, and vocational training. Technical education in Britain has sometimes been blamed for the failure of British industry to keep pace in modern times with Germany and the United States. It is true that British technical education does not produce as many highly trained routine engineers as did Germany from 1870 to Hitler, nor as many as we do. But at the level of research and invention, where science and engineering come together, and most certainly in "pure" science, modern Britain does very well. It would seem that the real causes of the comparative decline of British technology lie elsewhere than in the field of technical education.

The newer universities are all nonresidential, like the French universities for instance, and they do not have much social life of their own; Oxford and Cambridge in their constituent colleges are residential and, as all the world knows, they do have a very definite social life. It is nothing like "college life" in the Hollywood version, but it is not clear that life in American colleges is much like the Hollywood version. British undergraduates at Oxford and Cambridge study harder than they will usually admit; they actually play games a little more seriously, a little less informally than they appear to; they say they esteem more highly a First Class (graduation *summa cum laude*) than a Blue (a varsity sports letter); they take part in amateur theatricals, publish periodicals, join debating societies, form dozens of clubs and societies of all sorts devoted to philately, chess, abstract thinking, politics, and almost everything else that can interest man or boy. They are less openly and continuously interested in the opposite sex than Americans of their age, but they are by no means unaware of its existence. Indeed, though the sexes are separated into men's colleges and the much newer women's colleges, both Oxford and Cambridge are as *universities* coeducational, as are the provincial universities. All in all, even Oxford and Cambridge are more like a good American university or college than they are like anything else on earth. By and large, the Continental university sets out to train the mind, and lets it go at that; British universities, and in particular Oxford and Cambridge, attempt to mold their undergraduates to the full social life of the world that awaits them.

For some two-thirds of their undergraduates, much of this molding has been done already in the "public school." We come at last to this most praised and most damned of British educational institutions. The British themselves are not clear about the bottom line between the public schools and mere secondary schools; Eton is clearly a public school and on the other side a council school in a big city is clearly not, and the new County Colleges clearly will not be; but in between are many, mostly privately supported, which may or may not be. At any rate, there are many such schools which are to Eton, Harrow, or Winchester pretty much as a hill-billy or tank-town college is to Yale, Wisconsin, or California. For convenience, the British are usually willing to call a public school any school which is a member of the Headmasters Conference or of the Governing Bodies Association. Most, but not all, of these are boarding schools; perhaps half of them receive some grants or other aids from public educational authorities.

They number somewhat over 150 and they have about 100,000 pupils. Most of them are boys' schools, some few coeducational. Upper-class girls receive a similar training in separate schools.

Historically, the public schools have served to absorb the children of the newly enriched of the Industrial Revolution into the British ruling classes by giving them the proper accent, the proper classical book learning, the proper respect for sports, the proper sense of what is and what isn't done. Perhaps the most important thing to note about them is that they have done this not for a small aristocracy but, in the course of the nineteenth century, for a really very numerous upper middle class. Their end product is the English gentleman, about whom we shall have something to say in the next chapter, for the work of these schools is a social rather than a narrowly educational task. Even more than Oxford and Cambridge, the public schools do a job on the "conditioned reflexes" of their pupils, make them feel and behave in certain ways rather than think in certain ways. They do not, indeed, neglect the intellect, and the best of them today give a first-rate "liberal" education, in which science is by no means as much neglected as some of their critics maintain and in which critical thinking and judgment get a greater emphasis over mere accumulation of miscellaneous information than is usually the case in American secondary education. They have abandoned the Spartan canings and cruelties that made a Shelley so unhappy at Eton, though their modern Shelleys are still in revolt against them. You should not, in general, assume that descriptions of public schools in Victorian novels are today accurate descriptions of what goes on in them. Notably, they are much less sure of themselves than they used to be. Years of attacks on the "old school tie" have had their effect, and today the future status of the public schools is the subject of warm debate in a Britain where a great many fundamentals are being debated.

Even a brief review of education in Britain must find a word for Scottish education. The Scots have had a good press in the educational world; we all know the story of the Highland road mender who answered his English questioner, puzzled by his broad Scots, in Latin. It is true that in Scotland as in most Calvinist countries there has been a concern for popular education; it is true that the poor boy in Scotland once had a better chance to get an education than in England. Even the public school in Scotland is a relatively unimportant importation, an imitation of an English model, and not much better rooted than our American imitations of the same model in our Eastern states. Yet education in Scotland today is not more universal than in England. In a way, the Scots are living on their reputation. At its best, theirs was a rather narrow and bookish learning; and note also that the famous road mender was encountered on a Highland road—not in a Glasgow slum.

5. CULTURE, PRESS, AND RADIO

With the flowering of these educational institutions in British culture we have hardly to concern ourselves here— though it may be worth noting that both in Britain and in America the very word "culture" seems a bit under suspicion. It is certainly not commonly used in either country with the same naturalness it is used in Germany and France. The fact that they share a common language has made the literature of both countries available on both sides of the Atlantic. And certainly in the last century it has been a mutual interchange. An Englishman, Sydney Smith, did early in the last century make the famous remark, "Who reads an American book?" and the echoes of that remark persisted, to the embitterment of American intellectuals, long after it had any truth whatever. The truth is that Cooper, Hawthorne, Mark Twain, even Longfellow, have long been read in Britain. When we rediscovered Melville, the discovery shortly spread to the British Isles. The intellectual balance of trade was no doubt in Britain's favor until our own times; nowadays the interchange at what we may call the highbrow level is practically even; at the lowbrow level it is strongly in favor of this country, thanks largely to

Hollywood and Tin Pan Alley. Until very recently, we commonly knew more about British history, at least up to 1776, than the British knew about ours. In fact, save for a few books like the late Lord Charnwood's life of Lincoln, the educated Britisher read almost nothing about our national history. This is being rapidly remedied today. The war has brought a flood of books on America even in a British book market severely restricted by paper shortage, and instruction in American history is getting a foothold in the curriculum of British secondary and higher education.

For the understanding of Anglo-American relations, at least in the short run, the staples of culture are probably more important than the flowers. We shall have to say a word about the British press and radio.

British newspapers in normal times are uncensored, and the freedom of the press is one of the most sacred of national beliefs. The law of libel in Britain is, however, somewhat stricter than in America, and this may account for the fact that even their yellow journals are less unbridled than ours. They have their yellow journals, though they do not use that term to describe them—newspapers catering to the masses, and filled with news of crime, scandal, and other interesting abnormalities. No doubt at this level the British press is less "sensational" than ours at the same level, but the important point is that it is essentially at the same level—that of the masses. Like our own popular press, these British papers are really big daily magazines, read more for their "features"—sports, women's page, gossip, crossword puzzles, strip cartoons (under this name our comic strips have invaded Britain) than for their politics.

Politically, British popular newspapers run all the way from the middle-class Toryism of the *Daily Mail* and the imperialism of the *Daily Express* to the mild radicalism of the organ of the Labour Party, the *Daily Herald*. Many Americans complain that some of these papers are hostile to the United States. It is true enough that since 1945 British papers reflect the diversity of British opinion more completely than they could during the war, when a gentleman's agreement among the press kept criticism to a minimum. Some Britishers dislike us, and most Britishers feel that we are less than faultless. To complaining Americans they are likely to reply that theirs too is a free country; and they may add the argument that the antics of the *Chicago Tribune* can hardly be expected to pass unnoticed in Britain. There is certainly no reason why Americans should be alarmed at the attitude of the British press towards the United States; but it should be clearly understood that, since theirs is a great popular press, it is bound to respond to any important currents in public opinion.

Great Britain is small enough so that the great London newspapers can cover the whole country. London papers, including "quality" papers like *The Times* and the *Daily Telegraph* with circulations in the hundred thousands, as well as papers like the *Express* and the *Herald* with circulations of two millions, are national papers in a sense that none of ours, not even the *New York Times*, is a national paper. There are indeed a few influential provincial newspapers, notably the famous Manchester *Guardian*, but on the whole if you know what the London press is saying you know what is being said all over the country. This, of course, is not true of the New York press.

Like ours, British newspapers are great private capitalist enterprises, kept alive by advertising, and tied up with the whole business organization of the country. Like ours, they are therefore under attack by idealists of the Left, who maintain that they are not really "free." Even the idealists of the Left will grant, however, that the British press is not corrupt in the sense that the French press of 1939 was often corrupt. In this imperfect world, the professional ethics of British journalism is high. Finally, though Americans are often told in press dispatches that a paper like *The Times*, for instance, reflects an "official" point of view, no paper in Britain is a "government organ" in the sense that *Pravda* or *Izvestia* is a Russian government organ.

The radio in Britain is as much a staple of daily life as it is in America. Broadcasting in Britain is the monopoly of a public corporation, the British Broadcasting Corporation, controlled by the government. It is supported by taxes on receiving sets, and employs no advertising. Since most of its programs are broadcast on short waves, it is possible for Americans really interested in the matter to make for themselves the comparison between the British government monopoly and our own commercial competitive system. In both countries radio is concerned with the entertainment of the masses; in neither country, therefore, does the total output satisfy sensitive people with very high aesthetic and moral ideals. In both, selective twirling of the dials will in normal times usually produce some good music, some serious discussion. The size of the United States, and the freedom of our competitive system, probably allow the individual listener greater freedom of choice here than in Britain. The BBC is often under attack at home for its deliberate political neutrality—which its critics say comes down to political cowardice—for the lack of variety of its programs, for what its critics regard as a stuffiness and lack of enterprise which they maintain is inevitable in anything the government lays its hands on. There are British admirers of our own American system, though most of them dislike the advertisers' plugs, which after all would seem to be an inevitable concomitant of commercial broadcasting.

One thing should be clearly noted. By all the organs of mass dissemination of culture, newspapers, periodicals, books, radio, and the movies, there is going on constantly an exchange across the Atlantic which is quantitatively a new thing, and which has no exact parallel in history. In our own times this exchange at the level of the masses has been strikingly in our favor; at this level we export far more than we import. Indeed, many conservative Englishmen are alarmed by what they call the Americanization of Britain. They shudder at the sight of British children playing gangster; their ears are offended by the din of hot music fresh from Harlem; they are grieved by the increasing British use of American slang. To an American traveler their fears seem exaggerated. He cannot believe that Much Michingham will very soon become exactly like Kalamazoo of Kankakee. But it is certainly true that, thanks to modern agencies for the dissemination of culture—and in particular to the movies, for the British even under quota systems hanker for the product of Hollywood—ordinary people in Britain have become aware of many features of American life which they like, and which they would like to have for themselves. That many of these features—swing, slang, easy relations between the sexes, general social informality, cheap motorcars, electric refrigerators, central heating, the glitter, drive, and restlessness of Hollywood's America—seem to many thoughtful people on both sides of the Atlantic not at all good is certainly true. This is, however, merely to recognize that the fundamental problem of modern civilization, the full education of the masses, is essentially the same on both sides of the Atlantic. How far this still incomplete Americanization of the British masses will go no one can be sure; there still are, as we shall see in the next chapter, many real differences between the British way of life and the American. Meanwhile, it remains a fact that the well-worn expression, "after all, we speak the same language," is getting to be less a metaphor and more a literal description.

4. The British People

Many would say that our chapter heading is misleading—that there is no British people, but only British peoples, English, Welsh, Scottish, Irish, and so on. Historically we must admit that the English have been dominant in the making of the Commonwealth and Empire; but they are a modest people and in some ways a tactful one, and they have spared the susceptibilities of their partners by using when possible the relatively modern and somewhat synthetic term "British." Even so, they and others sometimes slip, and refer carelessly to "English foreign policy" or say that "England made such and such a treaty." Of course, the right word ever since the Union of England and Scotland in 1707 has been "British." Americans, too, should be tactful, and use "British" wherever the action of the whole state or society is involved. But there are limits. They did not sing "There'll always be a *Britain*"; and there is no such thing as "British" literature. There is another difficulty. "The British" will do as the plural noun, but there is no good singular. "Briton" suggests the blue-painted barbarians of old, and is faintly comic. "Britisher" is acceptable to Americans (and is used in this book) but it seems ugly to many in the British Isles. It has been suggested that "Englishman" is the best singular of "the British"—but not by Scots, Welshmen, or Ulstermen.

1. THE BRITISH MELTING POT

None of the constituent peoples of the British Isles are, by standards of modern ethnology, racially "pure." Ethnologists and archaeologists believe that there were several waves of invasion in very early times, even before the famous "Celts" arrived and that the Celts themselves were probably not a single race. They are in general agreement that the four-hundred-year Roman rule in England and Wales at the beginning of the Christian era meant no considerable additions from the Mediterranean to the human stock of the island. Until quite recently most historians have held, however, and many English laymen still hold, that the best-known invasion of the island, that of the Anglo-Saxons in the fifth and sixth centuries of the Christian era, killed off all the earlier inhabitants of all but the western fringes of England and the Highlands of Scotland, and substituted the tall, blond Germanic Anglo-Saxons. This view has in our own day suffered discredit from extra-scientific sources through the fact that two bitter wars with the Germans have made Englishmen somewhat less anxious than in Victorian days to be known as fellow Germans; it has also suffered, in the long run perhaps more seriously, from careful studies which show that over most of England the previous inhabitants, the Britons, were not wiped out as the Red Indians were wiped out in Eastern North America, but survived as a menial class, and eventually mixed with their conquerors. In Wales, in the Highlands, and in Ireland the Celtic peoples survived almost intact.

The Norman conquest of the eleventh century brought a relatively small amount of new stock to the mixture, but it made a great change in the ruling classes, and it profoundly altered English political and cultural institutions, tying them very closely with those of France. Indeed, for the next four centuries England and France were in some senses one country, and their ruling classes, in particular, mingled freely. The Norman was the last great conquest of England, but several small though important additions to the previous human mixture were made in the following centuries, notably of Flemish weavers in the Middle Ages and of French Huguenots in early modern times. Modern England was, especially in the nineteenth century, a haven for political refugees from the continent, and there has always been a slight inflow of foreigners brought by economic motives. But these have been mere trickles. The British melting pot—and for centuries it was a real melting pot—had long ago done its work.

It would no doubt be an exaggeration to say that the average Britisher glories in the fact that he is a product of race mixture. But in anything like the sense the term has for Nazis, the British are simply not "racialists." They do not even talk as much as they used to about contrasts between the Anglo-Saxon and the Celt. They have indeed as a people a very deep feeling that they are superior to other peoples, and that feeling has overtones of at least "white supremacy." But only a few extreme nationalists really hold that "niggers begin at Calais." The British, perhaps in part in reaction against the Nazis, do not base their sense of superiority on anything as philosophical and literary as theories of race. That may well be one of the reasons why their sense of superiority, even in these days when their Victorian world supremacy has gone, is still so strong and serene.

The foregoing generalization, like all those we shall attempt to make about the British, must not be taken as more than a very rough one. If, as Burke said, you cannot indict a nation, you cannot describe one either—at least you cannot make mathematically exact statements about one. It is clear that you can make no concrete statement about the attitudes and character and behavior of fifty million people on this earth which will hold for every one of them. You may say that the British are stolid and phlegmatic; you will not go far in direct experience with them, nor in indirect experience of them through reading their novels and their history, without encountering some who are voluble, excitable, even hysterical. Our generalizations in such matters must be rough approximations based on the average, on the common-sense, unarithmetical statistics our minds forge out of our direct and indirect experience.

Traditional stereotypes—the canny Scot, the hot-tempered (and preferably red-headed) Irishman, the Scandinavian square-head, the Latin lover—are dangerous because of their over-simplicity, which leads us to over-simplify international relations, to assume that a given course of action will have simple and predictable results, to be unduly angry with other peoples when they do not behave altogether as we think they should behave. Nevertheless they are important, first, because they form a sort of first approximation from which we can build up better and more accurate judgments; and second, because, in the present stage of human education, ordinary people still think about their neighbors mostly in terms of these stereotypes. For a long time, most Americans are bound to form their opinions of the British from Hollywood, the pulps, the popular press, the so-called "comic strips," and such-like sources rather than from the writing of Henry James, Madariaga, Renier, and Brogan. They are going to find their Britishers in Lord Plushbottom, Sir Sidney, Mr. Arthur Treacher's butlers, Sir Aubrey Smith's aristocrats, Bulldog Drummond, the cartoonists' John Bull; they will not commonly get even to the relative simplicities of Dickens, Kipling, and P. G. Wodehouse.

2. BRITISH NATIONAL TRAITS

Thus duly warned of the necessary incompleteness of such judgments, we may now attempt to describe some of the traits of the British as they come out in the British way of life. We have already noted that, though in the United Kingdom at least they are clearly one people politically, Wales, Scotland, Ulster, and even the various regions of England itself, have in earlier times been politically independent, and that history and geography have combined to stamp certain peculiarities upon them. All in all, from the point of view of the effective working of the political unit as a whole, these differences today are clearly of the same order as the differences between Vermont, Louisiana, and California rather than of the order of those between Russia and Poland; that is, they do not menace the unity of Great Britain. You will hear occasionally of movements for Welsh home rule, or even for home rule for Scotland, but they are not really serious. The usual pat reply of the Englishman to the suggestion of home rule for Scotland is that it would be better put as home rule for England, since as everybody knows the Scots run England and the Empire. The reply, though a humorous exaggeration, is not wholly without a basis, for the Scots, like many other people from "hard" countries—Yankees, for instance—have been conditioned to work, frugality, and ambition, and they do bulk larger in the annals of British politics and business than their mere numbers would indicate. On the other hand, the Welsh have kept more to themselves; Lloyd George is almost the only Welshman who has had a top role in recent British history.

There are also very real differences between classes in Great Britain. Indeed, it is probable that most American notions of the British are based on the behavior of the British upper classes. When we think of an English accent, it is usually that which Mr. Shaw calls "standard South English," or its exaggeration in the "Oxford accent." When we think of the strong, silent, pipe-smoking Englishman, it is again the upper-class Englishman we have in mind. At most, American folk-lore recognizes the "gentleman's gentleman" or the butler, who usually talks like a gentleman, and the Cockney, the London man of the people. Needless to say, these types do not exhaust the range of the British people; notably, we Americans pay little attention to the great numbers of middle-class English people in the North and Midlands, the guardians of the "nonconformist conscience," who neither drop their *h*'s nor intone in the so-called Oxford manner. We are, incidentally, a bit behind in the matter of the dropped *h;* the *h* is indeed still dropped in various parts of the island, especially by older and middle-aged people, but it is a striking tribute to the effect of popular education that among the young the dropped *h* is slowly but noticeably disappearing.

There are, however, a number of valid generalizations that

hold roughly true of all classes and all regions. First, we may say that the British are still as a people self-assured, serene in their national sense of superiority; or to put it crudely and negatively, that they have no national inferiority complex. They have been, at least until the present time of troubles which began for the whole world in 1914, clearly a great, successful nation, in Victorian times at the very top of the heap; or as the Nazis used to put it for propaganda purposes, but not without an element of truth, they were a "satiated" people. This does not mean that there were no discontented people in Britain, that there were no *individuals* with inferiority complexes; it means that as members of the great group, as members of a club or a team called the British Commonwealth and Empire, Britishers could feel that they shared in something the whole world admired or envied. The actual situation of Great Britain in the contemporary world is no longer that of "top nation," and the consequences of this change will be one of the most important matters we must consider in the later part of this book. But it would seem that psychologically the implications of this change have not yet penetrated far into British popular consciousness. Deep down, the British still feel pretty satisfied with themselves.

What we are driving at may come out more clearly if we use the method of contrast. There are peoples who are, *as peoples*, aggrieved, unhappy, who nurse unsatisfied ambitions, whose national pride is sensitive—peoples with national inferiority complexes. That they often, and perhaps usually, are morally justified in their attitude need not at this moment concern us; we are trying hard to describe, not to praise or blame. Though it will give offense to many good people to cite them, we may give as examples the Irish, the Poles, and thanks to the unhappy events of recent years, the once fairly serene and self-assured French. From a lofty and perhaps inhuman position of neutrality, these peoples look like problem children; they have to be handled delicately, like the patients which in a sense they are. The British afford no such problem.

They do, indeed, afford an opposite sort of problem. Their national self-assurance—especially if it is reënforced by various class traits into that effortless sense of superiority said to be the special stamp of Oxford and Cambridge on their sons—makes it extremely hard for foreigners to get along with them. Anglophiles like to point out that the British really aren't snobs, that it's only their manner, and that once you have broken the ice the Britisher, if not precisely a hale-fellow-well-met, is really a very decent fellow, quite willing to compromise, and in fact much easier to get along with than peoples more superficially pliable and accommodating. This is probably true of the great majority of Britishers—but the manner remains, and takes some adjusting to, as many an American government official or soldier in the recent war can testify.

Among the upper classes especially, British self-assurance takes the (to us) odd form of an incurable addiction to understatement. We Americans, save perhaps for a few backward Yankees, do our boasting openly and unashamedly; characteristically, what we have of folk literature is the tall tale—Paul Bunyan and his compeers. It may well be that our fondness for hyperbole often masks a certain lack of self-assurance. It is true also that our tall tales, as a Mark Twain tells them, for instance, are satirical attacks on pretense and vainglory. You can burst a bubble as well by blowing it up too far as by pricking it. But such matters are too foreign and too subtle for the Englishman to understand. When he hears an American talk big, he thinks the American is an offensive boaster. Similarly, when an American hears an Englishman apologize for almost everything, depreciate almost everything—especially things personal to himself—the American thinks the Englishman is a bit of a rabbit. Actually, the Englishman is just obeying a fashion no more than skin deep; when he says "Not much of a show, this" he really means in American "We've got a swell outfit." A social psychologist with time on his hands could no doubt delve pretty deeply into this matter, and come up with some interesting reflections; we may here be pardoned for noting merely that for the future of Anglo-American relations it really is a superficial matter. It is a good thing for people of both nations to note as one of the striking differences between the two—and then not exaggerate it by worrying about it. Above all, neither should try to imitate the other; in social intercourse between the two peoples, one may even say that the more picturesquely American an American is, the more he succeeds with the British; and, of course, the converse is true. Imitation here may be the truest, but it is certainly not by any means the most effective, form of flattery.

Second, and again consequent at least in part on the successful role of Britain in modern history, Britishers display a very wide toleration of individual differences among themselves, and even among others. The trait comes out most clearly as a willingness to tolerate, indeed it seems at times a willingness to encourage, individual eccentricities. If you wore a straw hat and a fur coat to a football game in America the odds are overwhelming that you would get the hat knocked off before you had gone very far; if you did the same thing at a varsity rugby match in England you would probably find that most people were trying rather uncomfortably, and certainly rather conspicuously, not to notice you at all; and even if you tried it at a more plebeian professional soccer match, you would probably meet nothing worse than a few jeers. Let there be no mistake— the British have some very rigid codes of behavior, notably the public-school code, and individuals who do not do the right things and avoid doing the wrong things soon find themselves rejected. But this fact does not produce as much leveling and uniformity as we observe in democratic countries like the United States and France, let alone deliberately totalitarian societies like Germany, first because the British upper-class code encourages variation, once a few essentials are complied with, and second, because the structure of British society is so definitely a class structure that lower and middle-class people can unashamedly have codes of their own.

The point has often been made: the British, socially at least, prefer liberty to equality. There is the individual liberty of the every-Englishman's-home-is-his-castle sort, the liberty that has its extreme in oddity and eccentricity. But even more important is the great freedom with which the British form voluntary associations. Such associations are perhaps quite as common with us, and they are in a sense a mark of Western civilization. Even in France, where there are supposed to be fewer of these group loyalties between the individual and the state, there are really many voluntary societies; Frenchmen too form leagues, clubs, and societies of all sorts, even a *ligue contre l'alcoölisme*. But the British still do an extraordinary number of things by voluntary association that with us are done by the government. Most visitors to England have noticed on shop counters the miniature lifeboats, with slots for coins, inviting contributions for a society which does what our Coast Guard does. The most generous of our soldiers in Britain have admitted themselves to be a bit worn out by the extraordinary number of good causes which have their special flag days (tag days); but the British go right on patiently putting a few coppers in boxes held out to them in the streets by young ladies, and receiving paper flowers, flags, crosses, and what-not for their lapels as a sign that once more they have done their duty. Hardly had the Allies got to North Africa in 1942 when advertisements appeared in *The Times* requesting contributions for a society for the protection of horses from their unfeeling Arab masters.

This last suggests a fact noted by many British critics, that many of these societies are devoted to good causes in lands not quite up to British humanitarian standards. It was a stock reproach made by British radicals in the last century that the men of Manchester would join societies for the protection of horses in Timbuctoo, but would not pay their own workmen adequate wages. The reproach was not quite unfounded, but it does not cut very deep. A vast amount of time and money has been spent by humane societies in the home islands.

This freedom of association suggests a third note in British life; the British do a lot of things voluntarily, or at least habitually, which in other societies require some form of state action, because they are essentially law-abiding, because the machinery of law on the whole works smoothly. This is conspicuously a product of their recent history, their recent successes. For the British have not always been law-abiding. On the contrary, in the eighteenth century they had, quite justifiably, a reputation for being unruly, riotous, hard to govern. To Frenchmen in 1780, serene in the apparent stability of their monarchy, the British were incurable revolutionaries who had cut off one king's head and chased another, had had to put down the Old Pretender in 1715 and the Young Pretender in 1745, had just made a mess of things in their North American colonies, and in that very year had indulged themselves in the Lord George Gordon Riots, when London was for three days in the hands of a raging mob—or at any rate, a drunken mob. The political stability of Britain is a comparatively new thing.

It has by now become fixed in habit, and can stand fairly big shocks; there is, for instance, the familiar tale of strikers and policemen playing football during the abortive General Strike of 1926. The British are occasionally somewhat priggish about their respect for the law. A young English exchange student in America during the Prohibition era used firmly to refuse cocktails with the remark that of course he drank when he was home in England, but that like all good Englishmen he believed in respecting the laws of the country in which he was a guest. He was not a great success in America. It is no doubt idle to speculate whether this respect for law, this willingness to abide by customary forms of settling questions by discussion and voting, could withstand a period of grave internal economic and political difficulties of the sort that certainly threatens Britain today. One thing, however, is clear; a long period of stability has given the British certain political *habits* which, like all human habits, are essentially conservative and are not easily eradicated; they have in their law-abiding habits, if not complete insurance, at least a kind of backlog against violent revolutionary change.

Whether these habits are so ingrained as to make slow evolutionary change too difficult is an even harder problem. For nearly two centuries, certainly, Britain has undergone, without serious political and economic violence, changes as great as any society has undergone. We have already pointed out that Liverpool is almost as "new" a city as Chicago. The process was not wholly without industrial violence—the anti-machine riots of the early nineteenth century, a whole series of strikes—nor wholly without political crises—the near-revolution of 1832 when parliament was first reformed in the direction of democratic suffrage, the Chartist troubles of the 1840's, the crisis over the powers of the House of Lords in 1911. But on the whole the process of change has been so orderly that we must list as a fourth trait of the British their reputation for conservatism.

Here, perhaps, their reputation is not altogether deserved. As tourists, we Americans note the survivals of medieval ceremonies, the Beefeaters at the Tower of London, the old castles and cathedrals, the half-timbered houses, the bewigged lawyers, the royal procession to open a session of parliament, the Renaissance heating arrangements, the hardly more than Renaissance plumbing. We note that the British are proud, in their usual apologetic manner, of all this surface medievalism. We hear them talk in the gentle tone of mock irony, which is the public-school way of boasting, about their incurable conservatism. And we are fooled—which is quite natural, since in these matters the British have already succeeded in fooling themselves. We do not readily seize the fact that much of this British reverence for the past is on a par with our own ancestor-hunting, our own reconstruction of Colonial Williamsburg, our own Mr. Ford's paradoxical devotion to the Early American he has done so much to destroy, our own worship of the Founding Fathers. It is, perhaps, no more than the necessary emotional counterbalance in a society undergoing all sorts of fundamental social, political, and economic changes. But it should not blind us to the reality of those changes: the Britain that produced the Mosquito bomber, that proposed the Beveridge Plan, that passed the Education Act of 1944, that attempted the great experiment of nationalization of banking, coal mining, and transportation, is not precisely old-fashioned.

No one can study the British people without encountering their pride in what they usually consider their superiority to mere logic. They are especially fond of contrasting themselves in this respect with the logic-ridden French. Once more, we are dealing with popularly accepted stereotypes. The land that produced Bacon, Darwin, and other great scientists has clearly produced logical thinkers of a very high order. But we need not here go into such complicated questions as whether or not British cultural genius has a depth not found in reason-loving Frenchmen. For us, the important point is the political implications of the British belief that they are superior to logic. If you define logic in politics as the pursuit of abstract principles to their bitter and uncompromising end, then the British are singularly free from addiction to logic in politics. They have had their abstract political extremists—William Godwin's *Political Justice* of 1794 objected to the orchestra leader's baton as a tyrannical interference with the individual liberty of the players—but as a people they have not since the seventeenth century followed political extremists. The British, perhaps even more than other Western peoples, are fond of their old and "irrational" institutions, such as the House of Lords, for instance, and they often use such institutions to give themselves the comfortable feeling of permanence in the midst of change; and they accept in practical politics compromise solutions which do not fully satisfy the expressed aims of active extremists. This is all the famous British superiority to logic comes to. It does not differentiate them as much from other peoples, notably ourselves, as many Britishers like to think it does.

A sixth note of British life is the hardest of all for Americans to get themselves straight about, hardest because in the eyes of the rest of the world we share this trait with the British; here, to understand the British we have to understand ourselves, which is always difficult. But if you read French, German, or almost any continental comment on the British, you will be struck with the recurrence of phrases like "perfidious Albion," "British hypocrisy," and so on. A distinguished Italian publicist is fond of saying, "When you hear the British say that they are no doubt dull and stupid, but at least honest, beware! They are about to double-cross you." Or take the famous phrase, "the white man's burden," for the Empire. British liberals and radicals have never been very fond of that phrase, and today you will rarely hear it from British lips save in irony—which may possibly be not altogether a good sign for the future of the Empire. But in Victorian days a lot of British-ers were really sincerely moved by the feeling that they were trustees for less developed darker-skinned peoples. To Germans or Frenchmen, however, India, for instance, hardly looked like a burden; or at any rate, it was the kind of burden they would gladly see their own country assume. We Americans were asked by some of our leaders, notably Senator Beveridge, to take up a similar burden after the Spanish–American War. But this phase of our national history proved no more than temporary.

There are a number of reasons why the British acquired this reputation for hypocrisy, but the main one is clearly this: Britain had managed to acquire a great deal of the world's wealth and territory. It is true that it was often said that Britain had blundered into Empire in a fit of absent-mindedness, but to less successful peoples this seemed hardly plausible. They thought wealth was usually acquired by rather shady means, and it seemed to them likely that the British had acquired it so. Moreover, the British really had as a people certain obvious virtues—law-abidingness, toleration, cleanliness—and many of them were on occasion a bit priggish. Hypocrisy and priggishness are not identical, but in their outward manifestations they are easily mistaken one for the other. In international affairs British statesmen and publicists always took a high moral tone in favor of the sacredness of treaties and the need for honesty and openness in international dealings; to which their European rivals would reply that strict adhesion to established arrangements is obviously to the advantage of those whom the arrangements benefit—that, in fact, the British were now moral because they were successful, and successful because they had once immorally grabbed so much. We Americans are likely to hear this last argument made against us quite a bit in the next few years—not inconceivably by a few Britishers, among others.

Self-assurance, willingness to tolerate eccentricity, great freedom of association, law-abidingness, a curious mixture of conservatism and enterprise, a reputation for distrusting logic which they do not altogether deserve, a generally high standard of public morality which has seemed to their continental neighbors not unmixed with hypocrisy—these are generalizations which hold reasonably true of all classes of the British people. But there are real class differences in Britain, and no one could write sensibly about that country without attempting to describe some of these differences.

3. CLASS DISTINCTIONS IN BRITAIN

In England there is one singularly clear-cut class line which is the most important of all, and which has no exact parallel in the United States—the line which separates gentlemen from those who are not gentlemen. We may anticipate briefly here what we shall have to consider at greater length in the latter part of this book, and point out that this war has strengthened in Britain a feeling which has been growing for a long time, that it is not really a good thing to have a society in which it is so easy even for a foreigner to tell who is a gentleman and who is not. In fact, the British tend a bit to avoid the word "gentleman" and almost entirely eschew "lady"; but the phenomenon is there, and you do not change it by using terms like "upper class," "ruling class," "possessing class," and the like.

A word of warning. We Americans do not get ourselves forward much in the necessary task of understanding the British if we tell them—and ourselves—that we have nothing like class distinctions in the United States. We have, indeed, produced one of the most cutting phrases in all the arsenal of snobbery; "She was born on the wrong side of the railroad tracks." And on what is perhaps the gentler side of such matters, it is clear that there are regions in Boston, Philadelphia, Charleston—and, in spite of the opinion of most Americans to the contrary, New York City—to which only birth can give access. But in America such matters do not worry even the self-made man, let alone the average citizen; in Britain they do.

In England, you can tell a gentleman by his accent. We all know that it is almost impossible for an American to acquire even a moderately convincing English accent; it is just as nearly impossible for an ordinary Englishman not born a gentleman to acquire a gentleman's way of speaking. It is not a matter of pronouncing one's *h's;* it is a far more delicate matter of vowel-quality, intonation, and rhythm. And accent is of course but the beginning—though it is by far the simplest single sign of membership, so simple that a foreigner with any kind of ear can recognize, even though he cannot imitate it. There are other signs—clothes, for instance, which are not always tweeds, and a whole set of ritual responses in the day-to-day routine of life, which can only be made properly automatic, unconscious, by early training. As in most societies, much of this training is done by the family; but in England—and this is the striking role of the public school—a much greater part of the training than is usual in most societies may be done in school.

For it is a commonplace of modern British history that, though at any given moment its upper class is so clearly defined that it may be not unfairly described as a caste, access to that caste from below is comparatively easy. The classic process is for the outsider to make good; making good is usually thought of, especially in novels and essays on English life, as making money, but it may mean no more than a modest penetration of university, church, bar, medicine, civil service, politics, press— any of the careers normal for a gentleman. Even in business, money-making need not be on a colossal scale. The outsider who has thus made good will find himself pretty well accepted, and unless he is an introvert much disturbed by his lack of the proper accent and other automatic responses, will not feel himself too much of an outsider. He will send his children away to school while they are still pretty young; the schools will give them the responses their parents did not have; the second generation, therefore, will be unquestionably accepted by their caste. Nearly two hundred years of this process in a state constantly growing in wealth and population have produced an upper class by no means small in numbers. The British census naturally does not deal with such matters, but it is clear that ladies and gentlemen must be numbered in the millions. You must not think of them as a small and oppressive aristocracy, even in a purely social sense; they are, if we may permit ourselves to be vulgarly American on the subject, a sort of glorified middle class.

They are not an absolutely homogeneous class. They display a great deal of individual variation, as well as those professional variations and group loyalties which are only beginning to be studied by sociologists. In many senses a British physician, for instance, is first of all a physician and only second a Britisher, or even a gentleman. Certainly those who during the war had the task of promoting good individual relations between our men in Britain and the British found that the safest way to start was to bring together Americans and Britishers who had the same vocations. There is, of course, at the top of the social hierarchy in Britain a titled aristocracy; but, just as with the upper class as a whole, assimilation of outsiders lifted to the peerage is relatively easy. The majority of British peerages today have been created within the last two centuries, and only a handful go back beyond Tudor times, that is, to the Middle Ages. Nobody can tell what has become of the famous Norman blood, but it seems to have got about as mixed as blood can be. There is also a very large fringe at the bottom of the inclusive class of gentlemen whose status, in spite of the clear sign of accent, is not altogether fixed. By and large, the career open to talents works for the continual enlargement of the gentlemanly class; it is, paradoxically, easier to go up than to come down. But there is a certain amount of downward movement, brought on almost always by economic failure; in the nineteenth century, much of this was taken care of by emigration to the United States or the dominions.

The clearest rift in the upper class is described by Mr. Shaw as that between "Horseback Hall" and "Heartbreak House." Horseback Hall is the hunting set, the people who play games, live in the country, provide the officer-class in Army and Navy (not nearly to the same extent in the Air Force), distrust the intellect and the arts, make up the "Die-Hards" of Tory politics. These are the people, caricatured no doubt unintentionally by Hollywood, who stand in American eyes as the typical English gentlemen. They are frequently by no means as unintellectual as they like to make out, and their wiser members are more resilient politically than they appear to be, but it would be foolish to maintain that even the Hollywood caricature is wholly without foundation. They are today over the whole class probably numerically inferior to the inhabitants of Heartbreak House.

Heartbreak House is the intellectuals, the people who read books and write them, who do a good deal of the work of governing, and who talk as much and as rapidly as any people on earth. They too live in the country as much as they possibly can. They are much less well known in the United States than the people of Horseback Hall, though Hollywood occasionally allowed the late Leslie Howard to play one of them. Like intellectuals elsewhere in the modern world, British intellectuals are in revolt against this unintellectual world, and some of them take refuge from it in the pleasanter world of their own ideas. But two world wars have disillusioned them, and to a certain extent toughened them. You will find in some of their weeklies the same symptoms of hyperacidity of the mind you will find in corresponding New York weeklies, but as a whole British intellectuals today are by no means in a mood of despair. They are more likely to live in Beveridge House than in Heartbreak House.

Most of the British upper classes belong in neither of these groups; they are just ordinary privileged men and women, most of them with responsible jobs and desirous of maintaining their position in the community. They are aware that their position is challenged by the demand of the masses for higher standards of living, and some of them are as frightened by the Red Menace as any members of the ruling class in other countries. But, if they are compared with their opposite numbers in most of Western Europe, they still seem like an effective ruling class. You will not find them panicky, as the ruling classes of the French Third Republic were panicky before the war. They are still willing to compromise, still willing to absorb outsiders. Their successful absorption of Ramsay MacDonald is perhaps too good a case in point; but in a quieter way they seem to be taking up much of the Labour Party. Finally, they display, despite what seems to many Americans the undue refinement of their manners, some of the toughness, the streak of iron, without which a ruling class in this harsh world is doomed. The English gentleman, much as it may pain innocent American Anglophiles to be told it, can still on occasion be ruthless—even Machiavellian.

This brings us to the real British middle class. The great majority of the people in the offices, stores, and government services, is still one of the world's great middle classes. Their economic position has been shaken by the inflation consequent upon two wars and by the scarcely corrective deflation of the Great Depression. But they have never suffered as the German middle classes have suffered, and like the rest of the nation they retain a good many of the Victorian ways—more, perhaps, than any other class in Great Britain. They still preach, and what is more, practice, middle-class morality. They are a perfectly literate people, but even in Scotland they are not a well-read people. One has the impression that, compared with the corresponding class in America, they are not very curious about the world they live in; they do not go to lectures, forums, and otherwise show as much interest in adult education as we do. And yet that is a very risky generalization. Cheap books, especially books giving surveys of serious subjects, are very popular in Britain nowadays. The British are even reading about the history of the United States, something they have never done before. They never have been quite as insular as the intellectuals who wrote novels damning them have made out, partly because it is a rare British family that has not some connection—through emigration, the merchant marine, or the navy—with the outside world. But they are, if you like, a type middle class, conservative, unimaginative, hard-working (in spite of their fondness for afternoon tea)—the well-known backbone of the nation. They were never, as a class, bold and enterprising. The bold and enterprising individuals who as inventors, entrepreneurs, and managers achieved the Industrial Revolution were exceptional persons, and they have usually risen into the ruling class. This process is still going on. Furthermore, the middle class as a whole, if not precisely rising in the world, is tending through education to get externally a little more like the upper classes.

The democratic process of leveling has also been at work among the British laboring classes—or, in a phrase no longer as frequently and as unselfconsciously used in modern Britain as it was in Victorian times, the lower classes. There are still slums in urban Britain and still poverty in rural Britain. But the standard of living of the British masses has clearly risen since the days when Hogarth painted the horrors of the gin-ridden proletariat of the eighteenth century and Dickens described the miseries as well as the humors of the English lower

classes in the nineteenth century. Not so long ago, the British
working man was known as boisterous, earthy, and addicted to
strong drink and rioting. He has not by any means been turned
into a dull, conforming, proper fellow, but he has been to a
certain extent tamed and disciplined by religion (eighteenth
and early nineteenth-century Methodism began his taming),
education, trades-unionism, and the modest, but real, protection of social security laws, which in Britain date from the
early years of the twentieth century.

The class is by no means uniform. On an economic basis, it
may be conveniently broken down into the more modest of the
white-collar (the British say "black-coated") workers, the
domestic workers, the rural laborers, and the industrial workers. It is this last group, now almost completely unionized,
that one thinks of first of all as the "British working man."

As in other modern economies, including our own, the white-
collar worker in Britain, clerical workers, retail shop assistants,
the lower grades of the civil service, and the like, tend to as-
similate themselves to the middle class, into which the more
enterprising of them not infrequently rise. They are not usually
unionized, and they are not as well paid as the skilled industrial
workers. They suffered greatly in the depression of the last
two decades, and they clearly caught some of the spirit of dis-
content common to their class in the modern world. They
were not, however, as were their German counterparts, won
over to a totalitarian philosophy. It seems pretty clear that the
votes of this numerous class of white-collar workers were for
the first time almost universally cast for Labour in July, 1945,
and determined the extent of the Labour landslide. But it
would be a great mistake to conclude that they have now become a well-disciplined, class-conscious proletariat in the
Marxian sense. They want social security, and for the most part
they are quite willing to have the government take a large part
in the economic organization of Britain. They cannot, however, at once throw overboard their heritage of middle-class
gentility, their middle-class habits of mind. It is probable that

in Britain as in the United States a great many of them should be classed as "independent" voters, and as one of the chief elements in the pendulum-like swing of democratic politics from Right to Left and back again.

The British servant class has long been dwindling under economic and social pressures of a kind not unlike those at work in this country. Even before the war, the servantless apartment and small house were taking the place of the big, old-fashioned nineteenth-century house. Under the rigorous mobilization of British manpower and womanpower during the war, domestic servants almost disappeared. They will reappear, but almost certainly in diminished numbers. The type, dear to novelists and to Hollywood, is too well fixed to die out entirely and at once. There will always—well, for a long time— be a Jeeves. But as a class with an important place in British life the old deferential British servant class seems to have died out. War service in the armed forces and in war industries has given them a new independence.

Britain is not, like France, for instance, a land of small farm-owners. The "farmer" himself may own his land, usually a farm of fairly large size for an intensive agriculture, but he is more likely to rent it on a long-term lease, or manage it for a big landowner. In any case, the "farmer" is a capitalist and a manager, and there are not many of them. The majority of rural England is made up of "agricultural laborers," landless men working for hire, not well paid or well housed in comparison with their urban fellow countrymen who have jobs, but still not a true rural proletariat, and much better off than their ancestors of a century or so ago. They are, of course, in so urbanized a nation, in a definite minority, but they are important in many of the farming counties of the South and Midlands. They are not a migratory class, but almost as fixed to their jobs as if they were landowners. They are good workers, generally sober and steady, conservative and provincial as such people are all over the world. But they too have been touched by modern conditions. Not so long ago, the rural workers really behaved as they were supposed to in Victorian novels. An American visitor at a "house" in an English village (there was one house, or at most two or three "houses," where the gentlemen lived; the rest were all "cottages"; the distinction was of a piece with that between an Anglican "church" and a nonconformist "chapel") found, even as late as after the war of 1914–1918, that the village men and boys tipped their caps to him, or touched their forelocks. By 1942, that deferential gesture had almost wholly disappeared. Again, it must not be assumed that the British countryman has turned revolutionist, that he wants to seize the land for himself, or make Britain into a land of collective farms on the Russian model. But, like his fellows in the cities, he wants social security and a higher standard of living. British war-time government control of agriculture seems to have convinced him that he can best get these things through some measure, at least, of continued government planning and control.

British industrial workers, skilled and unskilled alike, are now pretty completely unionized. They form the old nucleus of the Labour Party, to which they have long been faithful. Their leaders have been and are most important in the Labour Party, in which, though this may surprise some Americans, they are generally regarded as a conservative influence. Trades-unionism in Britain is of such long standing that it has acquired routines and habits. Its leaders are nowadays rarely revolution-ists, and indeed seem to many British intellectual Leftists to be merely another kind of bureaucrat. We must not exaggerate: the present temper of the British laboring men, leaders and led alike, is undoubtedly radical. The war has stimulated both their hopes and fears, and they have taken full part in the lively debate over the future of Britain which has come out of Army education and the general ferment of ideas in Britain. They do not want to go back to unemployment and the dole, and they do not want their children to have to fight another world war. They often call themselves "socialists." Indeed, it was not uncommon for a British soldier in an Army discussion group to preface his remarks with "Of course, I'm a socialist" —a remark one very rarely heard in corresponding discussion groups in the American Army in Britain. But it is significant that these British soldiers did not say, "Of course, I'm a communist," and only a handful of Britishers voted Communist in 1945. What they really want is a middle way between unrestricted private enterprise and full government control of industry. They believe they can get this and still preserve the British heritage of democratic individualism. Their present temper is radical, but not revolutionary.

Even in Victorian times, the British working man was not a very deferential fellow. He never, as Mr. Shaw so often pointed out, and most clearly in *Pygmalion*, completely espoused "middle-class morality." He remains an apparently incurable gambler, spending his money on football pools and race-track betting in a way his betters think unfortunate. He is fond of his pub, the "poor man's club." There is no American equivalent of the British public-house, which fulfills some of the functions of the corner drug-store, the pool-room, and the old-fashioned saloon in this country. Not that the pub is by any means a lower-class institution. All classes, especially in the country and in the small town, patronized the pub, which was divided into "public bar," "saloon bar," "private bar" according, presumably, to class lines it was difficult for a foreigner to appreciate, for very few Americans could ever figure out into just which one they should go. Britishers probably knew by instinct. But here too democracy is at work, and the newer pubs and roadhouses are often built without these puzzling compartments. The British working man is very fond of watching soccer football, as well as of betting on it. He by no means confines himself to genteel urgings like "Well played, sir," but can make as much noise as an American baseball fan. It is still, however, not British practice to bait the umpire.

The British working man shares many of the national traits we have already outlined. He has no national inferiority complex, and feels generally superior to foreigners, but rather good-humoredly, and without the acid of race feeling. He is tolerant, as human beings go, fond of and used to discussion, and not the stuff of which totalitarians are made. He is almost as fond of his garden, his fenced-off little semi-detached house, as ill at ease in huge communal housing (though such housing exists, and is increasing) as the middle class. Indeed, the trait stereotyped as "every Englishman's home is his castle" is at bottom quite as true of the working man as it is of other Englishmen. Urban life has made him more gregarious than the upper-class Englishman, but he is nothing like as gregarious as Russians, Germans—or Americans. And finally, he remains essentially a law-abiding person. Under a new depression, he may revert to his old rebellious self of the seventeenth and eighteenth centuries. But right now it looks as if the leveling process of British democracy, which has certainly been in part a leveling-up, has made the British working man too much like the rest of his countrymen to be a good revolutionary.

PART II THE BRITISH ISLES IN THE WAR

5. The Effect of the War on Britain

Six years of war have brought many and profound changes in all aspects of British life. They may well have prepared the way for that "revolution by consent" in Britain about which so much has been heard both from Britishers and from foreign commentators. But we must not lose perspective; not even total war means total change in a modern community. The social and economic changes now going on in Britain are part of a process which set in towards the end of the nineteenth century, when Britain's industrial supremacy began to be challenged by the rising power of Germany and the United States. This war has undoubtedly accelerated the process of change, and may well have given it here and there a new direction. But it has not accomplished the impossible—a complete alteration in the institutions, traditions, habits, and sentiments which make up the way of life of a great people. Some human ways change with an almost geological slowness, a slowness often masked by the tendency of publicists to use sweeping terms like "revolution." Indeed, it is not altogether misleading to say that as agents of social change wars and revolutions may be compared with earthquakes and other rapid forms of geological change. In societies as on the face of the earth, other slower and less spectacular forms of change are more important.

The final figures are not yet certain, but it is already clear that in human lives this war was not as costly to the United Kingdom and the Commonwealth as was the last. Even including civilian deaths from enemy action—some 60,000—the

figure of actual deaths will not exceed half of the 950,000
Commonwealth deaths in the armed forces of the war of
1914–1918. And as yet this war has had no aftermath of epi-
demic influenza. In almost everything else measurable by statistics, the cost of this war to Britain already far exceeds that
of the last war. Direct destruction in the home islands, confined in the last war to the almost negligible damage done by
Zeppelins and coastal shelling, has not been exactly measured
as yet. As good an index as any of its extent is afforded by
the estimate that there are over 4,000,000 dwellings in the
British Isles in need of some kind of repair because of enemy
action. Some of these dwellings are mere rubble, and irrepa-
rable; others have minor damage to windows or roofs, and
have already been patched up. But the sum total is staggering.
The damage to the wealth of Britain—to its "plant"—from six
years of neglect, of failure to do more than the absolute minimum of upkeep—may well be even greater. The British Information Services, in a pamphlet of 1947 entitled *Fifty Facts
about Britain's Economic Position*, estimates the total losses at
about $625 per head of the population, or about one-quarter of
the national wealth.

Yet Britain is by no means a land of "scorched earth." Its
countryside and its small towns and villages have been largely
untouched by enemy action. Even in Greater London the destruction is less than some alarmist American reporters have
made out. The incendiary bombings of 1940–1941 left large
areas, especially around St. Paul's, in a desolation like that of San
Francisco in 1906. Damage from V-weapons, though extensive, was scattered throughout the area of Greater London. No
one wishes to make light of the destruction total war has made
in Britain, nor of the sufferings her people have so courageously
borne. But the sheer physical damage done is not as extensive
as it is in areas where air warfare has been supplemented by
land warfare in Normandy, Italy, Germany, and Russia. The
economic cost of this war to Britain is very high, but it is not
so high that it cannot be paid by hard and intelligent work
and the British people are quite prepared to pay it.

1. INDUSTRIAL CONTROLS

The war has brought to Britain a whole series of changes which may be summed up as a tightening of the controls exercised by government over the activities—and especially the economic activities—of individual citizens. It should be clear at once that this is no war-made novelty, but part of a tendency clear even in the United States and which has been going on all over the world ever since those now far-off days of the early nineteenth century when most men in Western society assumed it as axiomatic that "that government governs best which governs least—and most cheaply." The war of 1914–1918 had already brought a great tightening of such controls—had, if you like to put it that way, brought Britain close to a form of "collectivism." There was after 1918 a rapid relaxing of these controls. The war, however, brought them back in even stronger and more efficient forms. War-time Britain was in fact a thoroughly regimented society, for the great majority of Britishers were convinced that only by such regimentation could they mass their strength against their enemies. It was, in a very real sense, a voluntary regimentation, and did not seem therefore oppressive to those who underwent it. To the problem—one of the key problems for the understanding of modern Britain—of how the British people feel about the nature and extent of "de-control" after the war we shall later return.

There is no need here to rake over the coals of controversy about Britain's slowness in getting ready for this war. History will probably be a little kinder towards the Chamberlain government than contemporaries can now be. At the very least, it must be recorded that the weapon that saved Britain and the world, the Royal Air Force, was forged in the 1930's. It really took Narvik and Dunkirk to galvanize Britain into total mobilization of her strength. Though beginnings were made after declaration of war in September 1939, most of the rigorous measures which marked a Britain wholly dedicated to the war date from the summer of 1940. It is not within the scope of this book to record these measures in detail; we must content ourselves with a general view of what they have achieved.

Through a series of National Service Acts and Essential Work Orders British manpower—and womanpower—were harnessed in military and civilian war work. Men from eighteen to forty-one and women from nineteen to twenty-four years of age were made liable to military conscription. Practically all able-bodied men and women not in the armed forces were liable to what must be called labor conscription. The system of directed labor, to give it a kinder name, was certainly not tyrannically administered, nor did it result in a Britain where every single healthy adult was doing war work. Married women with dependent children were not conscripted, and this of course is the most numerous group of women. The government sought to keep going as much as possible of the routine life of a modern society, so that one could find beauty parlors, small retail shops, department stores, movies—and even a few taxicabs. But all such services were cut to the bone, and many normal goods, such as household utensils and furniture, were manufactured in minimum quantities and only in "austerity" models, so that the market for them was almost wholly a second-hand one. The government did not hesitate to direct men and women into necessary jobs even though that meant moving them away from home. Statistics on these matters could be piled up at great length; perhaps the most enlightening one is the government's own estimate that by 1944 two out of three adults between the ages of fourteen and sixty-five were doing some kind of war work or were in the armed forces.

All this was not achieved without stresses and strains, without some public complaint, without some government mistakes. The simpler American Anglophiles do Britain a disservice by insisting that in Britain such things are done with superhuman perfection. They thereby fail to bring out the essentially similar nature of the democratic process in both countries.

There were wartime strikes in Britain, as there were in America; so far as we know, there were no wartime strikes in Germany, but the price paid by Germany for this exemption seems a trifle high. British strikes were not, however, long or numerous; that there were any at all did indeed give rise to many indignant letters to the editor and to some grumbling among the forces, but it seems clear that most servicemen and women, who in peace are working men and women, felt that a certain number of strikes is inevitable in a society based on free trades-unionism. In the first access of energy after Dunkirk it is clear that workers of all classes tried to do the impossible. All restrictions as to hours were thrown overboard, and twelve-hour daily shifts in a seven-day week were not uncommon. It soon became obvious that with all the patriotic will in the world, such hours were too much, and that total output lost rather than gained from exhausted workers. Working hours were reduced, but even in the sixth year of war a sixty-hour week for men and a fifty-five-hour week for women were quite usual. Mistakes were made in the direction of labor supply, especially in the vital coal industry. Indeed, save to dogmatists who blame everything on "nationalization," it is clear that many of the difficulties that now plague the British coal industry date from these war policies. Too many experienced young and middle-aged miners were taken for the armed forces, and their places filled with men who had quit the industry before the war. These had quit usually because they were not the most skilled miners, and as a result output suffered. By 1943 the government was obliged to select by lot some of the eighteen-year-olds who came up for military conscription and send them into the mines. It is asking a lot of lads who had dreamed of themselves in the blue uniform of the RAF to accept the hard, unpublicized work of a coal miner. Some few refused, and the whole matter was aired in press and parliament. But the government refused to yield, and—this does almost look like a revolution—some public-school boys went to work as miners. There were other difficulties. Remembering the grave inroads of 1914–1918 on the intellectual leadership of the nation, the government made a serious attempt to "reserve" from military conscription young men who showed promise in their studies, especially in the field of the natural sciences. Government never wholly gave in to the protest that such reservation was "undemocratic," but they yielded somewhat and it seems likely that in proportion to the total casualties this war will cause as great a drain on Britain's gifted young men as did the last.

Management in industry was put under government control as thoroughly as was labor. Firms producing nonessential goods were obliged to switch to the production of essentials. Those left in industries marginally essential—that is, producing consumer goods for normal human needs—were made to work at a minimum rate, to consolidate temporarily with other firms in the same industry, to move into joint factories and storehouses, thus making more space available for war industries. Supply of raw materials, both domestic and imported, was put under direct government control. Prices were fixed all along the line from raw materials to the finished retail product. Wages, too, were fixed, and foreign exchange rigidly controlled. The result was a remarkable stability of price levels. The threat of inflation exists for post-war Britain, as for most of the nations of the world, but grave wartime general inflation was avoided. Private businesses were not actually taken over by the government, but the whole economic process was so completely controlled that little "free enterprise" was left.

2. RATIONING

All classes of Britishers have for nearly ten years been submitted to a strict system of rationing which has covered almost all articles of food and clothing. Food rationing has been under the control of the Ministry of Food, a special wartime ministry;

all other rationing has come under the long-established Board of Trade. Both ministries have power of price fixing as well as rationing. The Ministry of Food has often gone the whole way towards what must be called socialism; it has bought stocks of food, both home-grown and imported, and taken charge of the whole process by which the food went to the ultimate consumers. But usually even the Ministry of Food has made use of the established commercial system, especially its retail outlets, and both ministries have relied heavily on the collaboration of the business community, which has been given with a willingness which is certainly in part due to the keen awareness of every Britisher that after Dunkirk there was no sense debating over bureaucracy, socialism, free enterprise, or any other ideological problem.

By the end of 1942, food rationing had been so successful that the Minister of Food, Lord Woolton, was next to Mr. Churchill the most popular man in the Government. It seems clear that the basic condition for this success was the popular knowledge that in the beleaguered and thickly populated island strict food rationing was essential. Those who indulge in the popular pastime of comparing to American discredit the working of food rationing in the two countries usually overlook the fact that in the United States this basic condition did not have anything like the same strength as in Britain. Other factors, however, undoubtedly contributed to the British success. The complete vertical control exercised by the Ministry of Food over the whole process of feeding the nation, and its unshared power of price fixing was one such factor. Another was the fixed-quantity rationing of basic foods, meat, milk, butter, margarine, cheese, and the requirement that the weekly ration of such foods be supplied through a regular retailer with whom the consumer was registered. This did a great deal to prevent "most-favored customer" privileges and under-the-counter sales. Flexibility was introduced by a limited-points system for canned goods. Supplies of bread, potatoes, and fresh vegetables were maintained in sufficient quantity so that they did not need to be rationed. The existence of a few unrationed protein foods—poultry, game, fish—and a few unrationed luxury foods which were free even from price fixing, like mushrooms, asparagus, strawberries, did not seem to arouse the anger of those who could not afford them. Restaurant meals were permitted without use of ration coupons, but the danger that this freedom would be allowed to give the rich a chance to eat which the poor did not have was averted by putting a price limit of five shillings —about one dollar—on all meals even in the most expensive restaurants, and permitting no more than three courses—soup or hors d'oeuvre, main dish, dessert. Permission granted to fashionable restaurants for cover charge, music, and the like rarely forced the price up over ten shillings. Moreover, the Ministry instituted cheap government-run restaurants, known as the British Restaurants, where food could be had for one shilling—twenty cents—for a three-course meal, and saw to it that industrial canteens with cheap meals were introduced in most war industries.

The result was that what food was available in Britain was spread more evenly over the whole population than it had ever been in peace time. It was not very varied food, but it had all the necessary calories and vitamins, and health statistics show that the British people have not suffered from undernourishment during the war. Indeed, everyone in Britain will tell you that the lowest 20 per cent of the population was better nourished than in peace time. This result, which seems fairly well established, has been brought about by the more equal distribution of meats and other proteins, and by a well-conducted campaign for the better use of vegetables and other "protective" foods. The Ministry of Food put front-page advertisements in the press, broadcast through the BBC, and used its own large staff of field workers to get the British housewife to make the best use of foods available to her. We are even told that British housewives have by this means been cured of their habit of boiling vegetables for hours on end; the cure has not yet spread to the average restaurant or hotel in Britain.

Clothes rationing was conducted by a point system based on the bare minimum of human needs; indeed both press and bureaucrats used to indulge in some obvious humor over the adjective "bare." An example of the standard taken, for instance, is the official estimate that a man can get on with one new suit every three years. Rationing was introduced, then, not merely to prevent a rise in prices and to procure a fair general distribution of clothing, but to discourage the production of clothing and make that much more productive power available for war goods. The result was a nation which in the sixth year of the war was certainly not well dressed. On the other hand, to an ordinary observer the British did not seem to deserve the epithet "shabby" some American reporters applied to them. Certainly one never saw them in rags. They seemed adequately, if not smartly, dressed.

There was a black market in Britain, but it was not an extensive one, and never roused public opinion. The courts early established precedents by severe fines and jail penalties, and this course was thoroughly approved by the people of Britain. It is certain that most Britishers have a holier-than-thou attitude towards what they think has been the practice of continental nations and of their American ally in regard to black markets. That their attitude is based on fact—for it is clear that British law-abidingness in general survived the temptation to illicit trading in rationed goods—unfortunately does not make it much easier for other peoples to put up with. Americans may console themselves with the knowledge that the British record was not perfect. There were black-market tailors who would put forbidden cuffs and pockets on men's suits, there were restaurants which served more than the statutory meals, there were ways of getting private motor-cars for forbidden journeys.

3. AGRICULTURE AND TRANSPORTATION

The farmer, still in most of the Western World nearest to the independence dear to classical economics, was during the war quite as much under government control as the worker and the business man. The Ministry of Agriculture took him firmly in hand, told him what he had to grow, even how much land he had to plow, regulated prices in collaboration with the Ministry of Food, and helped his labor supply with the sturdy young women of the Women's Land Army and with vacation camps for the harvest season. The results were extraordinary. Before the war Britain grew about 30 per cent of her food; by 1944 she was growing 70 per cent more than in 1939, or just over half her total food supply. Something like 7,000,000 acres of new arable, mostly in wheat and potatoes, were added, some of it submarginal land that had not been plowed for centuries; but the yield per acre was also increased on old lands. Though the great emphasis of the Ministry of Agriculture was naturally put on grains and potatoes, other foods were not neglected. Even tomatoes, of which the British people have become very fond in the last thirty years, were grown in greenhouses which used valuable coal. Eire helped furnish poultry, eggs, and meats which used to come from Denmark, Holland, and France. The milk supply was maintained at a level which permitted full supplies for children and nursing mothers, and even allowed at least half a pint a day for others. It is an interesting comment on the complex interdependence of the modern world that the remarkable addition to British arable which was the basis of all this agricultural achievement would never have been possible without the mechanical tractor. There were nowhere near enough draft animals available, and not enough labor to use them had they been available. The tractor saved the situation —and the tractor depended for fuel entirely on overseas production of gasoline and oil.

Transport was of course under strict control. Britain was

fortunate in being able to add to her own shipping many tons belonging to her allies, and these were all pooled. After the United States entered the war a combined board, as in the last war, directed all allied merchant shipping. On land, the British did not find it necessary to take over the railways, which immediately after the last war had been consolidated into four great systems. The railways themselves, in collaboration with the Ministry of Transport, made the many adjustments necessary for wartime operation. They were kept going with a minimum of new rolling stock, and with attention to upkeep confined to essentials rather than to looks. Americans who remembered the spick-and-span of British railways in normal times were at once struck with the unwashed windows and unkempt toilets of the passenger trains. But the essentials were not neglected, and though trains were always crowded and often late, the safety-record of British railways has been excellent. The public was urged to restrict its travel to unavoidable necessity; everywhere the traveling public was confronted with posters asking, "Is your journey *really* necessary?" It must be recorded that even the British public, conscientious and law-abiding though it is, did not wholly conform to such requests. Before the difficulties of rationing travel, however, the government recoiled. Absolute restrictions on travel were imposed only in certain coastal areas during the preparation for the invasion of the continent. Civilian motor travel in private vehicles was restricted from the start, and by the end of 1942 was limited to physicians, nurses, government officials and others to whom it was absolutely necessary. For ordinary motorists, gasoline was not rationed; it was simply forbidden them.

4. POLITICS NOT AS USUAL

Yet with all these restrictions, the Britisher was not deprived of what he has come to consider the normal democratic freedoms, the right to freedom of speech, of association, of election, of the press. We must not exaggerate; even with respect to these things, the ordinary citizen "knew there was a war on." The government had, and used, emergency war powers against individuals suspected of treason or sedition. Enemy aliens were rounded up, particularly after Dunkirk, and interned. Even so, a maximum of 23,000 out of 77,000 enemy aliens were interned, and many of these were subsequently released. Some of those interned were unquestionably good anti-nazis or anti-fascists, but it is not surprising that in the excitement of 1940 the authorities preferred to risk injustice to individuals rather than expose the country to the much publicized Fifth Column. Some native fascists, among them the notorious Sir Oswald Moseley, were also interned without benefit of *habeas corpus*. There was some public protest when Moseley was later released on grounds of illness, but on the whole the British people refused to get excited, and only a handful of British subjects were kept in confinement.

There were no general parliamentary or local elections during the German War but there were numerous by-elections brought on by death or retirement of individual members. By the "party truce" it had been agreed that the regular parties —Conservative, Liberal, and Labour—would not put up opposition candidates in a by-election, so that a Labour man, for instance, would be unopposed in a vacant Labour constituency. Actually, very few by-elections were entirely uncontested. The Commonwealth Party was not bound by the truce, and they managed to win four by-elections. Moreover, there was nothing to prevent any "independent" candidate from standing. By and large, the electorate conformed to the truce, and though there were over a hundred by-elections in the ten years of its life, the party structure of the Commons at the dissolution in June 1945 was still essentially the same as it was when parliament was new.

The truce did not entirely eliminate party politics from the press. Indeed, the British press was and is still clearly a free press. The government used its war powers to suppress only one paper, the Communist *Daily Worker*. That paper took in 1939 the line that war against a Germany that was obviously getting on well with Russia was wicked, and very few Britishers thought its suppression undemocratic. After June 1941 relations between Germany and Russia changed, and the *Daily Worker* was allowed to resume publication. It is true that the general tone of the British press was more subdued than in normal times. But this would seem to be the result of a sort of gentleman's agreement among journalists, an awareness of the need for national unity, perhaps also an awareness of the fact that the government could crack down if it wanted to. The government had, indeed, a weapon it could use without recourse to direct infringement of the freedom of the press; it controlled, as it controlled so many other commodities, the supply of paper, almost all of which is imported. The government does seem to have suppressed the violently anti-American French weekly *La Marseillaise*, published in London, by the simple method of refusing it paper. But it wisely refused to apply this method to the British press and the British book trade. Newspapers were reduced to a four-or-six-page format, and books and magazines appeared in a wartime austerity dress. Publishers were given so much paper; they could print on it what they liked, if it were not treasonous. Naturally there were complaints that publishers still preferred to print potential best-sellers rather than good solid works. But the best indication that the government did not manipulate the paper shortage politically is seen in the fact that the Left Book Club flourished all during the war. And the best indication that the war has not effected a complete revolution in British culture is shown by the fact that there are still new detective novels.

One of the most publicized effects of the war in Britain has been the further raising of the income tax until, in the very top income brackets, it takes 19s. 6d. out of the pound—that is, 97½ per cent—and averages 50 per cent. Here, however, the war has most clearly been no more than a culmination of a process that started even before the last war. Combined with very heavy death duties (inheritance taxes) the income tax has made it pretty well impossible for the owners of great estates to maintain them, and one by one these princely homes are reverting to the state or the National Trust to be maintained as museums, or are being taken over by schools, hospitals, and other institutions. The war has hastened leveling down at top levels, as it has apparently hastened leveling up at lower levels. But Britain is by no means a land of economic equality. There were in 1945 eighty persons with incomes after taxation of over £6,000, and 1,170 with incomes after taxation between £4,000 and £6,000. These numbers may seem incredibly few to Americans; but it must be noted that they refer to absolute *net* income after taxation and some allowances for expenses. There has been no general capital levy, though the effect of the death duties is that of an occasional capital levy. Under a lower income tax at the top brackets, which is possible though unlikely in the near future, the incomes of rich people would be greatly increased. Such people during the war have certainly been, in comparison with their earlier standard of living, reduced to a very bourgeois existence. That figure of fiction and fact, the old English servant, vanished almost completely, and has yet failed to reappear in numbers. The war unquestionably hastened, and the Labour victory unquestionably prolonged, a leveling, or, if you prefer, a democratizing, process in British life.

The war, then, brought government control to almost every aspect of British life. It multiplied government ministries and agencies, added thousands of civil servants to government pay rolls already filled with millions of men and women in the armed forces. It may, as many Britishers fear and many others hope, prove to be a firm entering wedge for something like permanent state socialism. But it must in fairness be reported that even in wartime Britain the atmosphere was not that of a totalitarian society. The ordinary man could, and did, complain about the government as much as he liked; there was no Gestapo, no government spying. The press could, and did, debate the fundamentals as well as the details of politics; indeed, even Mr. Churchill was not during the German war nearly so free from criticism as many Americans thought he was. The election campaign of 1945 was free and quite unrestrained. And even the huge machinery of control was by no means a purely bureaucratic one. The Board of Trade, for instance, has made full use of the coöperation of trade associations and other business groups—indeed, such use that it has been accused in Leftist circles of laying the basis for great private monopolies in many fields. Control of the supply of labor has been made possible by collaboration between the Ministry of Labour and the unions. The Ministry of Agriculture did not simply send out its own bureaucratic agents to dictate to the farmers; instead, it secured the aid of hundreds of voluntary local committees. Indeed, this war has seen a proliferation of the kind of voluntary associations, each equipped with its president and its indispensable "hon. sec'y," we have already seen to be so characteristic of British life. There was always a law in the background, right down to such routine tasks as fire watching; and there were always teeth in the law. But at bottom there was also consent and coöperation. The result was undoubtedly often something less than the perfect efficiency we were told by German propagandists characterized the administration of the war effort in totalitarian societies; but it proved adequate to the job, and it has left Britain still a land where government is government by discussion—among the whole people, not just among the bureaucrats.

The election of 1945 was in some senses the protest of a people who had put up with the miseries of war, and who were taking the first decent occasion to show that they hadn't liked them. It was also the expression of new hopes among millions of ordinary British, who wanted to build better on the ruins of the old Britain. The Labour landslide surprised many commentators in the United States, and even in Britain. Yet no one who had talked to the men and women of the armed forces should have been greatly surprised. The hopes and fears of ordinary men and women combined to beat Mr. Churchill. The nation was, and remains, grateful to Mr. Churchill, but it could not believe that he was in 1945 willing to make the great experiments most British people found necessary. The Labour Party, for the first time in its history, won a clear majority over all combined opposition groups in the House of Commons.

5. FUNDAMENTAL EFFECTS ON MORALE

The British, then, *organized* themselves for total war in a way that would have made an enemy of the state like Herbert Spencer shudder, but they did not precisely fight fire with fire—they did not become totalitarians to defeat their totalitarian enemies. The war had, of course, wider effects than those it had on the structure of their government. These wider effects on the whole spirit of the people we may for convenience analyze as effects that make for a sense of fear and weakness, and those that make for a sense of hope and strength. As always in such analysis, we shall be separating and cataloguing something that in human experience is not so separated, but inextricably and quite illogically mixed in human hearts.

To take first the sense of fear and weakness. No matter how nonchalant a front the public-school manner may demand, the British know they cannot win alone against a foe like Germany. What the *Luftwaffe* began the V-weapons finished. The British are aware that their island has in fact been invaded, and that the barrier of the Channel has already sunk to little more than the level of a good tank trap. The war of 1914–1918, though it shook the strategic complacency which had been one of the mainstays of British isolationism, did not by any means destroy the common belief that as long as the British Navy was supreme the islands were safe from invasion.

This war has almost wholly destroyed that belief. It would scarcely be an exaggeration to say that ordinary Britishers feel as *exposed* as ordinary Frenchmen did after the last war. This does not mean that their reactions will be exactly like those of Frenchmen in 1919, though some striking parallels are already discernible. The British have sent the victorious Churchill, as the French sent the victorious Clemenceau, to political defeat. Americans often say that Churchill has had a "raw deal." The British said the same thing about Clemenceau. Psychologically at least, there is something in the formula: As Britain was to France in 1919, the United States is to Britain in 1945. However that may be, it is certain that a primary concern of Britishers in their international relations will be a desire for military security—security in the popular mind certainly from the German danger first of all, but also security from any dominant European power or combination of powers that may arise. The British are not clear, and certainly not unanimous, about how that security is to be attained. But the important point is that they no longer feel geographically and strategically safe from hostile invasion.

To this sense of strategic insecurity must be added a less recent sense of economic insecurity. Britain never attained what the economists call Full Employment in the period between the two wars. Though through her newer industries in the South and West she made some progress in the late twenties and in the late thirties, she suffered almost as badly as we did in the Great Depression; and in the depressed areas of her old industrial greatness—in the coal, steel, shipbuilding and textile area—she suffered from chronic unemployment for twenty years. And although the war and its aftermath have for the moment solved the problem of unemployment, every Britisher who pays any attention to public affairs knows that Britain has had to sell a large part of the foreign investments which helped to balance her international accounts. He knows that her merchant marine has been decimated, that, even though she did not have to settle in the conventional commercial way her debt to us under Lend-Lease, she has piled up large balances owed to countries like Eire, Argentina, Canada, and India. He knows that since V-E day Britain has been obliged to borrow further from the United States and from Canada.

However little he may know of theoretical economics, the average Britisher has heard too often the cry "Export or die" not to be greatly worried by a dilemma he feels to be very real. He has been told by his leaders that to keep up the standard of living and to maintain full employment Britain will have to increase her exports at least 50 per cent above their level of 1938. He wonders how, in a world where even India seems able to compete with his textiles, where the United States and Russia have under the stimulus of war built up even greater and more efficient industrial plants, where even Australia has begun her own manufactures, Britain can achieve this feat. He has heard the comforting assurances of the Atlantic Charter as to the possibility of a return to unhampered international trade; but his mind is full of twenty years of economic warfare, of blocked currencies, bilateral agreements, international cartels, tariff walls, and a lot else which he may not understand very clearly, but which he knows adds up to something very different from the conditions which prevailed in the great days of Mr. Gladstone. It is no wonder that he has moments of doubt and fear.

But he also has moments of confidence and hope; and, since he is the heir of generations who built Britain up to greatness, it is probable that such moments still determine his basic attitudes towards the world. First of all, British pride and self-assurance have been greatly strengthened by the knowledge that for twelve months Britain stood alone against the Axis powers, and held them off—not only held them off, but risked the offensive in Africa, and won. The British are, as peoples go, a reasonable people, and free from obsessive nationalism. They will tell you—and they mean it—that they know they could never have beaten the Germans without the aid of

Russia and the United States. They are profoundly grateful for that aid. But they will rarely admit that they think that Germany could ever have beaten *them*, even had they continued to stand alone. The aerial Battle of Britain in 1940 has already taken its place in British sentiment with Trafalgar as a purely British victory; if to finish off this tyrant, too, other peoples have had to join the British, if this Trafalgar has had to be followed by another Leipzig, another Waterloo, there remains to Britain the glory of having struck, alone, the blow that stopped the tyrant in his tracks. As to the reasonableness and historical justification of such sentiments it is unprofitable for us to argue with the British. The point is that they have these sentiments, and that these sentiments protect them from that self-pity and sense of inferiority which, in nations as in individuals, make them querulous and intractable. With all their fears for the future, the British still have deep within them that unreasonable and unreasoning confidence in themselves with which long ago they faced the invincible Spanish Armada. A young lieutenant hastily summoned from training camp in June 1940 and put in charge of a machine-gun squad at a Kentish road block remarked in the relative serenity of 1943, "You know, for all they said, I never really thought I'd see Jerry coming up that road." The playing fields of Eton again? No doubt, but not a fake, not a bluff. That next time the Armada may land, that the "few" may not be enough, the British know well enough, intellectually, and even in a sense emotionally. Right now they are determined to guard against that "next time" by every means within their power, including most emphatically international organization to keep the peace. But they also share the feelings of the subaltern at the road block in Kent; they cannot quite see Jerry on English soil.

Their economic fears, too, are balanced, perhaps overbalanced, by a sense of hope born of what they have achieved in this war. They have seen unemployment vanish almost overnight. They know that they have demonstrated the ability of their industrial system to produce in quantity such efficient instruments as the Mosquito bomber and the Spitfire fighter. They know that in the midst of war they have managed by their rationing system to redistribute the national income in such a way that the health and standard of living of their poorer class has actually improved. They are saying, as indeed men and women are saying in America, "If we can do all this in war time, why can't we do even better in peace time? Need we ever go back to poverty, depression, unemployment, now that we know such things can be overcome by human effort?"

This is, like all folk beliefs, a simple belief, and it ignores great difficulties—and a good deal of history. The historian can hardly avoid a reference to the fact that in 1918 Britain was to be made into "a land fit for heroes"; he must remind himself of other and contrary folk beliefs, that

> *When the devil was ill, the devil a monk would be;*
> *When the devil was well, the devil a monk was he.*

Yet history never crudely repeats itself; and furthermore, the modern mind is inclined to believe we can learn at least from recent history. A great many people in all walks of life seem determined that we should not repeat the mistakes of 1918–1919—though that determination does take at times the somewhat simple form of doing exactly the opposite of what was done then. In Britain, the slogan "a land fit for heroes" shares the disrepute of all slogans of the last war; but the British want all the more firmly a land fit for ordinary men and women.

Even in our short perspective, we can see that behind the many similarities, indeed identities, of the two last world wars, there is a profound difference. The war of 1914 was begun in the midst of general prosperity in a world where men believed that peace and progress, if not quite automatically assured, were none the less somehow in the order of nature. The war of 1939 was begun in the midst of a by no means overcome economic depression, in a world which had never recaptured the hopefulness of the nineteenth century. All over the world, men in 1918 wanted something that seems to us very naive: they wanted to get back to pre-war days. This time, even in the United States, we do not want to go back to the pre-war days of the Great Depression. In Britain, this feeling is much stronger; they do not want to go back to 1939.

This British determination not to repeat what they feel were the errors of 1919 is clear in many ways—in none, perhaps, clearer than in the opinion, held by business men as well as by workingmen, that "de-control"—the dismantling of the complicated government machine built up to fight the war—must not be undertaken hurriedly as in 1919, must not, probably, ever be done as completely as it was then done. It appears as a determination to end once and for all the German menace, to so organize international relations that peace will once more become, as it was in the best hopes of men of the last century, the *normal* human expectation. It appears as a determination to grapple this time firmly with all the problems of internal and external affairs that proved so insoluble in the twenty years' truce. It appears in the landslide of votes which swept Labour into office in spite of the real gratitude most Britishers feel for the war services of Mr. Churchill.

What made the atmosphere of wartime Britain seem to a sympathetic observer to be so full of hope, in spite of the fears he could not help noting among the British people, in spite of what his historical sense told him of the relative decline of Britain as a world power, was the thoroughness and basic reasonableness—even good temper—with which a whole people thrashed out the problems of their future. This great debate is still going on in a Britain still subject to many wartime restrictions and hardships. And it is, as it has not been since the turbulent days of their great puritan revolution in the seventeenth century, a whole people debating. Britain was indeed in the eighteenth and nineteenth centuries fecund in political thought, a laboratory for political and economic experiment. But her great middle class had by the nineteenth century lapsed into intellectual dullness, timidity, smugness, at which men like Matthew Arnold protested in vain, and her lower classes had as a whole failed to respond, as the corresponding classes in France and in the United States responded, to the ideas of 1776 and 1789. All this has changed, and so rapidly that one almost begins to believe there may be something in the slogan "Revolution by consent."

Basically, no doubt, adversity has been Britain's schoolmaster, and the great success in this war of British army education, of ABCA (Army Bureau of Current Affairs), and of other educational schemes in the armed forces, is rather an effect than a cause. But, whatever may be the reason, the British soldier talked then, as the British civilian is talking now, about the Beveridge Plan, about education, housing, nationalization, Anglo-American relations, plans for world organization for peace, and read about such matters, too. The British people, if they no longer read parliamentary debates as much as they used to, are reading the more substantial White Papers of the government, reading their newspapers and periodicals, listening to the radio. It is interesting to note that the British equivalent of our radio "Information Please," the BBC "Brains Trust" program, does not get spot questions and ingenious factual puzzles put up to it by the public, but a series of profound, if often naive, questions on political, economic, and philosophical fundamentals. The Brains Trust is not asked which name occurs most frequently among the Popes, nor who was known as the Grand Old Man, but whether the doctrine of the survival of the fittest can be reconciled with Christian ethics.

The great national debate has come to no conclusion as yet; the election of 1945 has stimulated, rather than settled, it. But it is already clear that many Britishers have made up their minds about what they want, if they are not sure as to how to go about getting it. They want social security and full employment; and, as we have seen, they feel that the war has shown them that full employment, at least, is humanly attainable. They want, if not doctrinaire social equality, at least an end to the painfully obvious division of the British people into those who are gentlemen and those who are not gentlemen. They put great hopes in popular education to help eliminate such class distinctions, and indeed nothing is more the subject of widespread debate in Britain today than their educational system. Though they need more workers, they have raised the school-leaving age from fourteen to sixteen, or eighteen if the last few years are devoted to part-time work. Some of them want to abolish the public school of tradition, to come to something like what the French call the "école unique." Others want to keep the public school, but make it "democratic"—which sounds to an outsider at least like a contradiction too great even for the British to put up with. They want good housing, with all the nice things—even central heating—they have learned the Americans have in their houses. But they do not want flats (apartment houses) or any kind of communal living. The Englishman's home is still to be his castle, even in a Planned Society. They want (at least their old ruling classes and intellectuals want this—their great urban masses are more confirmed town-dwellers than you would guess from English novels, and are not much moved by the problem) to preserve in an even more industrialized Britain the "amenities" of the green and pleasant countryside of Merrie England. They want more motorcars, but they don't want ugly ribbon developments along their motor roads. They have admirable reports from special parliamentary committees set up to solve such problems of planning—Beveridge report, Scott report, Uthwatt report. They want to stay themselves and to be born anew; they want to be free individuals in a collectivist society. Mr. G. J. Renier, a Dutchman, once wrote an amusing little book, "The English —Are They Human?" The answer can no longer be in doubt. The British of today are most human, and in nothing more so than in their determined effort to attain that most human of desires: a way to eat your cake, and have it.

6. Eire and the War

The history of Ireland is recommended reading to all who incline to the view that small nations are unimportant in world politics. The truth is that all nations, great and small, are elements in the bewildering equation of international relations, and if you neglect a single element your equation will come out wrong. Some small nations are, of course, more important than others. The geographical position of Ireland in what Mr. Lippmann calls the "Atlantic Community" gives her a strategic importance comparable to that of a nation even smaller in numbers, Iceland. Fortunately, the role of that part of Ireland called Eire in the recent war was negative; if we were denied the use of her ports and airfields, the Germans too were denied use of them. There is, however, not the slightest guarantee that in another Atlantic war the neutrality of Eire could be maintained. Holland, Norway, and Denmark are sufficient witnesses to that fact.

1. THE IRISH QUESTION TODAY

Eire is also a classic instance of the survival against great physical odds of whatever it is that makes a people willing to fight and die for "independence." The odds against her, very slight in the middle ages, have steadily increased until in the twentieth century the United Kingdom had fourteen times the manpower of Southern Ireland, and an industrial power that dwarfed the almost wholly agricultural and pastoral Southern

Ireland. Yet it was in 1937 that Southern Ireland won an independence complete enough for all but the most fanatical minority of the Irish Republican Army. Why has the history of the Southern Irish been so different from that of their brother Celts in Scotland, Wales, and Brittany, who have all accepted, if not absorption, at least political integration into the larger unity of the United Kingdom or of France? Any answer would have to be a very long one, and could still not hope for universal acceptance as a satisfactory answer. The fact remains that in 1939 Eire was independent enough of the British Crown to be able to declare herself neutral in a war that threatened the very existence of Great Britain.

To understand the legal position of Eire we must go back to 1921, when after five years of guerilla warfare waged against them by the people of Southern Ireland, led by the Sinn Fein party, the British government signed a treaty with some of the rebels setting up in twenty-six of the thirty-two counties of Ireland the Irish Free State. The Free State was specifically granted the status of a Dominion within the Commonwealth —a status like that of Canada, complete self-government including the right to have diplomatic representatives abroad, but with the British Crown still formally at the head of the state. This was not enough for a large part of Sinn Fein, and after an abortive civil war against the Free State government, this part of Sinn Fein won by the ballot what they could not win by bullets. In 1932 their leader, Mr. De Valera, secured a majority in the Dail (parliament) and was able to carry through a measure abolishing the oath of loyalty to the King required of members of the Dail. There followed a tariff war with the United Kingdom, but in 1938 the British concluded an agreement with De Valera which put an end to this tariff war, turned over to Eire, the new official name for the Free State —it means "Ireland"—the coast defenses of Cobh, Bere Haven, and Lough Swilly, and said nothing at all about the oath or dominion status.

Britishers will tell you that Eire is still a part of the British

Commonwealth of Nations; a great many Irishmen will tell you that she is an independent republic. There are still a few legal threads tying Eire to the British Commonwealth. Of these the most important is the use by the government of Eire of the British Crown for the accrediting of its diplomatic representatives, and the consequent fact that citizens of Eire abroad and in the Commonwealth and Empire are still British subjects for purposes of international law. But within Eire all the attributes of sovereignty belong to the government of Eire, and none to the British Crown. Economic, strategic, and even cultural ties between the two countries are, however, by no means mere threads. They may yet prove strong enough to make possible a renewing of the political ties.

The great obstacle to such a renewal is the status of the remaining six counties of Ireland, which as Northern Ireland are still an integral part of the United Kingdom, and send members to the British parliament in London. Again, full understanding of this obstacle to Anglo-Irish reconciliation would require a long excursion into history. To the men of Eire an Ireland amputated of the Six Counties is intolerable; the Six Counties are to them an *Eire irredenta* which they must redeem. But most of the Six Counties does not want to be redeemed. Northern Ireland is two-thirds Protestant, and hates Catholic Eire with a seventeenth-century fury which hardly obtains elsewhere on this globe in relations between Protestants and Catholics. You may say, especially if you are a Marxist, that this religious hatred is no more than a mask for the *real* difficulty, which is the distrust of the Northern industrialists and business men towards the egalitarian peasant-democracy of the South. But you would not thereby alter the fact that this deep gulf in human feelings exists between North and South. The gulf may be crossed in time, but there are today few signs that it can be bridged in our day. In 1914 the men who ran Northern Ireland were about to take up arms against the British government rather than accept Home Rule for a united Ireland; and Home Rule, compared with the present status of Eire,

was very close integration into the United Kingdom. The
men who run Northern Ireland today are still men of the stamp
of the Ulsterman Carson and his English abettor F. E. Smith,
the gun-runners and rebels of 1914. Indeed one of the leaders
of 1914, become Lord Craigavon, was Prime Minister of Northern Ireland at the outbreak of the recent war. These men are as
irreconcilable towards the South as ever, and seem to have
the majority of the people of Northern Ireland with them.

2. THE NEUTRALITY OF EIRE

The Irish Question, then, is still unsolved. But it would be
a great mistake to conclude, as some Americans and many
Britishers have concluded, that the neutrality of Eire in this
war springs largely from the hatred felt by the people of Eire
for Britain. So far as it is ever safe to make such generalizations
about the sentiments of a people, it is safe to say that the great
majority of the people of Eire no longer hate the British. They
do not love them, but the old feelings generated by centuries
of oppression—most of it real oppression, the control of the
land by absentee English landlords—have gradually diminished
with the removal of English political and economic control.
The Irish peasant still has his grievances: he has his little plot,
but he would like to extend it by getting the lands of the big
grazers, who are no longer in the main English. Indeed, these
grazers are mostly Irish themselves. De Valera has done a lot
for the small farmers, and he has promised more. They are on
the whole loyal to him. They are, like peasants everywhere,
stubborn, narrow-minded if you like, and swayed by ideas only
when those ideas are, literally, part of the soil. They hated,
not England, but the English landlord; now that he has gone
England is hardly more than a remote, but not unpleasant,
abstraction. Indeed, the attitude of the Irish peasant towards
Britain and towards the war was at bottom much like the attitude of the French-Canadian peasants towards Britain and the
war—an attitude also much misunderstood in the outside world.

Neither Irish nor French-Canadians were actively hostile towards Britain, and neither were actively friendly towards Germany. Indeed, what little either people bothered to learn about the Nazis was not calculated to warm their catholic hearts. Both peoples are profoundly and incorrigibly self-centered and provincial. It is not a heroic attitude, and in this small world, not in the long run a very safe or sensible attitude. It has proved to be an attitude almost impossible for ordinary Britishers—and Americans—to understand, let alone sympathize with; in war time inevitably those who are not with us seem against us.

There is, of course, an unreconstructed minority of Irishmen in Ireland and in the United States who hate England with the old Fenian fervor. These are now definitely a minority which is no longer a serious disturbing factor in Anglo-American relations. There is also in Ireland, both North and South, another minority, that of the really fascist-minded. Such people do not hate Britain, except as they identify Britain with democracy; nor do they love Germany, except as they identify Germany with their totalitarian creed. Fascists and Fenians were in Eire during this war in an unstable and unnatural alliance against Britain. But they did not determine the policy of Eire, which was a genuine, if somewhat touchy, neutrality. In the long run, the sympathies of the bulk of the Irish people are with the democratic forces of the world.

These sympathies are strong enough so that, in a confused and unheroic way, the people of Eire wanted the United Nations to win this war. As individuals, something over two hundred thousand men and women of Eire have volunteered in the British armed forces. It is easy here to bring in some vaudeville crack about the Irishman always spoiling for a fight, but vaudeville is no substitute for understanding. Nor did mass economic pressure send these Irishmen to fight for Britain; Ireland is no longer a depressed area. Many of these Irishmen fought for Britain because they believed they were also fighting for Ireland. Yet Eire as a political entity refused to go to war, and De Valera, who is one of the world's ablest politicians, undoubtedly gaged public opinion correctly when he declared for neutrality. Eire was neutral for the same reason Holland was neutral in the last war, and Sweden and Switzerland in both wars: because small nations like to stay neutral whenever they can. And big ones, too.

They often can't. Eire has had a very close shave in this war. It is pretty clear now that the danger of a German invasion of Eire was never great, though this was by no means clear in 1940. In fairness to the government of Eire, it must be recorded that they made real preparations to resist such an invasion. They took up all road signs, they manned the coast defenses, they watched the German diplomatists and secret agents who took advantage of Eire's neutrality to establish themselves in that country. It is pretty certain that they would at once have summoned British aid had the Germans attempted invasion.

Such aid might well have come too late. Eire is hardly equipped to defend herself in regular warfare, though she is presumably still supreme mistress of the art of guerilla warfare. The real danger to the neutrality of Eire in this war came from the British and the Americans. The price in lives of Allied seamen we have paid for the neutrality of Eire can never be calculated. It is probably not as high as some alarmists make it out to be, for after all Northern Ireland was available to us for the protection of our sea lanes, but there is no doubt that the use of harbors and airfields of Eire would have given us a useful margin in the struggle against German U-boats, raiders, blockade runners and planes. Yet the price was paid. We have respected the neutrality of Eire. It may yet prove, for the peace of the world, an excellent investment.

The British people for the most part took Irish neutrality with a shrug. Some of them undoubtedly have a bad conscience about their past treatment of Ireland. Most of them simply feel that, whether justifiably or not, the Irish do in fact hate them, and that there is nothing they can do about it. A few Englishmen, unfortunately with access to the press, felt that it was foolish to coddle people as hopelessly unreasonable as the Irish, and that the solution was simple: away with all this rot about neutrality—nobody can be neutral in this war; go in and take the Irish harbors and airfields. These people wrote some very bitter and very unwise things, which were echoed in our press. But the British government, headed by a man who has said that he did not take office to preside over the breaking-up of the British Empire, stood firm and refused to violate the neutrality of Eire.

The British government have since 1921 made a daring gamble in Ireland; they have put everything on the chance that a reversal of a centuries-old policy might end a centuries-old feud, that a free Ireland might become a friendly Ireland. They have come nearer winning the gamble than almost anyone twenty-five years ago would have thought possible. To have gone back on the agreement of 1938 and seized the Irish bases would have undone all that has been achieved, and would have exposed the occupying British to the same kind of dangers from resistance movements to which the Germans in France were exposed. That, indeed, it would also have put the British *morally* in the same position the Germans were in is a fact which did not escape the attention of discerning Englishmen, and ought not to escape the attention of discerning Americans. De Valera, though he replied a bit testily to Churchill's testy reference to the neutrality of Eire in May, 1945, showed clearly that he appreciated the magnanimity of the British government in not violating Eire's neutrality.

Internally, Eire shows signs of attaining a stability foreigners were not in the habit of expecting from Irishmen. When in 1948 De Valera was beaten in a General Election, he had held power for sixteen years, one of the longest periods of power any democratic leader could claim. The new government under Mr. Costello was certainly no more to the Left, and no more anti-British, than Mr. De Valera's had been. And Mr. De Valera "crossed the floor" of the Dail to take his seat as leader of the Opposition almost as if he had been Mr. Gladstone at Westminster.

It is true that the unsolved question of Northern Ireland remains to plague Irish politics, and while it is unsolved there will be scope for the traditional Irish hotheads on both sides of the highly artificial border that divides the twenty-six counties from the six. But Mr. De Valera's republic—if it is a republic—shows signs of settling down. The land hunger of the peasants is still not wholly appeased, and the melodramatic habits bred into Irishmen by years of conspiracy, assassination, secret societies and disrespect for the law do not easily give way to the duller habits of men in a stable society. Yet the Irish peasantry is spared the great curse of many peasantries, the Italian, for instance, that of an excessive birth rate. Britain provides an excellent market for a diversified Irish agriculture specializing in products of high value, poultry, eggs, cheese, vegetables and the like, and such a specialized agriculture may lessen the current rivalry in Eire between the land-hungry small farmers and the big stock raisers. And Irish lawlessness has been much exaggerated. Though professional Irishmen will not admit it, the Irish really have absorbed a good deal from their long life in common with the English. Or perhaps they never were very wild. No one can travel in the two countries without realizing that they have a lot in common. The Irish, like the English, are not really very good revolutionaries—not social revolutionaries. There is still in Limerick a hotel called the Royal George. The Russians, who know what a revolution is, would never let a thing like that stand.

3. EIRE IN ANGLO-AMERICAN RELATIONS

There remains a necessary word about the Irish-Americans, who are more numerous than the Eire Irish. A generation ago, no one could write about Anglo-American relations without paying a great deal of attention to the part played by Irish-Americans in almost every phase of those relations. This is no longer true to anything like the same extent. To begin with, the hyphen itself in Irish-American is already old-fashioned. Americans of Irish stock no doubt still love the ould sod, and their eyes still moisten to an Irish tune. They still supply a backlog of anti-British sentiment in this country. But very few of them in 1939–1941 were, as very many of them were in 1914–1917, so anti-British as to be pro-German. A number of them have been vocally indignant at the neutrality of Eire in this war—a fact not unperceived in Eire itself. Time and space are gradually getting in their work, and separating Americans of Irish descent from the daily life of Ireland.

Ireland is still a factor in Anglo-American relations, but its importance is now in large part strategic. Neither we nor the British can afford to have a hostile Ireland, and for both of us a neutral Ireland is an expensive luxury. But the forbearance with which in general both governments have treated Eire in this war—save for our rather tactless and certainly unfruitful joint summons to the government of Eire to get rid of Axis diplomatic agents in 1944—may, it is permitted to hope, bring Ireland of her own accord to acceptance of the active partnership with the Western democracies to which history and geography so firmly bind her.

PART III ANGLO–AMERICAN RELATIONS IN THE PAST

7. A Brief History of Anglo-American Relations

We talk and write glibly—as we must—about "international relations." We say that the United States and Britain agreed or disagreed about this or that matter. But just what do we mean? Obviously we are not dealing with relations between abstract entities, even though it is convenient to use terms like the United States and Britain, or even, if we like elegant literary variations, Uncle Sam and John Bull, Downing Street and the White House. We are dealing with an immensely complicated web of interactions among human beings. There are relations between governments, which means relations among human beings actually in charge of government; and though these are often very distinguished people, it should not be forgotten that they are human beings like the rest of us. There are relations among travelers, students, business men who have dealings abroad. There are all sorts of transactions conducted by correspondence. International relations are a constant flow of men, goods, and ideas across seas and frontiers.

Not the least important part of such international relations is the sum total of sentiments and opinions individuals in a given country have about other countries and about their interactions. You who are reading this book are thereby taking part in international relations; what you think about Great Britain is a part of Anglo-American relations. Now it is easy to say that the common man never takes part in diplomatic negotiations, never receives ambassadors, never signs treaties. It is true that the democratic process is a lot less perfect, less automatic, less simple than it seems in the smooth assurances of platform-oratory. Nevertheless, in all human societies, and above all in democratic societies, what quite ordinary people think does get ultimately translated into action. You, as an individual, may not approve the current trend of Anglo-American relations. But your vote and your opinions help make history.

What is called diplomatic history is normally, and quite rightly, concerned chiefly with the record of transactions among governments. Treaty-making and diplomacy correspond in international affairs to lawmaking and politics in domestic affairs, and in both fields they must be the basic stuff of the historical narrative. In both fields, final decisions are made as a result of a most complex interweaving of human hopes and fears that go far beyond mere politics, mere economics, into the whole life of a people. We shall need to review briefly, not only Anglo-American diplomatic history, but also, as far as the difficulties of the study permit, what Americans and Britishers have thought and felt about one another during the last century and a half.

1. A CENTURY OF CONFLICT

The key to our governmental relations with Britain for over a hundred years after we achieved independence of the British Crown is the fact that we really pursued a policy of isolationism. It was not, of course, "autarky," isolationism in the sense of having no relations with the outside world; on the contrary, our relations were steady and important, and the State Department was from the very first one of the major departments of our government. But we did not make alliances, did not play a part in what is commonly known by the derogatory name of "balance of power" politics. There is indeed one important exception to this rule, the Monroe Doctrine, first announced in 1823.

The Monroe Doctrine was not, of course, an entangling alliance; but its effect was to withdraw both the Americas from the interplay of the balance of power among European nations. It was for the United States a genuine commitment to something more than strict isolationism. We had to make that withdrawal of Latin America from European expansion good, or those lands might have suffered the fate of Africa in the nineteenth century. As American historians have been quite willing to point out, we were greatly helped in making that commitment good by the fact that Great Britain backed us up with her diplomacy and her navy, at that time supreme in the world. That it was to Britain's interest to maintain markets for her goods in Latin America, markets that might have been lost had large parts of Central and South America fallen again under Spanish or Portuguese control, or been seized by some other European power, does not alter the fact that here British and American policy coincided. We have had only one real quarrel with Britain over the Monroe Doctrine, the Venezuela boundary dispute of the 1890's, and though at the time that dispute gave rise to a good deal of bitterness in both countries, it seems in retrospect to have been no more than a last flare-up of traditional antagonism between the two countries.

The antagonism, in spite of Britain's support of our major international commitment, the Monroe Doctrine, was real enough for over a century to involve us in a number of disputes with Britain, all save one of which were settled by diplomatic means. The Peace of Paris of 1783, which gave us our independence, left a number of difficulties between the two nations. Under the loose Articles of Confederation the thirteen separate sovereign states controlled their own commercial policy, and no effective commercial treaty between the United

States and Britain was possible. Britain had promised to clear her troops from Detroit and other posts in the Northwest Territory—the old Middle West—but she took advantage of the weaknesses of the new Confederation to keep them there stirring up Indian trouble and postponing American settlement of the region; the boundary of Maine was unsettled; there were claims of British Loyalists for compensation for confiscated property, which by the Treaty of Paris were referred to the separate states, which did nothing about them. Most of these difficulties were cleared up, after the new constitution had strengthened the federal government, in Jay's Treaty of 1794.

For it had become quite clear to the business interests of the new republic that we had to trade with Britain. Only from Britain could we obtain readily the financial capital, capital goods and manufactures to expand our own economy. Britain was a useful outlet for our surplus of raw materials. Jay did get the British to evacuate their garrisons in the Northwest Territory, he got the Loyalist claims dropped, joint commissions set up to settle the question of private debts owed to British creditors and to delimit the northeastern boundary, and he got trade with Britain placed on a basis of "reciprocal and perfect liberty." Our protective tariffs were yet to come. So great, however, was the hostility of the more radical of American parties, the Jeffersonian democrats, towards Britain that it was only very begrudgingly that the Senate mustered the two-thirds vote necessary to ratify the treaty.

This hostility played a large part in involving us in our first World War as an independent nation. In 1812 we joined Napoleon—though not by a formal alliance—in war against Great Britain. Our dilemma then was extraordinarily like our dilemma in the World War which began in 1914. We were already a trading nation, and we wished as neutrals to trade with the maximum freedom possible with all the world. Most of the world was at war, and both belligerent sides were attempting to blockade the trade of the other. Economic warfare is not a new thing. Both belligerents violated what we considered our neutral rights. As a matter of fact, in the earlier phases of the World War which began in 1792 and lasted with a few lulls until 1815, France, annoyed by what she regarded as our pro-British policy in concluding Jay's Treaty, was for a while more bullying than Britain, and in 1798 and 1799 we fought an informal and undeclared naval war against France. In 1807 Jefferson attempted a policy inspired by a despairing feeling of "a plague o' both your houses," and put an embargo on all American trade with either side. Neither Britain nor France relaxed their measures of economic warfare, and the only result of the Embargo Act was to leave American ships rotting at their wharves. It was repealed in 1809. In the next few years the British did us more damage than did the French, largely because the British were now beginning to win out over the French. Moreover, our war party had its eyes on Canada, which could not be won by a war against France. Actually Britain on June 23, 1812, re-voked, as far as American ships were concerned, the orders in council blockading the European coast. But there was no transatlantic cable in those days. On June 18 we had already declared war on Britain.

The war on land was not a success for the United States. We failed in the attempt to invade Canada, and redeemed our military glory only by the victory of New Orleans, fought, once more because of the slowness of transatlantic communications, two whole weeks after peace had been signed at Ghent on December 24, 1814. At sea our infant navy had some extraordinary individual successes which gave a great fillip to our national pride. The treaty left things pretty much in that state we are apt to think the dear delight of the diplomatists, the *status quo;* but since there was not to be another world war for a hundred years, and since the British navy was to act as an efficient, if interested, international policeman for that time, the problem of the freedom of the seas for which we had fought did not arise in an acute form until 1914.

There remained two border disputes. In 1842 the question of the northeastern border was finally settled with very little acrimony by the Webster-Ashburton Treaty. There are a lot of geographical questions involved, but the final results of the long dispute do not confirm the American folk tradition that American diplomatists are babes in the woods in their dealings with the wily British; we did very well indeed to get the Aroostook country. We came out equally well in the other dispute. By agreement in 1818 the Canadian border from the Lake of the Woods to the continental divide was put at the forty-ninth parallel, but the still quite unsettled country west of the divide was left open to joint occupation. In the 1840's, as Americans began to follow the Oregon trail to its end, the question of the boundary became acute. This was the decade of Manifest Destiny and the Mexican War. Our expansionists coined the slogan "Fifty-four forty or fight!" and for a while there was a fine verbal war with Britain. We did not get the Oregon country up to latitude 54° 40', which is the southern boundary of Alaska, then a Russian possession, and we did not fight. We settled peacefully for the prolongation of the forty-ninth parallel to the Pacific, thereby gaining from the British fur traders the still unsettled territory which became the state of Washington in addition to what became the state of Oregon, which we had begun to settle.

During our Civil War we came within a hairsbreadth of another war with Great Britain. The British government and the British ruling classes—though not the workers, not the middle-class guardians of the non-conformist conscience—were sympathetic with the South. Their motives were mixed; they did not like the upstart Yankees; they were not sorry at the prospect of two independent nations where one had been before; they had the idea that the Southerners were Anglican gentlemen not so different from themselves; the more idealistic among them believed that here was a case of what later was called "self-determination of peoples." The

British government a month before the first battle of Bull Run recognized the Confederacy as a belligerent, but went no further. There were two major crises in the course of the war. In November 1861 a Union vessel stopped the British steamer *Trent* at sea and took off Mason and Slidell, Confederate commissioners on their way to England. In international law, this was a clear and simple violation of neutral rights we had long defended for ourselves. Lincoln and his Secretary of State, Seward, had the courage to resist pressure from hotheads, and conformed to our standards of international law by surrendering Mason and Slidell. The other crisis arose over the depredations of the *Alabama* and other Confederate raiders which had made illegal use of British ports, a use at least winked at by some high British officials. Our government wisely did not press its case during the war, and in 1872 the Geneva arbitration was decided against the British government, who paid us an indemnity of $15,500,000.

After this storm, the Venezuela dispute of the 1890's was hardly a serious matter; it is important only as the last old-fashioned diplomatic row between the two governments. The Monroe Doctrine had not affected the ownership of the relatively unimportant possessions held by European nations in the areas to the south of the United States. One of these, British Guiana, bordered on the republic of Venezuela. A boundary dispute arose, which Secretary of State Olney summoned the British government to arbitrate. His language was something more than firm: "The United States is practically sovereign on this continent, and its fiat is law upon the subjects to which it confines its interposition." The British government was not used to being summoned. The Prime Minister, Lord Salisbury, replied by rejecting arbitration and denying that the Monroe Doctrine had any application in the case. It is possible that the terrific press row which followed in both countries served as a necessary means of letting off steam. At any rate, the British government shortly afterwards signed a treaty of arbitration with Venezuela, and was by the ensuing arbitration awarded substantially what it had claimed.

By the turn of the century the war of 1914 was brewing in rising antagonism between Britain and Germany. The threat of the growing German navy brought the British government to their first withdrawal from their position as world-wide policemen of the seas. They decided to share that task with us. In fact, they decided that the United States was a world power before we ourselves were altogether sure of the fact. In 1901 they concluded with the American government the Hay-Pauncefote Treaty, abrogating the Clayton-Bulwer Treaty of 1850 by which Britain and the United States had decided to control jointly an unfortified Isthmian canal when it should be built. The new treaty granted sole control of the future Panama Canal to the United States, and permitted us to fortify it. In fact, Britain reduced her naval establishment in the Caribbean to a minimum, allowing us to make it an American lake. After fortifying herself in the Pacific by an alliance with Japan she was ready—at least from a naval point of view—for the Germans.

2. A HALF-CENTURY OF COÖPERATION

The British government may have made the renunciation involved in giving up any part in the Panama Canal not only from an awareness of their need to concentrate their navy against the Germans, but also from an awareness that we felt strong enough to build and hold the canal alone. But they knew they were not surrendering their position in the Caribbean to a hostile people. For the turn of the century marks the beginning of the first substantially popular friendly relations between the two peoples. When we went to war with Spain in 1898 we discovered, somewhat to the surprise of many of us, that the British people were wholeheartedly on our side. Since we were clearly not the underdog in that conflict, the British gave up one of their national delights—

sympathy for the underdog. It is hardly true that we recipro-
cated by siding with the British in the Boer War which took
place immediately afterwards, but compared with the attitude
of the German government and the German people in the
Boer War, ours was friendliness itself. In the flow of com-
monplaces and slogans which is so useful an index in international relations, there began to be heard a new one—new at
least in the context of Anglo-American affairs—"blood is
thicker than water." It was to be heard again in 1914.

The United States came into the war of 1914, however, not
because of her new friendship for Great Britain, but for a
more traditional reason: defense of her position that, subject
to a number of definite rules, such as those covering contra-
band of war and "effective" blockade, neutral vessels in war
time may proceed upon their business. As in Napoleonic wars,
both sides committed acts we regarded as infringing our rights,
and President Wilson protested formally to both sides. But
nothing Britain did compared in seriousness with the unrestricted submarine war which Germany, after once abandoning it under pressure from the American government, resumed in 1917. We went to war in April 1917 because the
Germans were sinking our ships and killing our citizens. This
the British were not doing. It is true enough that from the
start American public opinion was for the most part with the
British and the French, and against the Hohenzollern monarchy. It is true that German violation of Belgian neutrality
outraged the moral sense of the great majority of Americans.
It is even true, as our de-bunkers of the 1920's constantly
reminded us, that Americans had lent large sums of money to
the Allies, and that the Allies had effective means for propaganda in the United States. Finally, it is true that as the war
went on it took under the high moral leadership of Wilson
the form of an American crusade to "make the world safe
for democracy." A war which we began under the traditional
—even, in a sense, isolationist—motivation of preserving our
neutrality rights, ended with the American government ap-

parently committed to full participation in the task of world government.

We did not take up that commitment. This is not the place to debate the reasons for our failure to join the League of Nations. Ratification of the treaty of which the League was a part hung on a very few votes in the Senate, and it is possible that had Wilson been more willing to compromise ratification might have been secured. It was not secured, and however much the accidents of personalities and of awkward specific issues may have entered into the final decision, it seems reasonably clear that the great majority of the American people, in spite of its immediate post-war enthusiasm for an international organization, had not yet been thoroughly and permanently converted to the belief that the United States should abandon its traditional policy of nonparticipation in the web of agreements—call it alliances, or call it League of Nations—by which the world is governed. We had not, as a matter of fact, even made an alliance with Britain and France during the war, which we fought as an "associated" power.

Relations between the United States and Britain continued after the war to be on the whole excellent. In fact, the British government itself had apparently never planned, as the French had planned, to set up a League of Nations with anything like sovereign authority. The British, like the American, conception of the League was a "voluntaristic" one. They would have liked to have us in it, but they found in practice that we, like they, wanted above all to restore the world, including Germany, to normalcy, and that we thought as they did that the old diplomatic methods would suffice. Though we were not in the League, American experts took full part in the negotiations by which German reparations were whittled down in the 1920's; indeed both the Dawes plan and the Young plan take their names from American negotiators. The British decision to stop payment on the interest on the debt owed to the United States can hardly be said to have helped Anglo-American amity, yet in the midst of the obvious world economic tangle the average American took it pretty well. At the Washington conference of 1922 Britain gave up her alliance with Japan, and in the very temporary settlement of the Pacific question and the problem of naval limitation there achieved, there were no major discords between ourselves and the British.

This close identity of British and American policy continued in the face of growing aggression by Germany, Italy, and Japan. Both Britain and America agreed to disapprove this aggression and to protest against it; they both agreed in practice to do nothing effective about it. Neither has any moral right to a holier-than-thou attitude towards the other in respect to the blame for letting the Axis powers get the almost fatal head start they got in the decade before the war. The press in each country has done some sniping at the other—"If only the British had backed up Stimson in the Manchurian affair"; "If the United States had been in the League, and backed us up in economic sanctions during the Ethiopian crisis"; and so on. But sensible people in both countries are quite aware that there is blame enough to be shared evenly.

As the World War drew inevitably on, the United States made a desperate effort to keep out of it—an effort which went so far that in the Neutrality Act of 1936 we voluntarily incorporated in our own legislation measures renouncing the rights for which we had gone to war in 1812 and 1917. When war broke out in 1939, American opinion was almost unanimously against Germany. In 1914 there had been the "hyphenated Americans," there had been a strong minority which for one reason or another was pro-German, or at least anti-British. But in 1939 any such minority was infinitesimal. We were still determined to be at best, however, no more than the arsenal of democracy. In the months following the fall of France in 1940, the government, with the great majority of the people behind it, took measures, such as the exchange of the fifty destroyers for Atlantic bases, which scrapped our previous neutrality legislation and brought us to the edge of, if not into, a shooting war. The Japanese did the rest.

In this war, the intermeshing of British and American agencies, military, civilian, and mixed, was far closer than in the last war. It represents, indeed, a degree of collaboration closer than anything ever attempted by two sovereign governments in modern times. Under General Eisenhower, staffs down to the level of army groups were completely interleaved. For the rest, the names alone of some of the operative boards indicate the extent to which the two nations have worked together: Combined Chiefs of Staff, Raw Materials Board, Munitions Assignment Board, Shipping Adjustment Board, Joint Aircraft Committee, Combined Production and Resources Board. By the Lend-Lease agreements we made it possible for the British—and others of the United Nations— to secure munitions and other supplies from us without making it necessary to attempt to settle up after the war by the rigid methods of cash accounting.

Politically, then, a rough chart of our relations with the British would show two wars, the Revolutionary War and the War of 1812, a long period of coolness, marked by crises in which the hotheads in both countries at least talked of a possible war, the Oregon crisis, the Civil War, the Venezuela crisis, and a turning point which coincides with the turn of the nineteenth century, after which the two nations fought on the same side in two World Wars. Our economic relations have been more stable than our political, but here too there is a definite trend and a turning point. Ever since Jay's treaty, each country has been one of the other's best customers. But for over a century, the United States sent to Britain chiefly agricultural products, cotton, wheat, meats and the like, and took from Britain in exchange manufactured goods (in spite of our tariffs after 1816), services such as shipping, especially after the decline of our merchant marine at the end of the clipper-ship period, and, not least important, investment capital. In fact, for a long time Britain stood economically towards the United States as a whole in much the same position the Philadelphia-New York-Boston area stood towards the trans-Appalachian west. Long after we attained political independence we were economically a colonial region. Our trade with Britain was one of the factors, though not by any means the only one, which enabled us to develop so rapidly into a mature nation.

After the Civil War our development towards economic maturity was rapid. We continued, and still continue, to send Britain cotton, wheat and meats. But our trade with Britain is gradually approaching the status of an exchange between two complex industrial economies, like that between Britain and Germany before Hitler. Furthermore, the War of 1914 brought about a striking change in our whole position in international trade. From being a debtor country we became a creditor country. The recent war has fixed this change even more definitely. In the international money market New York has taken the place of London. This does not mean that London is no longer important, that the City has gone out of business. But it does mean that there has been a major shift in a complex balance, that economically as in other ways the child has outgrown the parent. It means that the problems involved in our business relations with the British are quite different from what they were only forty years ago.

The cultural relations between the two countries have undergone equally marked changes. They have always been close. Americans have been traveling in Britain ever since colonial days, and these travels have always had in them something of the nature of cultural pilgrimages. Here again the relation between the United States and Britain has in this respect been something like that between, say, Kansas and Boston. A minority of Kansans have been so overwhelmed by what they find to be its delights that they become more Bostonian than the Bostonians; the great majority enjoy its crooked streets, eighteenth-century buildings, and seafood, and go back to Wichita thanking God that they live in a modern city. The same holds true of most American travelers to Britain. The British themselves came here in numbers only as immigrants, and their children were very rapidly assimilated. British lecturers were, however, long an important phenomenon in our cultural history. They always wrote a book when they went back, and as the names of Dickens and Mrs. Trollope will remind us, the record of their discomforts in our rough frontier civilization did nothing to make Anglo-American relations more pleasant. In British eyes the American Revolution did not greatly change our colonial status.

All this has greatly changed, although, since complete social change takes a very long time to work itself out, you can still hear echoes resounding down from the days of *Innocents Abroad*. One good index is the flow of students. Only so short a time ago as 1904, when the first American Rhodes Scholars went to Oxford, the flow was almost wholly one-way, from America to Britain. Now, with the establishment of the Commonwealth Fellowships and other funds to bring British students to this country, with an increasing number of Britishers coming at their own expense, the flow has become a two-way exchange. So too with serious literature, science, philosophy, painting, music, there is not only free trade, but substantially equal trade. As we have already pointed out, at less serious but not less important levels, in the movies, popular literature, popular music, the balance has so heavily turned in our favor since the war of 1914–1918 that many conservative Britishers are worried over the Americanization of Britain.

To sum up: whether you think in terms of politics, business, culture or just plain human relations, the United States has now outgrown its colonial status in its relations with Great Britain. By a common metaphor which has the weaknesses, for purposes of social analysis, of all metaphors, but which is here most useful, indeed indispensable, the child has now reached the stature of the parent. It is, indeed, quite a few inches taller. It would be ungracious, and probably inaccurate, to conclude that the parent is doddering to his grave. The analogy between the life of an individual and the life of a society breaks down before the fact that societies, if they have not been immortal, have in the past been able to achieve renewals, rejuvenations, which have hardly even metaphorical equivalents in the life cycle of an individual. In the long course of Graeco-Roman civilization, the Greek colonies, though many of them "grew up," did not wholly displace the Greek motherland, as a matter of fact, were ultimately merged with the motherland in the Roman Empire.

Our metaphor, if sociologically ambiguous, has nevertheless a real psychological value. The psychological relation between the parent and the child who has just grown up is often a very difficult one. On both sides, the recent past hangs with a heavy weight. Both parent and child find it hard to alter a relation which was once habitual, and which has changed so imperceptibly and yet so finally. Yet among individuals the necessary adjustment does usually get made, and well short of tragedy. The tale of Saturn and Jupiter remains a bit of abnormal psychology. We must hope that as between Britain and America the necessary adjustment will take a normal and natural course. But there are no grounds for believing that it will be an automatic adjustment. It will require the best and fullest capacities of both peoples.

PART IV   PROBLEMS OF THE PRESENT AND THE FUTURE

8. Economic Problems

The wealth of nations is an essential element in the health of nations—and in healthy international relations. We need not here involve ourselves in the essentially metaphysical debate as to the primacy of economic motives in human life. Popular distrust of economic theory is not wholly unjustified, for many professional economists have not yet achieved the close and effective collaboration with "practical" men which has, for instance, been achieved between medical research workers and medical practitioners. But we should take care not to throw out the baby with the bath; the economic knowledge the race has gradually accumulated is a good sound infant, and worth preserving. Just as a good physician knows he must adapt the lessons ("theories") of the laboratory to the complexities of a given clinical situation, so the good economist —and there are such—knows that he must adapt his theories to the political and psychological complexities of a given set of human relations.

One caution is especially necessary. We ordinary human beings do not expect from our physicians any single magical formula that will cure all our aches and pains, and bring us "perfect" health. Many of us do, however, seem to cherish the hope that our economists and statesmen can somehow evolve such a formula, for which the common name is "Utopia."

Economic and political health in this real world is as relative as personal health. We can hardly expect a world without some economic maladjustments, a world wholly without gluts or scarcities, without waste, without strikes, without at least occasional unemployment. But it is pretty clear that the 1930's were a period of relative economic ill health all over the world. We can—and it is clear that today public opinion in both Britain and America does—expect something much nearer economic health than the conditions of the decade before the war.

1. THE BASIC BRITISH ECONOMIC POSITION

The basic factor in the economic health of the United Kingdom is clearly expressed in a phrase one hears constantly in Britain in these days—"Export or die." The fifty-odd millions of people in the British Isles live in the style to which they are accustomed only because they take raw materials, a large proportion of which are imported, work them up into manufactured goods, and export a surplus of such goods to pay for the original imports of raw materials, and, of course, for imports of foodstuffs and manufactured goods as well. Overseas trade, a large and complex overseas trade, is, then, essential for the maintenance of the pre-war standard of living of the British people. No exact quantitative statement is here possible. If you assume—and it is an utterly unreal assumption— the British Isles wholly isolated from the rest of the world, it would probably be possible, with perfect economic and political planning and execution, for their present population to exist, but on a standard of living something like that of an oriental peasantry. No such British autarky—that is, autarky of the home islands without the Commonwealth and Empire —is in this world conceivable. It would, because of the lack of oil, non-ferrous metals, and other necessities of modern industry in the home islands, mean a lowering of British standards of living which the present generation of Britishers would not accept, *could* not, psychologically, accept. Nor is a mass emigration of millions from the British Isles a practical solution today. If, then, the British are to have their meat, tea, fruits, movies, radios, and motorcars, it really is for them a question of export or accept a lower standard of living. No good judge of human nature would deny that under these conditions there is more than mere rhetoric in the slogan "Export or die."

But the British want something better than their pre-war standard of living. They have been buoyed up to sustain the sacrifices of this war partly, at least, by hopes of a better economic future, hopes expressed in the Beveridge social-security plan, plans for full employment, for a dynamic economy that will result in a rising standard of living. To attain this, their economists and publicists are in general agreement that Britain will have to increase her export trade some 50 per cent over the pre-war figures at 1938 prices.

Now Britain attained her present high economic level by producing a wide variety of goods, almost all of which, except for coal, were manufactured or processed goods, better and more cheaply than any other people on earth. Historically speaking, Britain about the turn of the eighteenth century got a head start on the rest of the world in the use of machines for large-scale production. She could, for instance, buy raw cotton in New Orleans, move it in her own ships to Lancashire, spin it into thread, send the thread back again in her own ships, and sell it in New Orleans. At each stage in this process, some Britisher normally made a "profit," and some of these profits, canalized through the mechanism of banking and investment, went into more factories and more ships. Moreover, some of these profits went into investments abroad, into factories, railways, plantations, mines all over the world. Britain was not only the world's manufacturer; she was also the world's investment banker. Her material prosperity was achieved, not merely by the export of goods, but also by the export of what the economist calls the "invisible" items in the balance of trade, such as payments made by foreigners for the use of British shipping and returns from British investments abroad.

Two facts about this record of British economic success must be particularly noted, for they largely explain the difficulties now facing British trade. First, though in the last hundred and fifty years of Britain's economic greatness there have been in most countries tariffs and other barriers to *complete* freedom of international trade, still, on the whole, until the unhappy days of the Twenty Years' Truce, there has been something *approaching* international free trade. Moreover, Britain's comparative advantage—her low cost of production of key articles—was sufficient to enable her to leap over many tariff walls. Second, Britain's prosperity was itself largely dependent on world prosperity, on a growing population everywhere, on the whole complex of a dynamic world-economy which makes the last two hundred years unique in the history of mankind. But this very process, to which Britain as banker-investor contributed so much, meant that Britain gradually lost her unique position relative to the rest of the world. Thread began to be made in Willimantic as well as in Lancashire. The United States and Germany began to produce certain manufactured goods more efficiently—that is, more cheaply—than Britain. In our own times, this process of industrialization has extended all over the globe. There are very few important nations today with a purely agricultural or pastoral economy. Even in the British Commonwealth and Empire, countries like Australia and India have begun the process of industrialization.

Britain's economic prospects are therefore in 1945 very different from what they were in 1845. In a world where other nations, many of them with greater natural resources of their own, have built up manufacturing systems equipped with the latest machinery, and have acquired the necessary managerial and labor skills to maintain a mature economy, Britain cannot hope to maintain the absolute industrial primacy she once had in world trade. Again, the first condition of British prosperity, access to world markets through a system of world trade at least approximating to what the economist calls free trade, has broken down as a result of the international anarchy of the last few decades. To the relatively simple obstacle of the tariff human ingenuity, and in particular, Nazi ingenuity, has added a host of technical devices in restraint of international trade: quota systems, exchange control, bilateral agreements, export bounties, blocked currencies, out-and-out barter of specific commodities, government trading monopolies, even peace-time embargoes. Britain herself has by no means been altogether innocent of such methods. But we are not here moralizing. It is sufficient to record what everyone, however puzzled by the economic technicalities involved, knows well: the movement of goods and services across international boundaries has in the last few decades been subjected to all sorts of restraints unknown to the nineteenth century. Even a rough approximation to freedom of international trade no longer exists.

Finally, this war and the previous one have meant for Britain the loss of a good part of the invisible items through which she balanced her international trade—that is, paid for no inconsiderable portion of the imports which enabled her people to live well. She has lost through enemy action a large part of her merchant tonnage, and, though her shipyards are now the busiest in the world, she has by no means made up for her losses. She faces, moreover, competition from American ships built during the war. Her commercial aviation has been injured in the same way, and again she has had to witness the growth of a powerful American air transport under the stimulus of the war. But most important of all, Britain has been obliged, in spite of her American help through Lend-Lease, to dispose of much of her holdings abroad in order to pay for two great wars. This process, which is known technically as "disinvestment," has not gone quite so far as some loose journalistic writing has made out. It is not true that Britain has had to sell *all* her investments abroad. She has, for instance, managed to keep most of her extensive holdings in Argentina—a fact which should be kept in mind in considering British policy towards that country. All told, Britain *may* be able to retain about half of her 1939 holdings abroad. But against this must be balanced payments to foreign creditors, *not* including repayment of her 1946 loan from us. Payments to Canada, Argentina, India, and other countries may seriously reduce this total.

For those who like figures, the table gives the official ones, as given out by the British Information Services in October, 1947.

BRITAIN'S BALANCE OF PAYMENTS

(In millions of pounds)

	Overseas payments			*Overseas receipts*	
	1938	1946		1938	1946
Imports	835	1,110	Exports	533	890
Government expenditure	16	300	Shipping	100	150
Film remittances (net)	7	17	Interest	205	150
Other	150	235	Other	100	72
	1,008	1,662		938	1,262
			Adverse balance	70	400

The adverse balance for the year 1947 was by unofficial British estimates placed at 650 millions of pounds. This sort of imbalance cannot possibly continue for more than a few years. And these millions of pounds represent, of course, the food, the textiles, the tools which made life at something like the old standards possible for millions of British people. They represent, it is true, some money spent for American tobacco and American movies, among much else. If you are the kind of person shocked by such expenditures, you will probably not be moved by arguments in defense of the British. But all Americans, whether or not they approve, must try to get this clear: the British do not intend to give up their hopes for a high national standard of living (which would certainly include tobacco and movies). They know they cannot run adverse balances in overseas trade much longer. They know they must produce and export.

In spite of very encouraging improvements in many industries, Britain faces serious difficulties in production, not all resulting from the recent war. She is suffering in part because of the very fact of her early industrial primacy. Her average plant is older and less efficient than that of nations that came later to the machine, and her labor and managerial force, skilled though it is, less well formed for modern automatic machinery and modern productive methods. The situation comes out clearly in the cotton textile industry. A report of the recent British Cotton Textile Mission to the United States sums up: "With normal staffing British PMH [Production per Man-Hour of labor] is less than the American by approximately 18 to 49 per cent in spinning, by 80 to 85 per cent in winding, by 79 to 89 per cent in beaming, and by 56 to 67 per cent in weaving." The report reveals one essential reason why in this industry the American worker produces from one and a quarter to ten times what the British worker produces in an hour's work; it is not that the American worker is that much more active and intelligent, but that 95 per cent of the looms in the United States are automatic, and 5 per cent of the looms in Britain are automatic—and so on down the line of other processes. It is true there are other reasons—there usually are in matters as complicated as economics. One, less to the discredit of British industry, must be noted. The differential is partly one of product. Many British textiles are so fine that their production requires high skills, and therefore more time and labor.

No doubt the cotton textile industry—one of Britain's oldest—is relatively in a worse position than, say, her automotive industry. Yet, in the long run, her coal industry may prove even harder to rehabilitate than the textile industry. Coal mining was the first major industry to be nationalized, a step probably made easier because under private hands it had already

come to a very bad pass. Under government ownership, mech-
anization of the good mines and abandonment of the poor ones
may boost PMH in coal, especially if the workers' morale,
notably strengthened in the winter of 1947–48, continues high.
Britain actually will have in 1948 an exportable surplus of coal,
and has already enough coal to boost steel and electric production, and thus make export of heavy goods possible. The
extreme pessimists of 1947 are already confounded. Still, the
conclusion can hardly be avoided: as a whole, British PMH—
perhaps the best single index figure for large-scale production
—is notably lower than the American. The war has crippled
the industrial plant of her chief European rival, Germany, but
unless the victorious Allies decide to deindustrialize Germany
—a decision difficult to carry out consistently and over a long
period—the rebuilt German plant will have all the advantages
of modern invention.

Britain, then, has got to raise her PMH, and this means new
machines, which in turn means a large capital investment.
British financial and industrial leaders are fully aware of this
necessity. The report of the Cotton Textile Mission to the
United States had repercussions throughout the country. The
influential London periodical, the *Economist*, has long been
insisting that only by raising her PMH can Britain maintain
her exports at a level necessary to carry out the large social
reforms her people have been promised. The task, though difficult, is not impossible. British achievements in war industries
show that production can be made modern and efficient. But
the task of boosting PMH throughout industry in peacetime
will demand at home skill, energy, and good organization,
qualities the British have displayed abundantly in the past. It
will demand a willingness to make expensive changes in plant.
It will demand shifting of industries, perhaps almost complete
abandonment of such industries as the cotton textile. It will
demand again the enterprise and originality which produced
the original Industrial Revolution. It will demand for a time at
least the continuation of some kind of rationing, of postpone-

ment of that higher standard of living the British still hope for.

At this point, many Americans will add in their own minds: "and it will demand the kind of good management you can't expect to get from people that have gone in for government ownership of industry." So warm are feelings on this subject both in Britain and America that pleas for caution and compromise are likely to go unheard. We have already pointed out that three years of the Labour government have not meant the complete socialization of British economic life. The basic structure of British enterprise is not, in fact, very different from that of the United States in 1948. In neither country is there actually realized the fine freedom of enterprise familiar in classic economic theory; but in neither country is enterprise wholly in the hands of government officials. In both, large-scale industry, separation of management and ownership, close-knit ties between finance and industry, increasing difficulty in launching new enterprises, at least in big industries, increasing tendency to accept planning, even when done by the government, social security for workers, great power to trades unions —all these characteristics of a mature modern economy are present in both countries. Britain has so far nationalized but a small sector of her total economy. She still has big businesses, like Lever Brothers and the Imperial Chemical organization, and thousands of middling and small businesses. Her business men complain about government about as much as do American business men; in both countries business men do in practice get on fairly well with government. No professional economist would risk his reputation by using figures; but let us guess that, if Russian collectivization is 100°, and complete *laissez faire* (which never existed) 0°, then Britain may be at 60° and the United States at 45° or 50°. But these figures, even as guesses, are misleading. The American and the British economies are simply not worlds apart.

It certainly will not do to conclude that her modest nationalizations have made Britain's industrial comeback impossible. But she must have reliable trade outlets overseas for her exports.

The home market in the British Isles alone, though it can no doubt be expanded somewhat, is simply not enough. Her best choice, for her own good and certainly for the good of the rest of the world, would be a restored world trade, not indeed doctrinaire free trade, but a world with a reasonably stable monetary exchange, and without too many closed doors, a world trading as it did before 1914, not as it did from 1919 to 1939. Apart from this, there would seem to be but two possibilities: first, a more or less autarkic trading system of her own, the Commonwealth and Empire together with the Atlantic "rim" of Europe, France, the Low Countries, Scandinavia and their dependencies, welded into what is usually called the "sterling bloc"—or second, decline into the status of a small, self-sufficient and internationally unimportant nation. This last fate, which German radio propaganda beamed to Britain during the war constantly predicted for them, will most certainly not be accepted by the present generation of Britishers without a struggle. If they cannot get orderly world trade, they will make every effort to build up as strong and extensive a trading system, a "sterling bloc," as they possibly can. Some of them, indeed, recruited from both Conservative and Labour circles, really prefer the autarkic bloc. Their motives vary, but all these dissidents see Britain pursuing a policy independent, or at any rate more independent than now, of *both* the United States and Russia.

Most Britishers, however, want a restoration of orderly world trade. And most Britishers are convinced that the possibility of such restoration depends primarily on the policies to be pursued by the United States. They do not discount the importance of Russia, nor of Europe outside Russia, and they do not forget the immense potential of the Asiatic nations. But right now they are fully aware that the United States has emerged from this war in a position of industrial and financial primacy comparable to that the British once held in Victorian times. With some of the psychological implications of this British awareness of American primacy we shall deal in a later chapter. It is not pleasant to play second fiddle after you have led the orchestra. Some of the people who run Great Britain —though not at the present writing a majority of them—find the prospect of playing second fiddle so unpleasant that they are willing to fight a trade war with the United States to regain leadership. These are the people who regard the sterling bloc not as a less desirable alternative to world trade, but as Britain's best choice, indeed as her natural choice. Others, though they would like to collaborate with the United States and the rest of the world in restoring international trade in accordance with the aims of the Atlantic Charter, are frankly afraid that the United States will either withdraw into a sort of economic isolationism, or try to set up its own "dollar bloc" in the Western hemisphere and the Far East, or adopt a policy of out-and-out economic imperialism in an attempt to make the rest of the world economic tributaries of the United States. Still others, and notably many of the Keep Left group of the Labour Party, seem to feel that the price Britain must pay for helping the United States restore multilateral foreign trade would be the abandonment of the experiment in nationalization. They argue that the United States is consistently, from Greece through Italy and France to Britain, backing Rightist and undermining Leftist groups. That American policy does not in fact seem to be such, that the State Department has specifically pursued policies clearly in support of non-Communist Left groups where they are established, as in France, does not quiet the Keep Lefters in Britain. But in view of the activities of men like Colonel McCormick, it is clear that the balance of trade in misrepresentations between Britain and the United States is still to our discredit.

As a matter of fact, even Britishers who believe that the United States will support a restoration of genuine multilateral foreign trade are afraid that we will not do all that is necessary to promote a very high volume of international trade, a volume essential to Britain but not essential to us. They fear that going along with us will hold them back. That some of these fears may seem to most Americans ill-founded and ungenerous does not alter the fact that they exist in British minds.

2. THE BASIC AMERICAN ECONOMIC POSITION

You do not hear in the United States the slogan that we must export or die. It is true that most economists and many business men are convinced that if we are to have full employment and avoid recurrent depressions we must maintain, and indeed increase, our foreign trade. But American export trade, which in the 1930's was around 6 per cent of our annual national income, is a minor item in our national existence if we compare it to the British figure, which is around 33⅓ per cent. Even if America increases her exports, the economists hold that this increase will be accompanied by an increase in our national income, so that the *relative* importance of our foreign trade in our economy is not likely to be vastly increased in the near future. What this means is that millions of ordinary Americans, whose votes ultimately determine what our government does, do not feel, as do Britishers, that foreign trade is an immediate and vital part of our life.

But thousands of such ordinary Americans in, for instance, the shoemaking industry, workers and capitalists alike, have in the past showed an acute interest in protecting by a high tariff that industry from foreign competition. They are mostly concentrated in a few congressional districts. They have acquired great skill in lobbying and in other ways of bringing pressure to bear on their congressmen. Congressmen pressed by their constituents to vote for a high tariff on shoes have in the past been in the habit of agreeing with congressmen pressed by their constituents for a high tariff on sugar or textiles, on the basis of "you scratch my back and I'll scratch yours." The result has been a series of tariffs culminating in the highest one in our history, the Smoot-Hawley tariff of 1929, which is still in force, though its general level has been greatly reduced in practice by the series of trade agreements associated with the name of former Secretary of State Hull.

The United States, then, is traditionally a protectionist country. Our congressional government makes it easy for pressure groups to protect a particular industry by a process of vote-swapping; moreover, not only industrial groups, but also groups producing raw materials—sugar and beef, for instance—have shown this ability to make use of political pressures to insure that foreigners will not have free access to our markets. Indeed, some observers hold that nowadays farmers, stock raisers, and other producers of raw materials are perhaps more ardently protectionist than is much of American industry. Finally, to many Americans whose callings are apparently not directly affected by international trade, protectionism has become an article of faith—not as an economic theory, for most such people are ignorant of, or frankly distrust, such theory, but as a basic *political sentiment*. A great many Americans "believe in" protection—for the United States—as they believe in the Constitution. Not all Americans, of course; the tariff has been one of the great focal points of American debate ever since 1816.

That debate is right now at a critical point. No doubt writers on public affairs are overfond of discovering crossroads and turning points in the destiny of nations; but it really does look as if the United States had reached such a crossroads in its policy towards foreign trade. Sometime in the near future the American people, through its government, must choose between two roads, one of which leads to the restoration of international trade in something like its old nineteenth-century forms, the other to a continuation, and perhaps an accentuation, of the restraints and limitations to which such trade has been subjected in the last few decades. The metaphor is no doubt unduly simple. There are, rather, two *road systems*, which are not altogether without connecting byways, but which, like communications between mountain valleys, get further and further apart as one goes along them. The great ridge of the American tariff is today the watershed between the two systems. But here the metaphor breaks down, for we can make our own geography as we go; we can flatten the ridge. In the summer of 1945, with the acceptance by Congress of the extension of the Reciprocal Trade Agreement, we took a great step towards disposing of impossibly high tariffs. But it would be premature to say that this tariff issue is dead.

Americans are not used to the position of arbiter of international economic relations, and even today many good Americans are not really convinced that what we do in these matters must vitally affect the whole world. For well over a century after we attained our political independence we were in reality still a "colonial" nation economically; that is, we exported raw materials and imported manufactured goods and capital. We did indeed come out of the war of 1914–1918 as a great manufacturing nation and a creditor nation. We had already begun to export manufactured goods, and in between two wars we have lent much abroad. But we did not, until Mr. Hull's trade agreements, lower our tariffs; and these agreements came only after a world depression had already vastly lowered the size and value of international trade.

Just why does American policy make such a difference in the state of international trade as a whole? The answer lies in the *multilateral* nature of such trade in what economists are hopeful enough to consider its "natural" form. Now some international trade is bilateral; for example, Americans buy coffee from Brazilians and sell automobiles to Brazilians. Such a transaction *could* be carried out, between two governments at least, on a basis of pure barter, without any monetary medium of exchange whatever; as a matter of fact, in the parlous state things reached in the 1930's, the Germans came very close to such purely barter transactions. But our transaction above with Brazilians would still be a transaction between individual firms, and would need the mechanism of exchange of American and Brazilian money. Most international trade is, however, more complicated than the above instance. Americans might buy coffee from Brazilians, sell automobiles to Britishers, who in turn would sell textiles to Brazilians. This is triangular trade, a simple form of multilateral trade, and of course could only be carried on conveniently through some method of monetary payments. Actually, international trade of the classic nineteenth century sort is much more complicated than triangular trade; it is thoroughly multilateral, with firms in each country carrying on individual transactions in foreign trade with freedom to spend the receipts where they wish. These transactions add up to the country's "balance of trade."

There must be such a balance. Common sense as well as economics tells us that, short of a gift of its products to foreigners, what a country sells abroad must be balanced in the long run by what it buys from abroad. As a rich and generous country, we Americans have given our products to foreigners—witness our charity to the Japanese at the time of the Tokyo earthquake. In this war we adopted, in the form of Lend-Lease, the old British device of giving outright subsidies to allies who, we believed, were by their efforts against the enemies of America fighting for the defense of America. And we have since made advances in many different forms to many nations. Some of these advances have been outright gifts. But, in spite of what some of our demagogues say, our normal foreign trade—including exports financed by our commercial loans abroad—is not a form of charity. It is part of international trade, and it must in the long run balance.

Now the technical side of this balance, which involves complex theories of international monetary exchange, is bewildering to the layman. But laymen must make an effort to understand at least a simple form of economic technicalities. The economist may be in some senses in a position like that of the physician; he may—indeed in fairness to him we may admit that he does—have specialized professional knowledge of the body politic and economic that we laymen cannot have. But though a democracy can and must make use of experts in economics and even in less developed social sciences, it cannot abdicate in favor of the experts; it cannot say, "you're the doctor—go ahead and operate." After all, even in matters of bodily health, a good physician does not want his patients to regard him with superstitious reverence; he prefers a patient who knows enough to help take care of himself intelligently.

We may hope that simplification here will not be falsification. Broadly speaking, a country can balance its exports in international trade by accepting as imports goods of an equal value, or by making up for an excess of exported over imported goods by accepting the amount of the difference in money paid by foreigners—and this means by accepting gold, or foreign exchange, or temporarily an I.O.U. Similarly, it can balance an excess of imports by paying out gold or foreign exchange to foreigners. If trade in a country is in private hands, and this balance is made by accepting gold from foreigners, the imported gold will make money in that country more plentiful. With a great deal of money in circulation, prices will go up, native business men will find it increasingly attractive to buy goods in cheaper markets abroad and foreign business men will find it increasingly attractive to sell goods at the high prices prevailing in the markets of the gold-enriched country. By this process, the said country will gradually buy more and sell less abroad; it will correct its original imbalance of exports over imports, and, indeed, reach the point where it begins to send its gold abroad.

This is, greatly simplified, the classic theory of international trade. It will be seen at once that this "natural" balancing depends for its working on the free play of market transactions among business men in different countries. Governmental action, as we know well from experience, can do a great deal to alter the workings of this "natural" trade. It can lessen its volume by imposing tariffs; it can alter its channels by bilateral agreements and all sorts of devices; it can, as the American government has done, in effect impound an excess of gold imports, and thus, by taking the gold out of commerce, prevent or at least greatly diminish the rise of domestic prices which classical theory relies upon to correct an excess of exported goods over imported goods.

But most of these devices still leave at work at least some of the forces operating towards a "natural" balance of international trade. It is certainly possible to conceive conditions under which very little indeed is left of international trade as our fathers knew it. These conditions sound, and are, fantastic, but it is worth while considering some of them in order to get a clearer light on the problems ahead of us.

A country might entirely close its borders to all trade. This is what the economists call "autarky," complete economic self-sufficiency, and seems certainly to be as yet little more than a theoretical concept. Or a country might continue indefinitely to export more goods than it imported, accept gold in payment, and continue to impound the gold, or use it to pave streets. As long as other countries produced gold, this could theoretically go on. But not even the wisecrackers about our gold in Fort Knox can really suppose that this possibility is more than theoretical. Or a country might continue indefinitely to give away goods abroad; this is the most fantastic possibility of all. A country might, finally, maintain indefinitely the opposite kind of imbalance; it might regularly import more than it exported. This is not as fantastic as it sounds, and has occurred in history. When Rome, for instance, conquered Egypt it imposed a tribute, which took the form of shipments of corn, a large part of which was distributed free by the Roman government to its urban proletariat. A stickler for form might say that this was not an international transaction, since Egypt became a part of the Roman Empire. But the principle is clear. A nation can enslave another, and exact from the enslaved nation goods which are a tribute, not a return for other goods or services. Britain, too, has had an excess of imports over exports for generations, and this excess represents in part interest on investments abroad made long ago. Whether such payments are "tribute" is a nice question, but for the moralist rather than the economist.

All of the above extremes are in their pure form unreal and theoretical in the modern world. But each and every one has existed in a less extreme form as part of the complex of international economic relations in the contemporary world. Even the tribute—for what else was it when the Nazis forced on the peasants of the Balkans clocks and toys they did not want in "exchange" for the food and other raw materials the Nazis took? A brief aside at this point: trade between an industrial nation with a high standard of living, and a primitive "colonial" agricultural nation with a low standard of living, though for the pure moralist such trade may have some taint of tribute, is for the economist genuine trade; and even for the moralist, though the record of European trade relations with less advanced peoples is full of violence and injustice, it is difficult to deny that over the centuries this trade has gradually raised standards of living among such peoples, and has today spread industrialization all over the globe.

That a restoration of genuine freedom of world trade is to be preferred to any of the extreme forms of controlled trade listed above, or to any mixture or attenuation of them, we may take as axiomatic. That restoration depends so heavily on the United States that we may say that, if for the British the slogan is "export or die," for us the slogan is "import or fight another World War." The dilemma is not as pressing or as evident to most Americans as the British dilemma is to most Britishers, but it is just as real. And it means importing goods, not just gold, for as we have seen, gold importations cannot go on indefinitely.

But why cannot the United States, while *exporting* as it has done, limit itself to the *importing* of goods like Brazilian coffee, which it cannot produce itself, and which therefore do not compete with American products? The experts answer that that kind of importation is not enough, that the place of the United States in the great nexus of multilateral trade as it has been and may again be is too important for such limitations, that under such limitations the other advanced nations, including most emphatically Britain, would simply not have a sufficient supply of dollars to sustain such multilateral trading.

They point to the example of the 1930's, when the depression brought about a reduction in the amount of dollars put into the international pot by the United States through purchases of goods abroad, through payment for services, and through long-term investments, from more than *seven billion* dollars annually in the late twenties to less than *two and a half billion* annually in 1932. The effect of the catastrophic depression in the United States was like that of the proverbial stone in the mill-pond; the waves spread throughout the world. These same experts hold that, especially since the great additions made to our specialized industrial plant by the war, we must have an increased export of things like automobiles, refrigerators, radios, and similar products of our most efficient industries, or we cannot maintain full employment; and if the United States cannot maintain full employment, experience shows that under almost any conceivable system of international trade, let alone under the unbelievably complex system of mutual interdependence of nations that has been growing up since the first machine industry began, other nations cannot maintain full employment. We need hardly insist that again experience shows that extensive unemployment and world depression is one of the surest roads to war.

It is true that the United States need not—indeed cannot—make up all its present excess of exports over imports by imports of goods alone. The other highly organized parts of the world—save for Latin America—have all had wealth destroyed during the war, not increased, as with us. There just aren't goods enough available in most of the world, even were we willing to take them. Figures here are of dubious value, but one can guess without them. We might gradually increase imports of actual goods, gradually decrease outright subsidies to foreign nations (as the present ones to Greece, for instance), gradually increase tourist expenditures by Americans abroad, accept more foreign financial and freight services, take perhaps some gold or other "tribute," and finally produce something closer to a balanced international account. We should, how-

ever, under such conditions literally have to accept the responsibilities for being the richest and strongest nation on earth,
for being in 1950 what England was in 1850. We should have
to accept from abroad goods in payment of the interest due us
as bankers to the world. That means we should accept grave
political as well as *economic* commitments. The two are, in
this harsh world, quite inseparable.

But why not try something close to autarky, a nice neat
system in which we and our neighbors to the south and north
produce everything we need, and let the rest of the world go
hang? Americans should be made a bit suspicious of such a
program by the fact that it was precisely the program Hitler
himself urged upon us before November, 1942. Let there be,
he said, three great self-sufficient areas in the world—Europe
(Germany), Asia (Japan), and the Americas (United States).
There will be plenty of room for each, and none will ever
compete with the others, and at last there will be world peace.
History gives a clear answer to Hitler. States, even the greatest
and most self-sufficient states, are not the fixed things they
seem to be on the map, where they look as stable as so many
tiles in a colored mosaic; men, goods, and ideas have always
moved continually across the frontiers and oceans that look so
deceptively fixed on the map, and there is no evidence whatever that this process will stop nowadays when it can make use
of the airplane and the radio instead of wagons and sailing
vessels. Attempted autarky—that is, economic isolationism—is
also a road to war. To see why it is a road to war we shall have
to go beyond purely economic considerations for a moment.
The United States together with Canada and some of its Latin
American neighbors has certainly the material resources for
full prosperity under an autarkic system. But political and
psychological considerations make overwhelming the likelihood that any such autarkic great blocs as Hitler's propaganda
described (were they to grow up, they would not, of course,
be quite the ones Hitler wanted) would simply not stay put.
Creatures as mobile, imaginative, adventurous, and grasping as

human beings will no more obey the rigorous prohibitory measures necessary for full autarky, such as trade embargoes, than they will obey Volstead Acts. Archaeology and anthropology show us that in most primitive times men have indulged in "international" trade, even when "international" meant no more than "intertribal." Approaches to autarky have occurred only as a result of insurpassable geographical barriers, or of the pretty complete breakdown of law, order, techniques—in short, civilization. There are no insurpassable geographical barriers today, and in spite of the moanings of our prophets of doom, our civilization has not broken down. Modern men cannot attempt complete autarky and remain modern men.

We come back to the formula: for the United States it is "import or fight another world war." We have ceased to be in the world economy a colonial nation. We may have had economic greatness, like political greatness, thrust upon us; indeed, there are those who would say that *because* we have become economically great we have inevitably become politically great. But the fact is inescapable. We must face the responsibilities of this greatness.

The task will not be easy. One of the hardest parts of the task will be the making of the necessary adjustments in our economy by a permanent lowering of our tariffs to permit greater imports. The economist, when he is thinking in purely economic terms, can arrange matters nicely; suppose they do make inexpensive shoes more efficiently in Czechoslovakia than in the United States. Well, we make automobiles and electric refrigerators more efficiently than they are made in Czechoslovakia. Let us take shoes from the Czechoslovaks and send them our automobiles and refrigerators. This will mean, of course, that some American shoe factories will have a market so diminished that they will have to go out of business. But, says the economist, our motor and refrigerator factories will have more business—and furthermore, this increased business in such export industries will increase incomes of everybody connected with such industries, and thence will spread out over all demands for goods and services in the country. There will be plenty of room elsewhere for the displaced labor and capital that was driven out of the shoe industry.

Now the economist is not as hardhearted and inhuman as some laymen think him. He knows that it is asking a lot in human terms to expect men and women settled comfortably in Brockton or Binghamton to move out to Michigan, or convert shoe factories into some other kind of factory. He knows that even under modern conditions of semi-automatic or automatic machine production, it is not easy for workers and managers to change over from one industry to another. In his own terms, he knows that neither labor nor capital is perfectly mobile. But he can point out to the fact that even within our own country, and with little impulsion from abroad, the record of our dynamic economic history is full of examples of human hardships and displacements quite as great as any that will come from an alteration in our present tariff policy. The crumbling walls of small, water-powered New England cotton mills, the lilac-bordered cellar-holes of abandoned New England hill farms, are witnesses of past adjustments and conversions. New England has not—and even Yankees must conclude, most fortunately for us all has not—enjoyed tariff protection against North Carolina and Iowa.

Moreover, it should be possible to make the adjustments in our total economy, which *must* be made if we are to play our full part in an expanded world trade, in a more orderly and humane fashion than in the past of unrestrained private initiative and laissez-faire competition. There is, indeed, no occasion for easy optimism. Compromise between the traditional devotion of the American community to unrestricted private enterprise and the necessity—which really does seem in the light of historical development a necessity—for some government supervision of, and coöperation with, private enterprise will not be obtained without bitter debate. As we have already seen, the structure of our politics and our political traditions make tariff reform particularly difficult. A group of producers in a certain industry will piously and in full sincerity pass resolutions aligning itself solidly on the side of American participation in a new and better world organization to keep peace, will ratify the work of international conferences and United Nations Assemblies, and then work its head off to keep high tariff protection for its own products, thus undermining the economic basis without which no international political organization can work. Many American business men who made unfortunate investments abroad after the last war look with sour distrust on the possibilities of the foreign investment field; yet if the United States is to play the part in the world economy its industrial and financial strength requires it to play, we must, the experts tell us, lend dollars to get goods back from abroad. For dollars are today the necessary means of priming the pumps of industry in war-torn countries.

To sum up these basic economic generalizations: If the United States and Britain are to do their share towards reestablishing the kind of economic conditions in this real world, as they promised in words in the Atlantic Charter to do, the United States must adjust its import-export balance to suit its new position as the world's banker, and Britain must adjust its economy so that once more British goods are abundant enough, good enough, and cheap enough to sell in quantity all over the world.

3. THE POSTWAR BRITISH ECONOMY

Three years after V–E day no one can be confident that either nation will be able to carry out successfully these heavy responsibilities. In both, one may say without false optimism, many responsible people in all walks of life have given clear evidence that they intend to do their best to achieve this end. As for the United States, we have already assumed our first responsibility, that of lending and giving from our abundance to nations, including Britain, suffering from complex economic difficulties brought to a head by the war. We have done this from mixed motives, and, since we are a democracy, against the noisy protests of several minorities. We have done it, perhaps, a bit naively in that many of us have expected from the rest of the world a kind of gratitude most human beings are incapable of expressing, and perhaps of feeling. We have been decisively moved by hatred and fear towards the Russia of Stalin. But we have done it; we have primed the pump. The future alone can tell whether we can bring the priming to a necessary completion, and—much more important—whether we can adjust our economic life to the kind of international trade necessary to our position as the world's banker. Once the pump begins to flow, can we use our share of the water?

In this book our main concern must be with Britain's part of the task. Now it is still too early to estimate fairly how far Britain is on the road to recovery, and just where that road will lead. Moreover, the British experiment with nationalization, modest though it has been, has unquestionably complicated the situation—or, at any rate, has complicated our American diagnosis of the situation. For few of us Americans are unmoved to hope or fear by what is suggested to us by words like nationalization, socialism, collectivism. For most of us, what the Labour Party is trying to do is, regardless of their actual success in 1948, a Good Thing, or a Bad Thing. Nevertheless, an attempt at objective judgment must be made.

First of all, hardest to measure and yet most important, is the actual state of mind of Britishers about their prospects. Here, one can trace roughly a kind of chart: hope rising in the first months after victory over Japan; gradually falling as rationing and deprivation continued; rising again in 1946 as a few good things—gasoline for private driving, for instance—came back; a very bad fall as the abnormally severe winter of 1946–1947 and the rapid exhaustion of the American post-war loan brought on restrictions heavier in some ways than those of wartime; and a scraping of the bottom all during the summer of 1947. Bad news came pouring in on the British from all quarters, from India, from Germany, from Greece, from the home production front, until, as Mr. I. A. Richards has put it, the British people had a "Job complex." Like Job of the Bible, they felt they had lived in righteousness, and yet here was the wrath of God unloosed upon them. They felt hurt, bewildered, and blameless.

Then there came in the late autumn of 1947 a psychological upswing which seems to be still going on. Almost all observers are agreed that British morale is once more high, that the British now believe they really will some day get the good things of life they want so much. There is, as with all complex social phenomena, no simple explanation for the upswing. The mild winter of 1947–48 undoubtedly helped. Good news from the critical coal production front may have started what in this case one must call a benign circle of hard work and increased production in other industries. Perhaps it is merely that the human spirit, if it is going to survive at all, can only scrape the bottom of the trough for just so long, and must then start upward once again. At any rate, one must record that early in 1948 British morale is surprisingly good.

The concrete figures of production—which take some months to emerge from statisticians' offices—are perhaps not quite good enough to justify great optimism. Yet here, too, and in fields more readily measured, the charts are moving upward out of the lowest troughs. Steel at the end of 1947 had already reached a rate above the target for 1948, 14 million tons a year, in contrast to 10 million tons in 1938. Here the goal of 150 per cent of the 1938 figure has been nearly attained. Electric power has already reached 170 per cent of the 1938 figure. The newer textiles, such as rayon, have reached 134 per cent, though cotton and wool, which suffered from war concentration, are still lagging. And in these newer textiles the figures show an even more significant fact: a smaller labor force is producing a bigger output—PMH is going up. (In 1937, 72,200 workers produced 12.57 million pounds monthly average; in July, 1947, 61,700 workers produced 18.21 million pounds; the ratio of increased productivity per worker is from 174 to 295.)

Exports too are going up, in spite of the still very unsettled state of most of the world, and in spite of the fact that dollars are still extremely scarce, and that no other adequate currency for multilateral international trade exists. By the fourth quarter of 1946, for all exports, a figure of 111 per cent of 1938 had been reached; the target for the end of 1948, 164 per cent of 1938, may not quite be reached, but 150 per cent is almost certain. It begins to look as if the British could now *count* on being able to produce certain types of exports, especially now that coal and steel are so clearly on the upgrade. This will strengthen Britain's hand in diplomacy; it will give her, for the first time since the war, something to bargain with.

These figures do not mean that Britain is over the hump and in the clear. In the first place, the magic figure 150 per cent of exports at the 1938 level may well be too low. More important, the loss in investments abroad, the accumulation of debts abroad, may mean that Britain's international accounts cannot be balanced without further writing off of debts. Devaluation of the pound, a step long talked about, may yet be necessary to get Britain back into an economy where both ends really do meet. Still, and with all due allowance for the elasticity of statistics, even in the most honest hands, it is clear that British production is increasing.

With these increases in production of goods most necessary to strengthen Britain's internal and external position in the long run has gone, in recent months, a decrease of many kinds of what the beleaguered British are reluctantly obliged to consider nonessential spending and production. We have seen that in some respects the war brought an improvement in British diet. Milk, for instance, is now at 166 per cent of the 1938 level, even though it is still rationed. But, by and large, consumption of clothing, household goods, and food has been held back by deliberate government action—in fact, by diversion to salable exports—from the kind of rise one would normally expect after a war. True, as we have seen, at first some of the

American loan of 1946 was used to buy—at very high dollar prices—what might be called luxuries. The government has now pared such purchases to the bone. And yet the British people, with no more than the kind of grumbling that makes life possible, have accepted all this—one egg a week, twenty cents' worth of meat a week, strict rationing of clothing.

This is in itself an extraordinary thing, and a hopeful thing. Just as our American aid abroad, also a most hopeful thing, has been accompanied by bitter and public complaints and criticism in the United States, so this British foregoing of consumption to restore capital and production has been accompanied by bitter and public complaints and criticism at home, and by a certain amount of self-pity. It would be extraordinary, and perhaps not altogether hopeful, had this not been so. The silence and apparent unanimity with which the Russian people seem to have foregone consumption for the sake of production is simply not in the British—or American—tradition.

All in all, then, British economic conditions in 1948 hold the promise that Britain can keep up her end in the long and hard process of world recovery. Britain may, as we shall see, use her new-found confidence to strike out in directions not quite in accordance with the American blueprint for world recovery. And she may find that her present spurts in production, especially in coal and steel, cannot carry her over permanently into prosperity. Nevertheless, in a sound and now popular phrase, Britain seems to this writer a good "calculated risk."

Yet in fairness to the reader he must be warned that the above report of Britain's prospects is more favorable than most such reports today. Prophets, publicists, columnists, propagandists, government officials in both Britain and the United States, display in 1948 about as wide a range of opinion on this matter as can well be possible. To one doctor, the patient is at his very last gasp, if he is not already a corpse; to another, he is in the best of health, ready for normal life.

Now the pessimists hold that rising production and export

rates will not go up fast enough, will not reach targets; that aid under the Marshall Plan will not be enough; that therefore the British cannot possibly make even a plausible balance between national income and expenditure. They predict with some assurance that the British will devalue the pound—that is, of course, accept partial bankruptcy in governmental finance. They further predict that the necessity to economize will drive the British into still further retreat from their commitments in international affairs—to withdrawal of their troops of occupation from Germany, to abandonment of their less valuable strategic posts in the Middle East and Far East, to further curtailments in imports—in short, to something near to the status of a small power.

Should the worst that these prophets of doom foresee come about in the next few years, it is clear that Anglo-American relations would be fundamentally altered. The major problems would, indeed, be political rather than economic. British withdrawal would create a vacuum. This vacuum might conceivably be filled by the natives of the areas concerned. Such a generous solution seems extremely unlikely. The vacuum might be filled by international supervision, by the action of the United Nations. This idealistic solution seems also unlikely, but not wholly impossible. The vacuum might be filled by the United States, frankly the heir of Britain's political position in the world. This by no means impractical solution might well be a difficult one to get accepted by Congress, and it would require more political skill and honesty than, in the opinion of many of our critics, we have hitherto shown in international affairs. The vacuum might be filled by Russia. All we can be sure about is that it will be filled. For politics abhors a vacuum.

4. MONETARY PROBLEMS

We have hitherto considered in general terms the economic positions and capacities of the United States and Britain.

Policy in these very big matters no doubt gets determined in a series of critical decisions, such as the one we made when we granted the British loan of 1946. Yet much also gets decided in the give-and-take of daily intercourse and trade, in the decisions made on concrete problems, such as the monetary problem, in all the complex details of Anglo-American relations. We cannot in so small a space attempt to consider all these concrete problems. We can but sample, hoping thus to bring down to more concrete reality the somewhat general economic matters hitherto considered.

Foremost in the public mind among specific problems both Britain and the United States face is that of an effective international monetary system. Here the experts warn that the best medium of exchange is after all only a medium, that no monetary system can of itself cure a basically unbalanced, unhealthy trade. Nevertheless, satisfactory international monetary arrangements are certainly one of the prime necessities for maintaining such a balanced trade, and the importance given by the public in both Britain and America to the negotiations at Bretton Woods is quite justified.

It will be recalled that, though more than forty of the United Nations took part in the Bretton Woods conference, the materials on which the conference worked as a basis were the American White Plan and the British Keynes Plan. These plans differed, and though the conference arrived at a compromise between them, the differences remain as fundamental expressions of differences in the economic outlooks of the two countries, differences we must attempt to understand if we are to face intelligently the necessity for carrying out some such compromise as that arrived at by the Bretton Woods conference.

Briefly, the Americans tend to want to salvage as much as possible of the classic gold standard of earlier days; and the British tend to want to scrap the gold standard entirely. Now, as we have seen, the use of gold payments to settle balances among nations in international trade—that is, to pay for any nation's excess of imports over exports—would, in conditions of perfect freedom of international trade, work automatically. Under freedom of trade among private firms of different countries, gold importations by a nation with excess of exports would create *internal* changes first in prices and then in production in that nation, which would encourage imports and discourage exports; and conversely for a nation with excess of imports. This process is not a figment of the economist's imagination. It exists in many of the phenomena the natural scientist studies. He calls it a "natural tendency to equilibrium." Physicians used to call it the *vis medicatrix naturae*, the healing force of nature. If you are a healthy person, and your digestive system has a temporary excess of acidity, your body is so built that it will automatically start processes which will correct that excess.

But you still listen to the advertisers, and dose yourself with some kind of alkalizer? Well, old-fashioned economists would say, that's just the trouble with the world today; it has been dosing itself with all sorts of economic patent medicines, dignified with the name of "planning"—exchange controls, monetary depreciation, blocked currencies, quotas and the like, when it ought to rely on nature's simple regulative, gold. It is tempting for Americans, with their pioneer background of reliance on the blessings of nature, to take the attitude that what the whole world needs is less of the economic medicine of planning and more of the hoped-for economic regulative power of free individual enterprise. But it does look as if the present economic sickness of the world is too serious to be cured by a restored gold standard. For one thing, only the apparently healthy United States has billions of gold. For another, the patients are in no state of mind for such a heroic remedy—and any doctor knows that the state of his patient's mind is a basic element in his treatment.

For the gold standard is a heroic cure. We say that its working is automatic, but what does this mean in human terms? It means that, like the drastic application in the United States of lowered tariffs with which a return to healthy, balanced world trade on a straight gold standard would have to be implemented, its imposition would throw thousands out of work in certain industries, would bring about adjustments in prices and production that must be translated into the sufferings of uprooted human beings in order to be understood. The truth is that "natural" freedom of competition among countries and within countries is that of "nature red in tooth and claw," which, our grandfathers so fondly put it, was "very cruel, in order to be very kind." The world today—and that also includes the United States which has undergone the Great Depression—is not willing to put up with the cruelty. Every nation wants for its people security, full employment, a progressive, dynamic economy if possible, but an economy growing in an orderly way, without the great shocks of depressions. No nation is willing to jeopardize its own precarious economic stability by letting the economic policies of other countries have direct influence on its own economy. This would be true even under the kind of "natural" free competition classical economists postulate; it is even truer today when those economic policies may well, as the unhappy experience of the world since 1914 shows, take the form of veiled or open economic warfare.

The British and the American positions on international monetary problems are thus by no means poles apart. The American tends towards the pole of the gold standard, the British towards the pole of "managed" currency wholly divorced from gold, but both positions are in temperate zones where compromise is possible, not in the icy wastes of doctrinaire polar extremes. The American position in favor of relatively free exchange based on gold derives from many sources. We are economically the strongest nation on earth, and freedom suits the strong. We have a large part of the world's gold supply, and we would like to use it. We are the world's great creditor, and we hesitate before plans for an international managed or fiat money which might turn out to be a device for "managing" our good dollars into other people's pockets. Finally, the most important of all, we have what is in many ways the nearest thing to a major nineteenth-century economy on earth. We have, in spite of the New Deal, more economic individualism and less government control, less collectivism, than any other great power. Compare, for instance, the tightly organized British system of labor unions with our own, where the question of open versus closed shop is still debatable—and debated. We must recognize this condition as a current fact, not to be changed overnight, regardless of what we as individuals may want. Some Americans, perhaps a majority, think that our retention of much of nineteenth-century *laissez faire* is a good thing, that, indeed, we ought to have more individual freedom in business and less government "interference." Other Americans think that in these matters we lag behind other countries, and that we ought to "modernize" our economy by more central planning and government control of business. But the important point to emphasize here and now is that we have, as a nation, habits and traditions that incline us towards the orthodox, gold-standard solution of the problem of international monetary measures.

The British position in favor of an internationally managed medium of exchange divorced from the gold standard is also rooted in British conditions. Britain is, at least relatively, economically weak, and the weak distrust freedom. She has very little gold—not enough to pay the balances she owes to her own Dominions. She, and her customers, still need credit to restore the international marketing of goods that are now really beginning to emerge from factories, fields, and warehouses, and would like to be able to draw freely on some kind of money—call it dollars, pounds, bancors or unitases, or whatever you like—internationally acceptable among her customers. Moreover, Britain suffered under the gold standard in the 1920's and prospered (comparatively) after she went off the gold standard in 1931. Finally, and again most important, her underlying attitudes, her bias, if you will, lead her to trust, much more than the United States can, government controls, expert planning, a tempered collectivism.

What can, and already has begun to, bring Britain and the United States to agreement in spite of these differences of attitude is first of all a willingness on both sides to see the other's point of view, and to make necessary compromises, and second, the fact that American trust in individualism and gold is tempered by the very considerable modifications of doctrinaire *laissez faire* made in the last few decades in actual American business life, not only by the New Deal, but by our increasingly large-scale business enterprises themselves; while British desire to experiment in the ways of collective controls is tempered by a very strong residue, especially among her business men, of the habits and traditions of private economic initiative. Britain, be it repeated, is not a Marxian state.

The original British (Keynes) plan for an International Clearing Union with a huge capital of thirty-five to forty billion dollars of fiat money and the original American (White) plan for an International Stabilization Fund of much more modest dimensions and tied closely to gold were modified in discussion among experts of forty-four nations at Bretton Woods in July, 1944. Out of this discussion there emerged a plan for a Monetary Fund of about eight and three-quarters billion dollars, to which each member nation would subscribe a quota; of this quota 25 per cent would be in gold. The quota of the United States, which is the largest of all, is about two and a half or two and three-quarters billions. Each member is, for the purpose of settling its international balances (*not* for all items of its international trade), entitled to buy from the Fund in exchange for its own currency an amount not over 25 per cent of its quota in any one fiscal year, and in all not over twice the sum of its quota. Note that, though at any given moment under this plan the actual foreign transactions of a member country would not be tied to its stock of gold, the Fund as a whole is based on a gold reserve, and its functioning rests on a "bottom" of gold. The Fund is much smaller than the one the British wanted, and it provides more exchange flexibility and more controls than the one we wanted.

Like most compromises, it does not altogether satisfy anyone. Americans fear that it may yet prove an entering wedge for the draining away of our dollars into futile attempts by foreign countries to avoid economic adjustments made necessary by their plight (in brutal language, to avoid lowering their standard of living, or at any rate so reallocating their national income among their citizens as to mean a lower standard of living for their upper and middle classes). Britishers fear that the Fund will by no means be large enough to enable countries short of dollar exchange to get on their feet again.

Nevertheless, the Fund has already helped Britain, who can draw on it at the rate of 320 million dollars a year. Her first use of the Fund came on September 17, 1947, when she drew 60 million dollars. Indeed, if the new International Bank, which is only just getting under way, proves a success, Britain may find that very shortly she can actually pay her way. She may need relatively little under the Marshall Plan if all goes well; at the moment, the plan allots her a substantial part of the total to be expended in the first year.

The somewhat pathetic attempt the British made in the summer of 1947 to make the pound freely convertible into dollars —it had to be abandoned after six weeks because of the drain on Britain's scanty stock of dollars—and the French defiance of international monetary agreements by their devaluation of January, 1948 are clear indications that in spite of three years' hard work, the problem of dollar shortage in international trade—or, if you prefer it put that way, the problem of the achievement of a satisfactory international monetary standard —has not been solved. But, again, for all but the most impatient and the most idealistic (the two terms are by no means mutually exclusive), concrete, definite progress has been made since 1945. German reparations, the isolation of Russia and the Russian bloc, troubles in Asia, and a lot else can delay international economic stability. But the technical problem of money ought not to be one of the really difficult bars to such stability.

5. DIRECT ANGLO-AMERICAN TRADE

No matter how great the importance of Anglo-American agreement and coöperation in the general structure of international trade, their actual direct trade is the real test of how well they can get on together. Each has been, in the past, one of the best of the other's customers. As we have seen, the United States was for long after its political independence in a colonial economic relation to Great Britain. Even before 1914, that status had altered, and now trade between the two is trade between two highly developed industrial nations. Here again, figures may be useful, this time for the last normal year, 1939. In that year Britain imported from the United States goods worth 117 million pounds, 13 per cent of her total imports of goods. Of these, 34 million pounds represented foods and beverages, 27 million raw materials, and 56 million manufactured goods. In that year Britain exported to the United States goods worth 28 million pounds, 7 per cent of her total export of goods. Of these, 8 million pounds represented foods and beverages (a good deal of it Scotch whiskey), 4 million pounds raw materials, and 16 million pounds manufactured goods. Thus, manufactured goods is the biggest item both in British exports to the United States and in American exports to Britain.

This balance of trade in goods alone, 117 to 28, is almost certainly in long-run terms too much in our favor. Invisible items such as British shipping services to us, American tourist expenditures in Britain, and the like, bring the total account nearer to balance. But, especially as long as our American producers of cotton, foodstuffs and other raw materials have in Britain a market for which American imports of Scotch whiskey and British luxury foods like Huntley and Palmer's biscuits can hardly compensate, the balance of trade in goods between the United States and Britain will continue to be against the British—that is, they will import more goods from the United States than they export to us. Balance will have to be made up in the multilateral world trade of the two countries, as it always has been.

Even though such a balance is achieved through multilateral world trade—and this means, even when all invisible items are counted up, that Britain must export more to *some* parts of the world than she imports, and that the United States must import more from *some* parts of the world than she exports— even under such a prospective multilateral balance, it is probable that Anglo-American direct exchange of goods in the 1939 ratio of 117 to 28 in favor of the United States is unhealthy and cannot continue. Part of the remedy, as we have seen, is a lowering of American tariffs; more specifically in this case, a lowering of American tariffs on goods like woolen textiles, cutlery, crockery, men's clothes, and other goods for which Britain already has an established reputation, and which already enjoy prestige—snob value if you like, though the phrase is unfair—in the American market.

But the American tariff should not be made a universal whipping-boy. It usually takes two to make any kind of maladjustment. If Anglo-American direct trade is out of joint, part of the blame lies with the British, who have not sufficiently modernized their plant to produce efficiently. Their archaic methods of production are probably their major difficulty. But they have also in many cases not made their products sufficiently attractive to attract foreign consumers. Maybe human beings ought to prefer sound, long-lasting merchandise even if it is unattractively packaged and very obviously made for utility rather than for looks. Maybe the whole race is being misled by modern commercial methods—to be frank, by *American* methods—to prefer looks to utility. A good many of us would prefer a kitchen knife with an ugly brown wooden handle and a blade that cuts and can be sharpened to a kitchen

knife with a bright shiny plastic handle and a rustless blade
that cannot even cope with a potato. But for better or worse,
we seem to have gone in for quantity production of all sorts of
good-looking things that wear out quickly and keep sales up.
The British in this as in other respects are less "modern" than
we. If they want our domestic market, and indeed other
markets, they will have to cater to our tastes. They will have
to give up Victorian solidity and go in for at least a bit of
modern window dressing. This, to judge from the motorcars
they build for export, they are beginning to do.

No better illustration of some of the concrete difficulties of
direct Anglo-American trade can be asked than that afforded
by the problem of the movies. Here is an industry in which we
got a pronounced head start, whether because of the climate
of Southern California, or American initiative, or American
advertising, or American female beauty. Anyway, we got the
head start, and with it the economic power to attract the best
foreign directors and stars as soon as they had world reputa-
tions. We have raided the British for years with particular
severity, especially for actors and actresses. British audiences
even before the last war showed a fondness for the Hollywood
product which the aesthetically moral may deplore, but which
the rest of us will just accept as a fact. During the war, the
British government severely reduced the number of pictures made by the British movie industry, in accordance
with its general policy towards nonessentials. But movies
helped morale; therefore American imports were actually increased.

On the other hand, the British were slow in starting their
movie industry, and though in many ways they caught up
with us technically and in some respects passed us artistically,
they never did succeed in turning out a run-of-the-mill product
which would sell in the American market. The American
movie industry is, of course, not exactly an example of textbook American rugged individualism. It is at least a semi-
monopolistic industry, an example of what the economists call

oligopoly, within which competition is not quite the kind of competition Adam Smith and our current politicians talk about. The Hollywood industry has always said, and still says, that British movies don't go over in America, save for an occasional "Thirty-nine Steps" or an astounding "Henry V." The British, they say, go in too much for simple things, for bird watchers and flower gardeners, for Victorian humor, dowdiness, understatement, in short, for the world of Jane Austen and Anthony Trollope, from which Americans have already been frightened away by the attempts of their high-school teachers to attract them to it. American critics, who do not themselves make or market movies, sometimes claim that the Hollywood trusts, with their control over theaters, deliberately keep British movies out of this country, and that therefore Americans can't really tell whether or not they do like them. At any rate, relatively few British films come in, and many American films go out. The result: some Britishers owe Americans a balance in dollars.

The British paid 72 million dollars for American films in 1946–47, and this money in a sense came from our loan. Naturally they could not afford such an outlay, and Americans (outside the movie industry) were among the first to criticize them for so doing. The British have tried putting a quota on the number of films imported from the United States, and they have tried taxing very heavily the profits made by American film companies on the showing of their films in Britain. This last step was greeted from Hollywood with the cry that such taxation was confiscatory, and for a while there was a kind of Anglo-American film war. But cooler heads have already got to the work of compromise. Britain itself has now produced a movie magnate on the Hollywood model, Mr. J. Arthur Rank. The British movie industry is livening up, improving as an industry if not as an art. British movies are beginning to be seen more often, at least in our big cities. And with an improved international economic position Britain may be able to let American films compete freely on the British market. It is true, as we have insisted before, that we shall have to import *something* British. Perhaps, since the male animal is conservative in such matters, we can increase our importations of British woolens.

6. COMMERCIAL AVIATION

There remain for consideration, before we can close this necessarily long chapter, certain problems of Anglo-American economic relations in which governmental action is quite as important as it is in the making of monetary and banking arrangements. We may take as typical of these problems two which are, or have recently been, very much in the public eye: first, that of commercial aviation, which, like all forms of international transportation must be a close concern of governments; second, that of the oil industry, which may be taken as typical of an essential industrial—and strategic—raw material which is not found in Great Britain and which threatens to run short in the continental United States.

At Chicago there was held in the late autumn of 1944 an international conference on commercial aviation which was perhaps the least satisfactory in its outcome of recent international conferences. In the absence of Russia, and of course of Germany and Japan, the United States and Britain dominated the conference. The original plans of the two countries were at least as far apart as the White Plan and the Keynes Plan; but unlike Bretton Woods, Chicago reached no compromise. The conference ended with the United States and Britain agreeing, none too cheerfully, to disagree. Technical questions—provisions for international codes of safety in the air, signals, airport standards and the like—were settled satisfactorily; but the economic—and political—questions were not settled. An international interim commission of twenty-one is continuing the study of the issues involved, and there will probably be held before long another conference which will attempt to achieve a settlement.

The threat, and at present rather more than the threat, of an open split between the United States and Great Britain exists in the field of commercial aviation. The focal point of the disagreement is over what is colloquially known as the "fifth freedom" of the air. But pessimists who howl mournfully that nothing was done at Chicago should note that, in addition to its achievement of technical agreements and its establishment of the interim council, the conference did show that the United States and Britain, who can carry with them most of the other nations, save perhaps Russia, *are* agreed on enough freedoms to lift international commercial aviation far above its pre-war status. Notably, the four freedoms accepted in principle by both countries add up to transit rights, including right to refuel and repair, in any country that accepts the international agreement. Again with the enigmatic exception of Russia and her satellites, it seems likely that we have got beyond the days when a country could forbid a foreign commercial plane to land in its territory, or even to fly over it.

The "fifth freedom" the United States wants is the right for a commercial airline to deposit and pick up without restrictions freight and passengers in any country along a clearly defined and reasonable through route, *for a destination outside that country*. An American line, for instance, from New York to Moscow with stops at Glasgow, London, Paris, Berlin, and Warsaw would have the right to take passengers from London to Paris. It would not have the right to take passengers from Glasgow to London. Nor would it have the right to take a zigzag line, including say Marseilles and Milan en route, thus deviating from a through line for the purpose of picking up local traffic. Britain does not, as a matter of fact, wholly oppose this fifth freedom; she does, however, insist that it be *restricted* by specific agreement as to number of flights and volume of traffic. She wants to limit freedom of competition by assigning quotas which will protect her own lines from what she thinks will be, at least for a rather long period of transition, unfair American competition.

To Britain, it looks as though the United States wanted free commercial competition in the air because American aviation has come out of the war so strong that it could, in a free market, offer cheaper rates and better service everywhere on the globe, and thus force her own lines out of business, or make it necessary for her to provide them with a prohibitively high government subsidy. In fairness to Britain, we should admit that in view of the present state of commercial aviation in the two countries, her fears are by no means unreasonable. To the United States, however, it looks as if Britain, under the influence of a weakness which she ought to be able to remedy, were proposing quota and other restrictions the net effect of which would be to limit commercial aviation to a small-scale luxury trade, and hamper its development into a major form of world transportation.

Strategic considerations further complicate the problem. Their chief importance right now is a psychological one. The British—not to mince words—are frightened. They cannot possibly now have the hopeful, friendly, indeed naive *feelings* about what goes on in the air, which Americans, who have never been bombed by hostile airplanes, have. In spite of his justified pride in the RAF, the average Briton's heart does not leap up when he thinks of aviation. Indeed, deep down within he may well feel about airplanes that the fewer of the blasted things about the better. His government can hardly avoid being influenced by his feelings. But their official policy is to maintain a strong air force, and though it is no doubt true that civil planes cannot be converted into military planes, the factories that make them can be easily converted to the production of military planes and the trained personnel makes an invaluable reservoir of manpower; and furthermore, civil planes as military transports are of major importance in global warfare. The British want to maintain at all times as strong a civil aviation as possible. They believe that at present at least they cannot maintain such a civil aviation in open and free competition with American commercial airlines. Therefore they want a quota system; they want, in fact "protection." Americans, mindful of their own tariff history, ought to try to restrain their virtuous indignation over this British attempt to fly in the face of economic laws.

Just as the problem of moving pictures brings out the specific details of human tastes and habits on which international trade in part depends, so this problem of civil aviation brings out the larger aspects of national policy on which international trade also depends. Here, the formula for us would appear to be *force oblige*. The idealistic solution of the problem of world-wide aviation, which was indeed actually proposed at Chicago by Australia and New Zealand, would be an international authority charged with the actual operation of international airlines, and given authority superior to any national authority. It is pretty clear that the world is not ready for any such abandonment of national "sovereignty." Our own proposed "fifth freedom," which is certainly not without its idealistic aspects, may well be the next best thing, and we may well be able to make a start towards it by agreement with the British. But to attain that agreement we shall have to allow for British fears and weaknesses; we shall have to accept some qualifications on complete freedom of competition, allow British airlines some minimum of assured business. Meanwhile, we have gone ahead signing "five freedom" agreements bilaterally, trilaterally and indeed as multilaterally as we can with nations that will accept them. These are mostly Latin American nations, and we have had precedents for such action in the earlier development of Pan-American airline services. The danger from this policy, from the point of view of those who wish to see a genuine multilateral world trade is that, if the British are not somehow brought in, they may go ahead and build up by separate agreements their own aviation bloc. Such a bloc would be undesirable for the same reason that the establishment of semi-autarkic dollar blocs and sterling blocs would be undesirable. Their rivalry would be a constant threat to peace.

It is possible that the International Civil Aviation Organization (ICAO) which emerged ultimately from the Chicago meeting, and which was formally organized in May, 1947 at Montreal, may under the auspices of the United Nations give a genuinely international solution to these problems. Meanwhile, the British have managed to secure some of the transatlantic trade for their British Overseas Air Corporation and Anglo-American rivalry in the air is not at the moment serious. But the basic problems of air commerce between the two countries remain unsolved—which for two pretty empirically disposed peoples is perhaps in itself a solution.

7. OIL

Oil as a potential cause of strife between the United States and Great Britain came into somewhat undue prominence during the course of the war when a proposal for an American-built and American-owned pipeline from Saudi Arabia to the Mediterranean, sponsored by the American government through the Petroleum Reserves Corporation, was aired in the press of both countries. Fortunately, the course of the war took a turn for the better, the immediate need for the pipeline ceased to seem pressing, and a rather hush-hush Anglo-American conference of oil experts in 1944 allowed the proposal to drop for the time being. The hue and cry that arose at the time, however, shows that Anglo-American economic relations are subject to sudden tempestuous disturbances. Some Britishers saw in the proposed pipeline not merely an American attempt to secure additional reserves of oil against the possible exhaustion of our own, but an outright attempt of Yankee imperialists to muscle in and get a political protectorate in the Middle East. Some Americans saw in the British protests evidence that Britain was not only planning to hold on to every shred of political and economic power she had anywhere, but that she was planning to work on us in oil the same kind of squeeze she and the Dutch had worked on us in rubber through the Malayan and Netherlands East Indies monopoly of a decade ago.

Wiser heads have at the moment prevailed, and from the Anglo-American conference there may yet come, as that conference recommended, an international oil conference, which one may hope can be integrated under the Economic and Social Council of the original Dumbarton Oaks proposals. For, like all the important economic issues between the United States and Britain, oil is really an international issue. Effective Anglo-American agreements in this as in most other issues can only be a basis for wider international agreements.

For extremely important oil beds exist in small and weak countries, some of them "backward" countries; further exploration may find oil almost anywhere in the wilder parts of the world. A free scramble among the great and middle nations for such oil beds can lead, whether it is conducted by private companies, by private companies aided by their governments, or—as in Russia—by a government monopoly, to exploitation of backward countries, to the stirring up of their internal politics to the point of endemic revolution, to conditions we know by experience to be one of the surest seedbeds of wars. In the present state of the world, the traditional American policy of the Open Door—equal opportunity for all consuming countries to import oil from a given producing country—seems to be the best solution.

The policy of the Open Door should not, however, mean that a country is open to exploitation. It should be open to guests, not to masters. And this means that the host country should have definite rights, preferably under international guarantee, to regulate conditions of labor in oil fields, to guard against rapid exhaustion of supplies, to safeguard its royalties, and in general to keep its house in order as it sees fit.

The orderly international regulation of the oil industry will be difficult; indeed, if such regulation can be achieved for oil, it ought to be attainable for other strategic materials in possible short supply, such as rubber and the alloy metals. For the oil industry is traditionally a romantic industry, speculative in the extreme, and subject to unpredictable variations of supply. It is, moreover, an industry in which the small man stands no chance; he cannot afford the capital expenditure necessary to get started. Oil, therefore, tends towards large-scale production which easily becomes monopoly or semi-monopoly. Given half a chance, experience shows that such great companies in the major producing countries will try to overcome the variations and uncertainties traditional in the oil industry by getting together privately—with or without, but usually with, the aid of their governments—and agreeing on production and market quotas, prices, and the like. The net effect is almost always higher prices to consumers, and greater, or at least steadier, net profits to the companies.

8. CARTELS

This kind of international agreement among well organized producing companies—usually monopolies or semi-monopolies—is known as a *cartel*. We come at last to one of the great problems of Anglo-American economic relations, and one which will serve to sum up this chapter, since the problem of cartels underlies most other specific problems of such relations today. Do not ask for a rigorous definition of the term "cartel." The word has long ago passed from purely technical use into the language of everyday life, where, at least in the United States, it has acquired sinister overtones, much like those surrounding the term "trust." For the economist, a cartel is an agreement between firms in the same branch of trade limiting the freedom of these firms in the production and marketing of their products. A cartel is not the same thing as a trust. A cartel is a kind of treaty among firms which preserve the form at least of their independent existence; a trust is the incorporation of several firms into a super-firm. A cartel is a league of firms; a trust is a single sovereign firm, however complex its structure. For the common man, however, both cartel and trust are Big Business organized in restraint of trade. He tends to think of the trust as Big Business operating domestically, the cartel as Big Business operating internationally. This usage, if not strictly in accordance with the economist's terminology, is convenient for our purposes. We may agree to call a cartel an arrangement among firms of two or more countries to limit the free play of supply and demand in their business at home or abroad or both—but not necessarily to the same degree. This is an extreme or "polar" definition, but it is useful because it makes obvious the fact that some degree of regulation—that is, limitation of the free play of the market—is inevitable in international trade. It would be convenient if we could only say that such limitations achieved through international governmental regulation of trade—such, for instance, as international legislation on conditions of labor—were progressive and good, but that limitations achieved through agreements among firms—such, for instance, as exchange of patent and process information between certain American and German firms before the war—were reactionary and bad. Unfortunately, you can't unscramble governments and private firms in contemporary international cartel or cartel-like activities. Government-owned enterprises have actually participated with private companies in international agreements restrictive in nature.

The real issue, then, is not one between the impossible poles of absolute unrestricted international free-trade and absolute restriction of such trade—say by the organization in each of the independent nations of the world of foreign trading monopolies on the Russian model and the organization of these into a sort of world super-cartel—but rather one of the complex and constantly changing adjustments of conditions of international trade among nations in no one of which is the balance between private business enterprise, little and big, and government regulation or ownership of business ever exactly the same.

Now by and large it is true that in Britain the temper of the business community and of government experts—the "climate of opinion"—is today a good deal more inclined towards the pole of collectivism than towards the pole of unrestricted private enterprise; and in the United States the climate of opinion is inclined rather towards the pole of private enterprise and free competition of individuals and firms, in the domestic as in the international field. But we must take care not to see this as an opposition of black and white; we must avoid the dangerous formula of "either . . . or." Britain is not a collectivist country; the United States is not a country of small independent producers competing among themselves in pioneer freedom. Both countries in fact are seeking for a middle way between private enterprise and government intervention.

The danger is that Americans, not only ordinary citizens, but also business leaders and economists, may fall into the habit of assuming that whenever in specific economic negotiations the British propose a restriction (as in commercial aviation) they are seeking, if the affair is primarily a governmental one, to impose "socialism" on us, or, if the affair is primarily one of private firms, to make us join a wicked "cartel." On the British side, the danger is that whenever we propose greater freedom of competition (again, commercial aviation will do as an example) they will form the habit of assuming that we want a fine free-for-all, from which, since we are a very rich and powerful nation strengthened rather than weakened by the war, we shall inevitably emerge with the lion's share. What we all want, British, Americans, and the rest of the world, is the increased production modern technology can give us; and then, if it would still be impossibly Utopian to talk of every nation's share of that production as a lion's share, it would nevertheless be true that the share of a much humbler quadruped under such condition would be greater than the lion's share of the pitifully shrunken production of the 1930's.

Here too there is the possibility that Anglo-American differences over cartels can be adjusted in an international organization. In the preliminary work for the International Trade Organization under the United Nations, agreement was reached in the summer of 1947 to set up a commission to pass on infringements of fair trade practices by cartels. All will depend, of course, on the way in which good and bad cartel practices are defined in the daily rub of actual cases. One may still hope that here, as in the general problem of restoring international economic order, the American representatives will not attempt to put into practice the nicest forms of economic free trade taught them by their college professors thirty years ago.

9. THE POLITICAL IMPLICATIONS

The classical economists would still seem to be right; the best way to get the most out of the resources of this earth is to make full use of the varied "natural" and acquired skills of all peoples by allowing them to specialize on what they produce best, and exchange freely these products in multilateral trade. We have throughout this chapter emphasized such trade as a goal that both the United States and Great Britain can work for to their mutual advantage. But this goal is no easier to attain than the political goal of organized world peace with which it is so closely tied. It will not be attained at once, nor without setbacks. Though, as we have pointed out, political and psychological considerations make it extremely unlikely that the United States could pursue even a modified economic self-sufficiency for long, there is little doubt that she could protect herself for a while in an era of international anarchy by settling down in her own and adjacent quarters. Britain, however, could not maintain anything like her present standards of living by such a withdrawal. At the very least, she would have to trade with—that is, be able to draw on the economic resources of—the Commonwealth and Empire or adjacent Europe, or both. Even under best conditions of multilateral trade, some economists are pessimistic about Britain's ability to solve her problem of balance of payments. In the face of their difficulties, there is little wonder that some Britishers do not even want to try to get the best solution—healthy multi-lateral world trade, but are willing to content themselves with the perhaps safer, but shrunken and restricted, prospects of a cartelized "planned economy" in a sterling bloc. We Americans are hardly in a position to tell them not to be so timid.

For, though the American instinct against restrictions of output is a sound one, we should be honest enough to recall that we too did a certain amount of "plowing under" in not very distant times. We should be aware that domestic trade practices restrictive in nature—that is, like those of cartels—are a commonplace of American economic life. The truth is that when times are bad and men and nations are distrustful of one another they will in desperation take all sorts of restrictive measures to guard the little they have—even to the paradoxical extent of destroying part of what they have so that the rest will be more valuable to its owners, if not to the community. In a time of troubles each nation, and each group within a nation, will try to protect itself from outsiders by quota systems, cartels, and a hundred other devices. The science of economics can help us greatly to increased production and better distribution, but it cannot provide a magic formula that will get us out of our present difficulties. The skills we call political are still essential if we are to build a better world.

It is not, of course, that economic and political considerations are mutually exclusive or antithetical. Neither makes sense without the other. Neither really "comes first." But problems of Anglo-American economic relations cannot be settled, even though economists and business men of both countries can come to agreement on technical matters, unless the two countries can establish mutually satisfactory political relations in a world of generally orderly and decent international relations. To come back once more to an analogy from human physiology: the role of economics may be compared to that of diet in human health. We must have a well-balanced, varied, and abundant diet if we are to get the best out of life on this earth. If we start with good health, such a diet may well be in itself enough to keep us healthy. But if we have fallen into a state of nervous and physical exhaustion, complicated by serious organic disease, no good physician would hold that the best of food would in itself restore us to health. We should need rest, medicine, good sound psychological therapy, perhaps even a bit of surgical attention. The world today has been through a very serious illness. It is, one may hope, on the way to health again, but at the very least it is now no more than convalescent. Diet—economics—will not alone bring it back to health; it needs the full therapy of politics. To leave the metaphor and return to our facts: in a world where there is no accepted rule of international law, where each nation fears its neighbors, each will try to protect itself by economic restrictions. You cannot have an expanding world-trade in the midst of international anarchy. We come, then, to the problem of what Anglo-American political relations can do to diminish the international anarchy.

9. Political Problems

Somewhere in the train of events leading up to almost all wars you will find a disputed territory—the Polish Corridor, Bosnia and Herzegovina, Trieste and the Trentino, Alsace-Lorraine, Texas. One nation wants a piece of land another has got, and goes to war to obtain it. There is no use disputing over the question as to whether the aggressor nation is moved by political or economic motives, whether it is out for "power" or "wealth." The fact remains that territorial disputes are one of the simplest and most obvious causes of war. There are certain regions which have long been danger zones of dispute between powerful states. Such, for instance are those two European fragmentation zones of small and middle-sized states which separate the German nation from its French rival on the West and its Russian rival on the East. In the five hundred years of modern European history you can find involved in almost every one of its dozens of wars some bit of land on a rough semicircle looping down from Danzig to Trieste and back to the mouths of the Rhine and Scheldt.

There is no such zone of fragmentation and dispute between the United States and Great Britain. As late as 1840, no one could be sure that the northern frontier of the United States would not form such a zone. We had invaded Canada unsuccessfully during the War of 1812. The boundaries of Maine and of Oregon were still in dispute. But the difficulties were overcome and today the "three thousand miles without a fortification" which form the land and lake boundary between the

United States and the British Dominion of Canada is a comforting platitude of after-dinner speeches. This does not mean that there are no problems, and no threat of future problems, in the triangular relationship of the United States, Great Britain, and Canada. But it does mean that one of the simplest and surest causes of war, boundary disputes, are at present no threat to Anglo-American relations. Niagara Falls is no Danzig, Aroostook County no Alsace-Lorraine. It is, indeed, possible to go further, and say that no important group in Great Britain wants to raise the British flag, or a Dominion flag, anywhere on earth where the American flag flies now; and that no important group in the United States wants to raise the American flag where the British or a Dominion flag flies now. Our mutual enemies in this war recognized this fact when they stated in their propaganda that both Britain and the United States are "satiated" powers. Problems of the degree of British or American political and economic "influence" in various parts of the world do indeed exist; but neither power wants any of the other's land in the sense that Nazi Germany wanted the Sudetenland.

1. THE ATLANTIC AND PACIFIC BASES

There is one possible exception to this rule, one territorial problem in Anglo-American relations which might conceivably come to be a territorial dispute. That is the matter of American air and naval bases in British territory. With the consent —indeed with the delighted consent—of the imperially-minded Mr. Churchill, the United States secured, before Pearl Harbor brought us into the shooting war, Atlantic air and naval bases on a ninety-nine year lease from Great Britain. These bases extend on an arc from Labrador and Newfoundland to the island of Trinidad off the coast of South America. Existing leases enable us to make full use of these bases until the year 2040, which in 1948 seems a long way off. The United States does not, however, "own" in strict juridical sovereignty even those portions of British territory occupied by the bases, let alone the whole of Bermuda, Antigua, Trinidad, and the rest.

There is a current of opinion in the United States, by no means unrepresented in Congress, which wants to go beyond these ninety-nine year leases and annex outright some or all of the Atlantic bases. The annexationists present a variety of arguments. Chief among them is the assertion that American national security demands outright ownership. A mere lease-hold, they say, is not enough. The British are right there on the scene, and though we may hope that we shall never quarrel with the British, we can never be sure we shan't, and therefore we can never really be safe. You may call them American bases, say the annexationists, but they will in fact be shared with the British. There are bound to be, as there were during the con-struction of the bases, all sorts of administrative difficulties, if not more serious political difficulties, with the local people as long as they are not American citizens. Anyway, the annexa-tionists conclude, the British owe us a lot, morally as well as economically, for our support in this war. The least we can get in return for Lend-Lease and the lives of our boys is a few square miles of land essential for our national safety and of no real use to the British—in fact, a source of economic and strategic weakness to the British.

It does not seem that at present there is anything like a strong annexationist sentiment in the United States as regards these bases. The arguments above cited are typical of American jingoes, isolationists (who are often jingoes not so much in disguise as in a different mood) and professional Anglophobes. There are plenty of signs that the American public is emerging from this greatest of wars in a mood far more generous and in-ternationally coöperative than that of the minority which is willing to risk a quarrel with Britain for the outright owner-ship of the Atlantic bases. The strategic necessity for American retention and most efficient use of these bases is, of course, axiomatic with professional military and naval men. Such pro-fessionals in America as elsewhere are not infrequently likely to consider strategic considerations as overriding political considerations. Many of them would like to own the bases outright, without having to make and keep making adjustments with the British. But our government has hitherto carefully avoided sponsoring a demand for outright ownership, and the public has not been worked up to any excitement over the question: you hear no slogans like "Fifty-four forty or fight!"

On the British side, there is sure to be a deep and widespread resentment against any proposal to cede British territory. Cession to a triumphant ally would seem in some ways worse than cession to a triumphant enemy. The Atlantic bases are a beautiful example of the great importance of sentiments—irrational sentiments, if you like—in human affairs. American annexationists are right in saying that the Atlantic bases are by no means economic assets to Great Britain. A large part of her Caribbean possessions has been for some time a depressed area, and a continuing problem to her Colonial Office. Indeed, an Anglo-American commission has been created to find ways of restoring prosperity to these once-rich lands. Bermuda, if no liability to the British, is a tiny island group dependent largely on the North American tourist trade. Newfoundland has been in grave economic difficulties. Even strategically, it may be argued that Great Britain as long ago as 1901, when the Hay-Pauncefote Treaty between Britain and the United States virtually recognized the Caribbean as an American lake, decided that she must in face of the German threat gather in her widespread navy and abandon claim to world-wide supremacy. Why should she object to the logical conclusion of this withdrawal by abandoning the Atlantic bases to the United States?

But Britishers do object. Trinidad may be no more to most of them than a bit of red on a world map which has a lot more important bits of the red color mapmakers seem by convention agreed to use for the British Empire and Commonwealth. They don't want to give up even the tiniest and most expensive blob of red. Reason, commonsense, and economics will not

budge them. Once national pride—national egotism if you prefer bad names—attaches itself to a bit of rock, desert, or jungle,
men will, if necessary, fight foolishly and heroically to try to
hold it.

We must not exaggerate. American annexation of the
Atlantic bases is no more than a possible threat to Anglo-
American relations. It has not yet come into actual politics, and
the odds are that it will not in the immediate future. Even
were the American government to press for annexation of
some, at least, of the bases, it is by no means impossible that
a British government might be willing to let them go under
conditions not too wounding to British pride. But under the
best of such conditions, the United States would be almost certain to rouse in Britain popular feelings that would threaten,
if not put an end to, Anglo-American coöperation. It would
seem to be the part of wisdom for the United States to put
up with something less than absolute sovereignty over the
bases, even though such sovereignty would make their military
and naval use much more convenient for us, and try to get the
best out of the present leases. They have already served us very
well, and will continue to do so. Only a hostile Britain, a hostile
Canada, could impede our use of the Atlantic bases; and the
surest way of making those countries hostile to us would be
for us to go in for landgrabbing at their expense. It would be
very hard indeed for an American demand for the islands to be
so couched as not to seem to Britishers and Canadians landgrabbing.

The United States during the course of World War II established land, air, and naval bases all over the globe. Most
of these bases in Britain and France have, of course, been duly
closed, and we are keeping only those necessary to the supply
of our army of occupation in Germany. But, until better relations with Russia are established, we shall want to keep some
sort of hold on our air routes to the Middle East. At present,
there is enough left of our close wartime coöperation with
the British so that the problem of liquidating our bases in the
Mediterranean and in Africa does not seem serious.

Ascension Island, the British-owned rock in the South Atlantic between South America and Africa, is in some ways a case apart. The importance of this island, which we made into a great airfield for our African supply-route to Russia, the Middle East and India, has only recently emerged from wartime secrecy. The island is in some way in the same category as the Atlantic bases. It is essential to the defense of the Western hemisphere under modern conditions of warfare, and we are bound to take measures to see that it cannot fall into hostile hands. Most of the Pacific bases we have built up beyond Hawaii are either in islands formerly mandated to Japan or on the territories of our Pacific allies, Great Britain, France, Australia, New Zealand, China. What to do with these bases is part of the whole Pacific problem, in which Britain has an obvious interest, and to which we shall come shortly. Meanwhile, it should be pointed out here that at least one of the islands taken at great cost of American lives, and often mentioned as a suitable permanent American base, belonged not to the Japanese occupier, but was mandated directly to Britain. This is Tarawa. Americans who announce that henceforth Tarawa is ours ought at least to have the grace to add, "with Britain's consent." If our naval experts decide that we must have Tarawa, it is likely that Britain will relinquish her claim to the island. But we should realize that in international law— and morality—its status is different from that of Japanese or Japanese-mandated islands like Iwo Jima or Saipan.

With the exception, then, of certain air and naval bases, there are no direct territorial conflicts between the United States and Britain. Neither wants territory belonging to the other. There remain, however, possibilities of conflict over the disposition of former enemy or enemy-held territories, and, in a world where the best obtainable international organization will still leave some sixty-odd "sovereign" nations, the possibility that Britain and the United States will fall into the kind of rivalry suggested by the term "spheres of influence." Both these possibilities must be considered.

2. ENEMY-HELD TERRITORIES AND THE TRUSTEESHIP PROBLEM

This time there are no German overseas colonies to give trouble. The Nazi empire was entirely in Europe. In the disposition of its constituent parts both Britain and the United States have a great, but not a direct, interest. The problem is essentially part of the whole problem of what to do with Germany, to which we shall come later. But the disposition of Italian and Japanese overseas possessions presents problems of the kind faced, not too successfully, in 1919. On the reversion of some parts of the temporary Italian and Japanese empires to the independent nations they formerly belonged to, both Britain and the United States are presumably agreed. Ethiopia, indeed, has already been reconstituted. Japanese-held China will become Chinese again. Yet even Ethiopia is no independent nation in the sense that Switzerland, for instance, is independent; and most of the lands from which the Italians and the Japanese have been driven bring up clearly the problem of colonial, dependent, backward peoples—Eritrea, Libya, Malaya, Borneo, and the rest.

We have come to the problem of the treatment of such peoples all over the world. Lands in 1939 under the Italian or Japanese flags form only a small part of the territories of dependent peoples—Libya and Italian East Africa, scattered Pacific islands once belonging to Germany and under Japanese mandate since Versailles, earlier Japanese conquests like Formosa and Korea. China has a historic claim to Formosa, Korea was until 1910 at least semi-independent, and Ethiopia was actually a member of the League of Nations; but the rest of these lands may be considered as disposable. Not so, of course, the recent Japanese conquests of lands "belonging to" Britain or a Dominion, Holland, France, China, the United States. These are much less clearly disposable.

Nevertheless, to many Americans, and we must admit, to be fair, to a certain number of Britishers, Dutch, and French, the opportunity seems present for a general settlement of the whole question of dependent areas. Since the term "mandate" has shared the discredit that has come upon all the works of the men of Versailles, advocates of a thorough reform of the system of colonial governments have adopted the term "trusteeship." Now the world-wide ramifications of the problem of treatment of dependent areas, its complexity and delicacy, make it one of the most serious of contemporary problems, and one which has so far been approached rather gingerly by the trusteeship experts of the United Nations. It is one on which the United States and Britain are obviously not wholly agreed. In neither country is there anything like unanimity, but by and large we stand at present for a large measure of reform, for the establishment of as far-reaching international trusteeship as possible, for the gradual but steady preparation of backward peoples for eventual independence; and Britain, followed by the other European colonial powers, stands *on the whole* for the present colonial system, with each colonial power managing its own possessions in accordance with its own conscience and its own sense of international morality, duly but perhaps a bit indefinitely meshed in with the trusteeship provisions of the United Nations.

At the level of interchange of comment in press and radio the question unfortunately lends itself to the kind of mutual reproaches that are so easy when we think of nations as individuals—as, alas! we all have to do, no matter how aware of semantic difficulties we may be. The United States, we hear from Britishers, is being self-righteous about trusteeship. She hasn't, and doesn't need, dependencies. She'll take good care to see that even an independent Philippine Commonwealth won't be too independent; and besides, she isn't talking about trusteeship for Hawaii, the Virgin Islands, and Puerto Rico. Until the United States practices what she preaches, they maintain, she shouldn't be so damned pious about British sins in Hong Kong and Singapore. Britain, we hear from Americans on the other hand, is the same old unregenerate imperialist she always was, selfishly grinding down subject peoples to enrich herself.

The two nations are fortunately not as far apart on this question as they would appear to be from such mutual reproaches among their citizens. The American government has never espoused the extreme point of view of the idealists who think that we can seize this occasion to do away altogether with the old colonial system, abolish all "empires" and the vested rights incorporated in them, and set up a single international authority over all dependent peoples. The American navy—and it is almost certain that the majority of the American people back their navy in this—is firmly set against accepting any international trusteeship over the bases we shall acquire from Japan. If only for this reason, we shall be forced into some sort of compromise. On the British side, though there are certainly a few die-hard Tories who want to preserve their Empire exactly as it was, the Labour Party, the Young Tories, and the great majority of independent voters are fully aware that changes must be made, and have already made many of them, notably in India, Burma, Malaya, and Ceylon. They are sensitive to American criticism, and they do not want to appear to be yielding to American pressure. They do not want to scrap the Empire—not even the Labourites want that —because they are patriotic Britishers and because they are fully aware of the economic and strategic value to Britain of these overseas territories.

Only a very rash person would try to predict just what will happen to dependent areas all over the globe. Even the peace treaty with Italy, ratified by the American Senate in June, 1947, specified merely that Italy was to renounce her African possessions. The Dodecanese Islands are clearly to go to Greece; Russia's claim to part of Libya no doubt further complicated the problem of the disposal of these Italian colonial possessions. Some at least may possibly go to Britain, outright or as lands under trusteeship, though at the rate at which Britain since 1947 has been trying to get rid of overseas burdens, no one should be sure that she would accept Libya. The Italian colonies were an economic burden to Italy, and they would almost certainly be an economic burden to Britain. The Italians may yet get some of these lands back, as a reward for good behavior. We may have the extraordinary spectacle of land that no one—save the Russians—seems to want. Or we may even have a real experiment in government by the United Nations.

3. SPHERES OF INFLUENCE: THE MIDDLE EAST

This, and the problem of the disposition of Japanese conquests, brings us squarely to the problem of possible Anglo-American conflict, not over annexations or even over trusteeships, but over that vague but very real extension of national power known in the jargon of international politics as spheres of influence. The term is imprecise, and usually derogatory; but if we keep in mind that such influence means at a minimum economic measures setting up the kind of "bloc" we have already seen as a major threat to world trade and world order, we shall not go far wrong in our use of the term. There are three main areas in the world where the threat exists that Anglo-American competition for trade—which is inevitable, and can under proper conditions of restraint be good for both countries—may become rivalry, damaging to both countries and to the peace of the world, for "spheres of influence." The areas we have in mind are the Middle East, the Far East, and Latin America.

The Middle East we may here define broadly as the irregular quadrilateral whose four corners are Turkey, Persia, Ethiopia, and French North Africa. This old Moslem core-land, once more advanced than most of Europe, felt little, or none, of those extraordinary forces that gave Europe the leadership of the modern world—the Renaissance and the Industrial Revolution. As a result, for the last few centuries every European power that counted, from Spain to Russia, has pursued its "interests"—there are harsher words for this pursuit—in the Middle East. Spain is long since out of the scramble, though even Spain clings desperately to a bit of Morocco. Germany's bid, fresh in our minds as "Berlin to Bagdad," is finished for the present at least. So is Italy's. France clings forlornly—and to most of us, annoyingly—to the last shreds of her influence in the Levant, and faces a serious native problem in North Africa. Russia, indeed, seems far from finished in the Middle East. Those who hold—and they include many Britishers—that Stalin's Russia is pursuing traditional Tsarist aims in foreign policy, fear that Russia intends to "penetrate" the Middle East in the time-dishonored fashion. Britain herself, under varied pressures, has decided to withdraw from Palestine; but it would be a great mistake to conclude that Britain intends to abandon her "interests," her "sphere of influence" in the Middle East.

Britain cannot withdraw altogether from this area. You simply cannot destroy that much history overnight. Britain has two major interests here, among a host of others: the Suez Canal, about which it is enough to say that Britishers *feel* towards it as we feel towards the Panama Canal, and oil, for which the region is an important source of supply. She will not, especially with Russia in the offing, hand over the task of protecting the Suez Canal to a weak power like Egypt, nor will she give up her rights in the production and transportation of oil in the Middle East.

Moreover, the whole region is stirring with the desire of its peoples to catch up with Western civilization. If you are a pessimist, you may well fear that these nationalistic stirrings in the Middle East mean that the cycle we of the West have perhaps begun to emerge from—industrialization, labor troubles, economic and political rivalries among so-called independent nations, racial and religious quarrels—will all have to be gone through there, to the great detriment of international order. If you are an optimist, you may hope that the Middle East can skip a few stages, and emerge fairly soon as a modern well-governed federation, a United States of the Middle East. At any rate, the recent modernization of Turkey and the rise of nationalism in the Arab states holds a promise as well as a threat. If Great Britain, as the dominant outside power in that region, can use her position wisely and temperately to promote the union and enfranchisement of these long-exploited but clearly gifted peoples, if she can moderate without suppressing their aroused nationalisms, if she can avoid the temptation to secure monopolistic privileges for herself, thus closing the door to international trade, the Middle East may not be what it threatens to be, a plague zone and breeding ground of world wars.

The thorniest immediate problem in this part of the world is that of Palestine. This would seem to be the kind of problem for which there is no immediate solution—not even a solution like Alexander's cutting of the Gordian knot. Yet some of us human beings can face with patience, hard work, and by no means hopeless research an immediately insoluble medical problem like that of cancer. Some of us should be able to face the Palestinian problem.*

Britain after the Four Years' War undertook to hold from the League of Nations a mandate for Palestine, which had been yielded up by its former masters, the defeated—and alien—Turks. The mandate was for the benefit of the existing population, mostly Arabs, and for Jews who were to migrate then to the old homeland. How far Britain was committed by the famous "Balfour Declaration" to the task of turning this mandate ultimately into a fully sovereign independent Jewish national state is a question that has been bitterly debated for years. The fact remains that Jewish immigration enriched Palestine with men and money, but left it divided among Jews and Arabs; and the Arabs, under the Turks last in possession of this history-ridden land, saw themselves men-

* For a full discussion, see Ephraim A. Speiser, *The United States and the Near East* (Cambridge: Harvard University Press, 1947), pp. 192–219.

aced by the growing wealth and numbers of the Jews. With the increased burdens put upon her by the recent war, Britain found her commitments in Palestine excessive. Psychologically, too, the British were worn out. They felt, and feel, pretty virtuous about their behavior in Palestine. To an ardent Zionist, such feelings may seem hypocrisy; but the British honestly feel, for the most part, that they have held a just balance between Jew and Arab. Recent events, indeed, have made most British anti-Jewish and pro-Arab. Pressure from displaced European Jews to enter Palestine, where their presence would have further altered the balance in favor of the Jews, and, behind this, pressure from powerful Jewish groups in the United States, made the British position even more unbearable.

After many debates, commissions, investigations, and a general expenditure of much energy, and even of good will and intelligence, as well as of less agreeable human traits, we have seen today the attempt to apply the remedy of partition between Arabs and Jews. In 1947, with the United States and Russia in the unusual position of agreement, the Security Commission of United Nations decided that, on the British relinquishing the mandate, Palestine (which is just a bit bigger in area than Vermont) would be divided into two sovereign parts, with Jerusalem itself an international city. In March, 1948 the United States went back on its decision, and returned the whole matter to the United Nations for reconsideration. At this writing, it is by no means clear what will actually be done. The Jews on the whole accept partition, since among other gains they can under this system regulate their own immigration problem; the Arabs inside and outside Palestine are in bitter revolt. There is still violence in the Holy Land.

For the purposes of this book, one need only record that the British withdrawal is apparently a real withdrawal; they do indeed intend to protect their oil interests and the Suez Canal, but of Palestine they have had their fill. Many Britishers would not be too unhappy—would indeed have a touch of what the

Germans call *Schadenfreude* *—should the United States, here as elsewhere on the globe, be forced into taking over Britain's responsibilities. We had clearly a major part in the decision of the United Nations for partition. We made, as Mr. Walter Lippmann is fond of saying, a commitment. It remains to be seen whether or not we shall back up our commitment by some firm and persistent form of action. We cannot keep reversing ourselves.

For, though to the wearied internationalist it might seem only just if Jew and Arab in Palestine could be left to settle their own affairs, it is certain that in fact the question of Palestine is a question that concerns the whole world. There remains the possibility that some kind of real international action—at a pinch, an international army of the United Nations—might maintain order in Palestine until Arabs and Jews could at last agree. This would seem to be the most hopeful course of action. In spite of the bitter heritage of the last few years, Jews and Arabs might conceivably agree without outside tutelage and intervention. Or, disorder continuing to be endemic in Palestine, Britain might stay, or go back. Or the United States might assume a new trusteeship for Palestine, backed by money and men. Or Russia———. But the possibilities are many, and no one is quite wise enough to be sure which ones will come into being. Right now, it looks as if the United States had undertaken a responsibility that should sober us all a bit, and make our idealists a little less certain that the world can be run best by breaking up the British Empire.

4. SPHERES OF INFLUENCE: THE FAR EAST

The history of Western intervention in the Far East is briefer, but in its broad lines not very different from that of Western intervention in the Middle East. We may define the

---

* Carlyle translated this "mischief-joy." It is a pleasure at the suffering of others.

Far East as the islands and lands adjoining the immense area of the Western Pacific. This region is much bigger, and politically and culturally much more varied, than the Middle East. It has produced one great modern power, Japan, and one potential great power, China. But, however great some of its cultures, it has historically been subject to penetration by Western energies armed and spurred by the Industrial Revolution. And it is now stirring with the desire to catch up with the West, and to put an end to this penetration. You may feel it regrettable that people who produced Confucius should wish to follow Adam Smith, Henry Ford, Karl Marx or worse prophets; but they do so wish.

Now, we Americans feel that we have on the whole had a good record in our dealings with the peoples of the Far East, as indeed we have. But it must not be forgotten that we too have had a share in the historical process of the penetration of the Far East by Western industrial civilization. We too have had lands under our flag—the Philippines—in the Far East; we too have enjoyed extraterritoriality and other privileges in China; we too contributed armed forces to the suppression of the Boxer Rebellion. Morally, our share in the struggle for spheres of influence in the Far East is better than that of any great nation; but we have taken part in the struggle. Britain is in deeper than we are. She had, until she lost it to the Japanese, sovereignty over Chinese territory in Hong Kong. She, or Australia, had possessions in Malaya, Borneo, New Guinea, inhabited by backward peoples for whom it is hardly reasonable to consider, as it is reasonable to consider for the Filipinos, independence. Her Far Eastern economic interests were great, and because of her dependence on export trade, of greater importance to her than ours were to us.

Again, however much many Americans may wish it, proposals for the immediate liquidation of this heritage of Western penetration of the Far East are not acceptable to the British—nor to the Australians, French, and Dutch. The idealistic solution is clear: absolute sovereignty, with no vestige of foreign rights over customs revenues, for a China to whom not only Manchuria and Formosa, but Hong Kong, Shanghai, Macao and the other treaty-ports have been restored; an independent Korea; an independent Philippine Commonwealth; a great Indonesian international trusteeship for *all* Central and Western Pacific Islands, the Netherlands East Indies, Malaya, and French Indo-China; an independent Siam. Against international trusteeship for *all* the islands our own navy has already made a firm protest. Britain, Holland, and France have already opposed with vigor the proposed international trusteeship for Indonesia.

Three years after the surrender of Japan, it is by no means clear what solution will be adopted for these problems of the Far East. At this writing, Viet Nam is still resisting the French in Indo-China; and, though a treaty has been signed, the final settlement between the Dutch and their former Indonesian subjects has not been worked out. One suspects that some kind of equilibrium, short of independence, will be reached in these regions. The war certainly meant that one could not go back to the *status quo* there; but it did not mean that European powers would never more come back to that area, except perhaps in the benign form of international trustees.

The Queen of Holland will rule or reign in the New United States of Indonesia, and the Indo-Chinese may yet have to accept membership in the French Union. The British have certainly gone far in retreat in this area. They have given dominion status to India, to Pakistan, to Ceylon (in the latter reserving a naval base), and they have given Malaya practically Home Rule, though again they hold on to Singapore. But they are not, as the sentimentalists sometimes claim they ought to be, wholly out of the Far East and Southeast Asia. They are still —like Russia, like the United States, like weary France—behaving the way a great power should: they are keeping spheres of influence. Even the independence granted to Burma by the British in 1948 looks a little like Cuban independence. The Burmese are "free," but the many ties, economic, cultural, and political, that held Burma to Britain were not cut overnight.

The trusteeship system, like much else in the complex institutional development of the United Nations, is still being worked out. As early as the New York meeting of the General Assembly at the end of 1946, France, Belgium, and various members of the British Commonwealth filed terms of acceptance of trusteeship for lands held under mandate from the League of Nations. The Charter of the United Nations (article 79) says that such terms "shall be agreed upon by the states directly concerned." It can well be imagined that the phrase "states directly concerned" gave trouble. Here, as so often in such cases, strict interpretation—the easiest—will probably be followed. There is not yet time and space for a John Marshall to work within the United Nations.

And so, the complaining critic can say, "new trusteeship is just the old mandate under a new name—and both are fakes." For the man who will have perfection or nothing, trusteeship is clearly nothing. But to the historian, at least, trusteeship marks a slight but appreciable gain over the mandate system, just as the United Nations marks a slight but appreciable gain over the League of Nations. The new has a little, if only a very little, more of a federal government and less of a mere alliance or confederation.

At any rate, Britain and the Commonwealth have accepted the trusteeship principle, and will not be the major obstacle, one guesses, to its extension towards the idealist's goal. Britain will certainly go part of the way with us towards the idealistic solution, and the other colonial powers will probably follow. China can no longer be treated as a much less than sovereign nation. Some measure of international supervision of colonial administrations in the Far East, extending to territories not affected by the former mandate system of the League of Nations, should be attainable. If we cannot, as seems likely, get the full open door to such colonial possessions, we should be able to secure Britain's coöperation for the open-door policy in China, Korea, Burma, and Siam—and the Philippines. But, if these nations are to be really independent, no other nation could prevent their putting on tariffs and other forms of trade control. Nor could an international authority do this. There are more ways than one of shutting a door; most obviously, it can be shut from the inside as well as the outside.

The important thing is that, in the Far as in the Middle East, the United States and Britain should in fact cease to play the game of spheres of influence and should collaborate to maintain full and free conditions of international trade. This will be difficult in the Far East, perhaps the more difficult as the Chinese and other nations attain real independence. They may in the enthusiasm of triumphant nationalism choose to adopt towards the Anglo-Saxon peoples a policy of "a plague o' both your houses." They are more likely to try to play us off one against the other. They have had long experience of such a policy, the natural weapon of Oriental peoples in their struggle against Western penetration. Such a policy may well be shortsighted; it may, as folk wisdom has long since noted, result in the substitution of King Stork for King Log. But it is too natural, and too habitual in the Far East, not to tempt the Chinese. Russia, of course, threatens in the Far East as elsewhere, but not yet quite enough to make American and British interests and policies there identical.

The United States and Britain are, then, in a sense rivals in the Far East. To keep that rivalry within bounds will require all the commonsense and moderation both peoples can muster. The danger here is that the United States, urged on by the Chinese, will take a very high moral tone with the British, and insist on the rapid liquidation of all British interests, economic as well as political, in China. The British will not like this, especially since they themselves have so long been used to taking a high moral tone with others. The general problem may come to a head in a specific point, as such problems usually do. In this case, the point may well be Hong Kong. British possession of Hong Kong is an affront to Chinese pride, much as British possession of Gibraltar is an affront to Spanish pride. Gibraltar, however, has great strategic value, and almost no economic value. Hong Kong has great economic value, and—though in spite of recent experience British strategists may deny this—under present conditions of warfare relatively little strategic value. It is inconceivable that Britain should relinquish Gibraltar; it is just possible, especially if the whole Pacific problem were so settled as to seem to her to be otherwise satisfactory, that she might give up sovereignty over Hong Kong to China. But British Conservatives have already indicated that they intend if possible to hold on to Hong Kong for a time at least, that they feel this business of getting out of China overnight is being overdone. And the Labour Party, if it has withdrawn from Greece and Palestine, if it has yielded much in India and Burma, has not yet given up Hong Kong.

5. SPHERES OF INFLUENCE: LATIN AMERICA

A third region of potential Anglo-American rivalry is Latin America. The problems here are indeed quite different from the problems in the Middle and in the Near East. Though—and this may surprise some Americans—a great many continental Europeans assume offhand that Latin America is simply an old-fashioned "sphere of influence" of the United States, the British very generally do not; or if they do, they have been tactful enough not to say so. Britain has, save for the flare-up over the Venezuelan boundary with British Guiana in the 1890's, accepted the Monroe Doctrine. The potential difficulty here is rather economic than political. British trade with, and investments in, Latin America were before the war more considerable, at any rate south of the Caribbean basin, than ours. Britain could take from nations like Argentina the cattle, hides, and grain that we could not take without raising a rumpus among our own producers of these goods. This war has forced upon Britain a partial, though by no means complete, liquidation of her investments in the region. It has meant

the continuation of exports of food and other raw materials
from the region to Britain, and, indeed, because of the shutting
off of other sources of British supply by Nazi domination of
countries like Denmark, their increase. Not only has Britain
continued to take most of Argentina's beef; she has, for instance, contracted to take the whole of the sugar crop of the
Dominican Republic. But British *exports* to Latin American
countries have dried up to a mere trickle as British industry
was turned to the production of materials of war. In spite of
the fact that American industry too has been turned to war
production, our industrial capacity has proved so great that
we have been able to fill, partially at least, the gap in Latin
American imports produced by the virtual cessation of British
exports to Latin America—and, incidentally the complete cessation of German and most other European exports to the
region. A single instance: before the war, 38 per cent of Costa
Rica's imports came from the United States, 23 per cent from
Britain, 23 per cent from Germany; during the war, 81 per
cent of Costa Rica's imports have come from the United States
alone. The figures would vary for each Latin American country, but there can be no doubt as to the fact that during the
war the United States took Europe's place in the supplying
of manufactured goods to Latin America. The end of the war
has not altered the trend; the United States exported an average of 485 millions of dollars' worth of goods to Latin America in 1936–1938, 1,263 millions in 1945, and 2,100 millions in
1946.

The British are naturally worried about the restoration of
their Latin American export trade, all the more essential to
them, since, as we have seen, they *must* raise their export trade,
and Latin America is an almost irreplaceable market for their
exports. The problem is potentially a political as well as an
economic one—as, unfortunately, are most economic problems.
In a nutshell: Britain has substantially abstained from political
meddling in Latin America—that is, she has respected the spirit
as well as the letter of the Monroe Doctrine—in part at least

because she has had satisfactory economic relations with the countries of Latin America. If she finds that she cannot restore those relations, and especially if she comes to feel that not her own ability to produce efficiently, but the policy of the United States, even though aided by that of Latin American countries, is preventing such restoration, she is bound to be tempted to try political pressures. Outright defiance of the Monroe Doctrine by Britain is unthinkable; but more subtle methods are possible. We have only to think of Argentina to realize what some of those possibilities are.

Americans who pride themselves on their realism may say at this point, "Well, we got that Latin American trade fairly, didn't we? It's Britain's hard luck she lost it. You don't think we'll just hand it back to Britain on a platter?" It might, however, be well if we could be a bit less harshly realistic in this matter. Some of our new export trade to the south we shall undoubtedly keep. Some of Britain's export trade will flow naturally back to her, not only because even in economic activities habit and tradition are strong forces, but because Britain can take from Latin America greater quantities of food and other raw materials than we can. Moreover, since we are reluctant to take most Latin American raw materials of non-tropical origins, some sort of triangular trade among the United States—Europe—Latin America seems absolutely essential. And the ideal solution, as for all aspects of Anglo-American trade rivalry all over the globe, would be the gradual building up of a dynamic economy in Latin America, a rise in her population, her industrial as well as agricultural production, and her standards of living, so that under free and orderly international trade Britain's total exports to Latin America, though *proportionately* less, would be *absolutely* greater than before the war. But there will be a time of transition, during which the United States would be wise not to press in Latin America, certainly not by government action, the very real trade advantages over Britain it has gained in this war. Until there is enough to go around, we shall be wise to share what there is—

a formula which holds true for Anglo-American economic relations all over the world. It will be a hard formula to apply in Latin America, since we have for long wished to increase our export trade with that region. And let us not disguise the difficulty. "Natural," unbridled competition in the Latin American market between American and British private firms will not, especially in the transition period, automatically arrive at a reasonable sharing of the market. We shall have either to accept some agreement between private firms, for which the bad name is "cartels," or some degree of government control, for which there are all sorts of bad names.

6. THE TREATMENT OF JAPAN

Next there comes the nexus of problems the United States and Britain must face in their relations with the defeated Axis powers. Japan presents the simplest of these problems. The dissolution of the Greater East Asia Co-prosperity Sphere opens up the Far Eastern question, which we have already treated in its major aspect—that of the gradual liquidation of the "colonial" situation brought about by the penetration of that area by the industrial civilization of the West. As for the treatment of Japan proper, there is as yet no evidence of any serious rift between British and American policy. Both countries at the Cairo conference agreed, and reaffirmed at Potsdam, that Japan is to lose all her overseas possessions, including Korea, and to be reduced to the lands she had before she started her imperial career in the Sino-Japanese War of 1894. Both countries are agreed that Japan must be disarmed. Both wish to end the menace of a revival of Japanese imperialism. In neither country is there apparent yet agreement as to how this last end is to be achieved. Undoubtedly public opinion in the United States was during the war far more aroused against the Japanese people than was public opinion in Britain. You would hear much more often from Americans than from Britishers assertions like "There's only one way to treat those bastards—kill 'em all off." But soldiers of both countries have a tendency to get to like the ex-enemy peoples whose lands they occupy. Now since the British are not occupying Japan and we are, it is conceivable that British public opinion is today harsher than ours towards the Japanese. At any rate, it is clear that there will be no conventionally Carthaginian peace with Japan.

The problem is sometimes put, for Japan as for Germany, as a choice between a "hard" and a "soft" peace. For neither country is this simple polar distinction an adequate one. What you find in actual discussions as to the treatment of Japan is a whole series of proposals from extinction to forgiveness and help for a "democratic" Japan. There are those who hold that the population and productive capacity of Japan have been so reduced that it will be possible for the Allies, with a minimum of regulation, to keep Japan to a poor, subsistence economy incapable of further harm. There are those who hold that, since even at the best—or worst—there will probably still be some seventy or eighty million Japanese in the homeland after the peace, Japanese economy can be regulated by Allied or international supervision so as to produce manufactured goods for peace, but not for war. There are those who believe that to get a stable Japan capable of eventual coöperation in world organization, it is essential to retain her basic folk-ways and economic structure, and in particular Shintoism and Mikado-worship—if not Bushido—and that these elements of Japanese life can be divorced from militarism and imperialism. There are those who believe that we must aid the Japanese to a full radical revolution, to the establishment of a Western model of government necessary to the development of a truly democratic society which can be integrated eventually into the society of free nations. Though in a sense in abeyance during General MacArthur's reign, these basic issues still exist.

You will find representatives of all these points of view, and of detailed variations of them, in both the United States and

Britain. There are unregenerate groups in Britain—the same groups who believe that the day of spheres-of-influence rivalry in the Far East is by no means past—who cherish not so very far back in their heads the hope that Britain may be able to use Japan as a "balance" to American power in the Pacific, and who will therefore press for a soft policy towards Japan. But short of a complete breakdown in Anglo-American co-operation for world peace, and the resultant establishment of British and American "blocs" (the new name for the old balance-of-power politics), it seems likely that Britain and the United States can agree on a policy towards Japan which gives us substantially what we decide we want.

7. EUROPE

This is a big world, and Europe is not the greatest part of it, either in area or in population. We Americans are nowadays in no serious danger of assuming that as Europe goes, so goes the whole planet. We are, perhaps, in danger of underestimating the importance of Europe. After all, all the world wars have started in Europe, and that continent *must* be reasonably stable and prosperous if there is to be any real prospect for a lasting peace in the world. The test Europe and its problems afford to Anglo-American understanding is perhaps the crucial test.

If one were to judge, for instance, from Russian comments, the United States and Great Britain are still in 1948 closely tied together in more than conventional alliance—against Russia, of course. Actually, as anyone who takes the trouble to read what gets printed in Britain and the United States can tell, there are many important groups in both countries who disagree with Anglo-American policies in Europe. Many Americans would have us altogether out of Greece, and as soon as possible out of Germany. Many British would like to come to some accommodation with Russia, regardless of American plans. No more than during the war is Anglo-American collaboration silent, smooth, automatic.

And yet, basically it is of course collaboration, and a much closer one still than has been customary among former allies in earlier world wars. The cynic will point out that the collaboration against one foe has been transformed into collaboration against another at least potential foe; and that the old rule of international politics, that only fear and hatred unite sovereign states, still seems to hold. The realist will as usual admit that there is some truth in the cynic's position, but he will hold that there is ample evidence that the British and Americans are working together freely and with good will for the most part to help Europeans reëstablish a continent of Europe fit for civilized men and women to live in.

On concrete problems at issue, the British and the Americans have usually stood together. They agreed that Greece should not come under the kind of Russian influence—we are trying to avoid abusive terms—exercised in the rest of the Balkans, and that agreement stood the test of Britain's economic and military withdrawal from Greece and our consequent assumption of burdens there. They agreed sufficiently on a German policy to establish a joint economic and political administration of their two zones of occupation in Germany, thus giving to the newspapers of the world the amazing neologism "Bizonia." They are approaching the French to produce "Trizonia." They have been in substantial agreement with the United Nations. They have usually been coupled by commentators, even by commentators who insist that there are really only two powers in the world, the United States and Russia; so that these commentators commonly speak of the Anglo-American side of the famous iron curtain, and so on.

It is impossible here to treat in detail the joint and several problems facing the United States and Britain in their relations with all the European states. Moreover, other volumes in this series will treat these matters in their direct relations with American policies.* Here we can merely consider very briefly Germany as the great test of the ability of the United States

* See especially the Dean, Deutsch, and McKay volumes, on Russia, Germany, and France, respectively.

and Britain to work together towards the solution of a major problem vital to both, and then consider, again very briefly, the attitudes towards British European policies of certain important groups in present-day Britain.

Even though the two masters of Bizonia seem in agreement as opposed to the Russians and the French, it is clear that the spectrum of opinion as to the future in Germany in both Britain and the United States runs a very wide range from "soft" to "hard." It is clear, as a matter of fact, that even within responsible governing groups in the two countries there is by no means unanimity as to the treatment of Germany. Some day the historian will have, perhaps, the necessary documents to explain just how the actual policies of the two countries were put together from the most varied of sources. But now we can only generalize as to the evident direction of Anglo-American policy in Germany.

That policy looks now a little nearer the extreme of "soft" than the extreme of "hard." Certainly we are not carrying out the Morgenthau program of "pastoralizing" Germany. It seems unlikely, though still not quite impossible, that we shall accept the French program for a Ruhr separated politically from Germany under an international government and devoted to the economic rehabilitation and strengthening of France and the Low Countries. We and the British seem determined to let whatever part of Germany we control become a going concern industrially, and as much of a democracy as circumstances, mildly aided by British and Americans who still believe in "reëducation," will permit. We have lost our first fervor for de-nazification, and we have lost our earlier fears of a restored and wicked Germany, no doubt because we have come to fear Russia more.

Everything seems to conspire towards an Anglo-American policy towards Germany in which much will be done by doing nothing, much will go by default, much will be done at cross purposes, and but little according to the hopeful "plans" of 1944 and 1945, at which so many British and American govern-

ment agencies labored so hard. But, unless the line that separates Russian-occupied Germany from the rest of the country
becomes a permanent gap, it seems now that Germany will
in fact come out of the war rather better than seemed likely
three years ago.

No doubt the obvious reason is also the main one: Britain
and the United States do not feel like alienating their zones
of Germany as long as Russia seems a menace to them. But
there are many other variables in the equation. American
business men, British business men, and the deliberately unsen-
timental generally, incline to the belief that a strong Germany
is necessary, not only against Russia, but in and of itself as the
base of a prosperous Europe. Many Americans and British of
the occupying forces, following the precedent of the last war,
have come to like the German people, and to grow very sentimental over them. There have always been many Americans
who believed that the Germans might some day see the light
and follow our democratic example. Although most British are
somewhat less hopeful in such matters, there is an old tendency
in the Labour Party to hold that the German heart really beats
in time with the Social Democrats, that the nucleus of the
German people is sound. Finally, both peoples, if peoples may
be so described, are fairly good-natured and little inclined to
hold grudges. Neither has had an *irredentum*. Both find it
fairly easy to forget, if not forgive, the Germany that seemed
so wicked in 1944. It is true that the very real weakness of
Germany today is an element in this attitude.

And yet only a few years ago it looked to many observers
as though the formula, the United States is to Britain this time
as Britain was to France in 1918, would hold for attitudes
towards Germany. Frenchmen in 1918 feared and hated Germany, as indeed they still do; Englishmen in 1918, their country
still uninvaded, still undamaged, did not really fear Germany.
It would seem that this time, bombed and blasted England
would show some of the signs of group fears towards Germany
the French had shown earlier, that England's foreign policy

would be centered on the problem of making Germany incapable of doing further damage. Yet in 1948 one can only report that this is not so. Relatively few British seem to hold strong, let alone obsessive, fears of a revived Germany. Most British seem persuaded that the villain next time will not be Germany. Since most Americans share these views, it is not really surprising that the two countries, on the whole, have been able to maintain a joint policy in and towards Germany.

Yet, in the larger problem of Britain's place in Europe, there are signs that important groups in Britain do not quite accept what seems to be Mr. Bevin's policy of close coöperation with the Americans. It goes without saying that the handful of British Communists believe that everything the two have done in common since V-day has been wrong, and that the British government has been wholly at the beck and call of the United States. But the Communists in Britain do not count. More important is the Left of the Labour Party, which has had to swallow a good deal since 1945, and nothing more indigestible than the fact that socialist Britain was lined up every time with capitalist America against the fatherland of collectivism, the U.S.S.R. Many of these Leftists were—and are—pretty anti-Stalinist, but they were almost as strongly against the land that nourished people like Henry Ford, Herbert Hoover, and Robert Taft. They have said and printed some bitter words, but until recently they seemed hardly able to influence British action directly.

They still do not seem in themselves a very powerful force, but they may find allies, and their program is one that may prove very attractive to many Britishers as Britain emerges from the doldrums. They are by no means a disciplined group, and they have yet to focus on any one leader. Nevertheless, one may take Mr. Richard Crossman as a good sample of their attitude, and indeed as a possible leader. Mr. Crossman, an Oxford don who has turned to politics, is a parliamentary chief of the "Keep Left" group of the Labour Party. His basic idea seems to be that Britain, by economic and insofar as possible political union with France, Italy, the Low Countries, Scandinavia, and as much of the rest of Europe as proves virtuous, social-democratic, and willing, will, with the help of the British Commonwealth, be able to stand up against *both* the United States and Russia, and avoid the present degrading dilemma of choosing between dependence on one or the other.

Mr. Crossman insists that he and his followers have no crude notions of making a British superpower to rival in conventional international politics Russia and the United States. Quite the contrary. He takes a somewhat patronizing attitude towards both Russia and the United States, in his mind, two somewhat overgrown and infantile powers which are not yet cured (as he seems to hope Britain is cured) of the puerilities that make for world wars. He would have Britain, with the help of near-by Europe and the Commonwealth, strong enough to stay out of what he sees as the coming Russo-American war. Such strength can only be attained by a free-trade area large enough to permit the very latest economy to function. Such an economy the United States and Russia have, but Britain by itself has not and cannot have it alone.

Moreover, Mr. Crossman admits to another motive for building up this third great economy and its own free-trade area and domestic market. He does not think that the official American policy of restoring multilateral world trade—with Britain sharing—can work, partly because he does not believe Americans will make necessary adjustments of tariff and other needed changes in economic policies, partly because he frankly distrusts American economic imperialism, and thinks that, however kindly our State Department may be, the business men who run America are really out to wreck the promising socialist experiment started in Britain.

Now these ideas, in their commoner form of vague distrust of the United States as a reactionary power still run by "Wall Street," are widespread but not very effective among British socialists. Crossman has made them sharper, has made them into a platform. The five-power pact of Brussels has seemed to some a first step towards realizing them. Their realization would, of course, set up a British-French, or Western European, center of power which, supported by large overseas possessions and partners, might actually develop into a third superpower. That such a center of power could actually stay neutral in another world war, that it would prove anything but another major rival in world politics, seems unlikely. There is no evidence that the peoples of England, France, and Western Europe are really wiser, more mature, more peaceful, than the peoples of America and Russia. They may at the moment be more tired. But that is a different matter.

The real danger of such a policy as Mr. Crossman's is the attractiveness it might possess for many British Tories, and for other plain Britishers, as comparative prosperity returns to the islands. Even liberals like Mr. Crossman have under the test of responsibility been known to abandon idealism and end up as good fighters in a vulgar cause. Stripped of the piety of his aversion to war, his program sounds extraordinarily like an attempt to revive the greatness of Britain. One half expects to learn that Mr. Churchill has joined the Keep Left movement.

Something like Mr. Crossman's dream may well come into reality should American plans for restoring multilateral world trade, at least outside the U.S.S.R., fail. Or, to put it another way, if Britain cannot prosper under the Marshall Plan, she may in self-defense attempt to build up an economic and political system independent of both the United States and Russia. It must be repeated that every historical precedent shows that such a "third superpower" would not be the virtuous, neutral, indeed somewhat unwordly society Mr. Crossman imagines. It would develop its own nationalism, its own sense of consecration. Of all the prospects of horror to come which our publicists take delight in raising, none can be much worse than this: an autarkic Russian complex of nations devoted to self-worship as true Communism, an American complex devoted to self-worship as true Individualism, and a Franco-British complex devoted to self-worship as true Socialism.

The temptation for two—any two—to unite against the third would be very great indeed. And all three would feel obliged to try to pry loose weaker or less devoted members of the other complexes. The pressures that would be exercised in such natural zones of contention as the Argentine, the Near East, India, and China are frightful to contemplate.

Actually, the present British government has given no sign that it wants to cut loose from the United States. It has indeed leaned definitely towards the United States rather than towards Russia, though it has tried hard to avoid being what its enemies call it, in varying stereotyped phrases, a mere slave of American policy, a stooge, a Charlie McCarthy, a satellite, and a lot else. It has insisted that the Commonwealth should be a going concern. It has been firm in its refusal to abandon the Ottawa agreements (which provided for "imperial preference," that is, lower tariffs within the Empire for members of the Commonwealth) unless and until the American plan of restoring real multilateral world trade free of unreasonable restrictions becomes a working reality. It has been most careful of French susceptibilities, short of giving in to the French view on the Ruhr, and has announced that it wishes close economic and political relations with France and with Western Europe generally. Yet the Labour government waited three years before committing itself to so definitely anti-Russian a step as the Five-Power Pact among Britain, France, Netherlands, Belgium, and Luxemburg signed at Brussels on March 17, 1948. The pact itself is clearly a consequence of the Marshall Plan. Britain has concluded conventional alliances, quite openly, with both Russia and France, directed against a renewed German aggression. The British government has shown itself fully aware, as the British people are now aware, that the British Isles are no longer in any important sense isolated from the continent of Europe. It knows that European problems must seem more real and more pressing to Britishers than to Americans. But it has done nothing that seriously conflicts with announced American policies. We conclude, as we began, that in spite of all stresses and strains, Britain and America are still in apparent agreement on the main line of their policy towards the distracted continent of Europe.

No one can say with confidence how the British people, apart from their government and their publicists, feel in what is for them the major question: must we choose between the United States and Russia, and if we must, how shall we choose? Clearly only a minority—though a somewhat bigger one than the 100,000 voting Communists—wants to embrace Russia and dismiss the United States. But there are infinite gradations from this position to that of the minority—also very small—for whom the United States can do no wrong. Probably the strongest group basically hostile to the United States—or at any rate to the present foreign policy of the United States—is represented by the Keep Left group in the Labour Party and its followers. The Tories may not like us, but they hate and fear the Russians. Indeed, some British outdo American conservatives in Russophobia, which in Britain is of great age, not new as with us. Probably the ordinary Britisher feels most of the time that we are rather a more natural and more suitable choice than Russia; but he wishes he didn't have to make the choice. It should be obvious that the whole alignment of powers in 1948 is not nearly as fixed and stable as most commentators make it out to be; and in that alignment the Anglo-American alliance is no fixed granite block. It looks firm enough today, but it will not persist automatically.

8. DOMESTIC AFFAIRS IN ANGLO-AMERICAN RELATIONS

We have in a hasty survey swept through the world to trace the more important problems of Anglo-American political relations. There remains a class of problems, by no means the least important, and indeed in many ways the most evident and pressing to ordinary people in both countries, that of the attitude of each to the domestic affairs of the other. In a per-

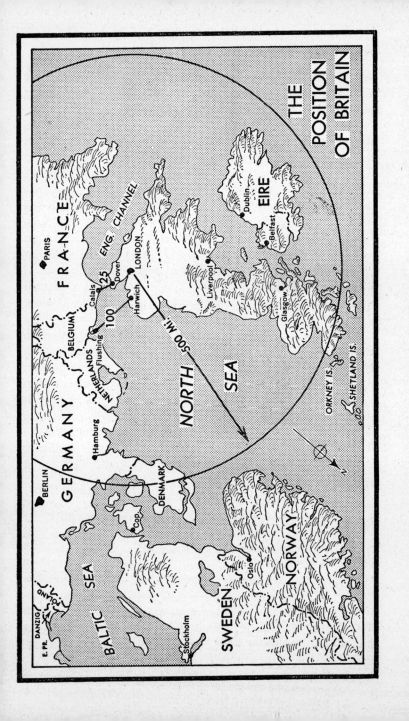

THE POSITION OF BRITAIN

FRANCE

PARIS

ENG. CHANNEL

Dover
25
Calais
LONDON
100
BELGIUM
Flushing
Harwich
NETHERLANDS
500 MI.
GERMANY
Hamburg
BERLIN

EIRE
Dublin
Belfast
Liverpool
Glasgow

NORTH SEA

ORKNEY IS.
SHETLAND IS.

DENMARK
COP.

BALTIC SEA
DANZIG
E. PR.
POLAND

SWEDEN
Stockholm

NORWAY
Oslo

N

fect world no doubt neither of us would concern ourselves with what is going on in the other's yard, but in this world we do —and usually with what is going on in the other's *back* yard.

Not since the unwise partisanship of the British ruling classes for the Confederate cause during our Civil War have the British come close to anything that might seem like official meddling in our affairs. As we have seen, they accept fully the political implications of the Monroe Doctrine. They may regret the extent of American influence in Canada—though not half so much as do the stalwarts of the Canadian United Empire Loyalists—but they have accepted it. Franklin Roosevelt was a hero to the British people, and in 1944 many of them made no bones about declaring that they did not regard Mr. Dewey as a hero, and that they hoped he would be beaten. But in general the Britisher takes no sides in American politics—he doesn't as a rule know much about them—and most certainly his government does not take sides in American domestic issues.

The British government does, however, maintain in the United States an increasingly elaborate system for securing information on American opinion about Britain and for disseminating to Americans information about Britain. This information is quite naturally information favorable to the British cause, and we might as well agree to call it propaganda. Now there is nothing wrong or unusual in this practice. We ourselves during the war, through our Office of War Information and the Public Relations Officers of our army, began to disseminate American propaganda in Britain and, despite some Congressional opposition, the Voice of America is still heard over the air. Partly as a heritage of the debunkers of the 1920's, who made out British propaganda as a leading factor in getting us drawn into the First German War, partly as a constant obsession of American Anglophobes, the touchiness of Americans to British propaganda activities in their midst has come to have a certain importance in Anglo-American relationships. The British government is fully aware of that touchiness, and their experts in propaganda have on the whole walked circumspectly. There is a small group of Americans who regard the mildest and most inoffensive British exchange student in Classical Archaeology as a British agent. But it seems likely that most of us really have come of age in international politics, and that the wickedness of British propaganda in the United States no longer bedevils Anglo-American relations.

It is indeed Americans who have done the major share of interfering in what the British regard as their domestic concerns. That interference has indeed not been official and governmental, or at least not executive and diplomatic. We must remember that to Britishers, who are usually very unclear about how our government works, what a senator or congressman says, sounds very official. (So of course does what a member of parliament says, but government members are under very good control, and what a back-bencher says doesn't usually get much publicity.) And then there are our countless societies and pressure groups, who manage to seem to foreigners at least semi-official. All told it makes quite a chorus, which has for years been calling attention to the evil doings in Britain's back-yard. There is no British stereotype corresponding to "twisting the lion's tail"—though it may be evidence of America's attaining full growth in the eyes of Britishers that when in January 1945 the London *Economist* replied with a sharp counterattack to American criticisms of British policy in Greece someone suggested that this was "pulling out the eagle's feathers."

Our own generation saw the Irish Question almost vanished as a public concern in the United States. Then the Indian Question came to take its place. Freedom for India used to be one of the favorite causes of American Leftists of all shades, and they would join a committee, go to a luncheon, and sign a resolution any day for India's sake. We have perhaps been rash in our use of the past tense in this matter. But just as American Leftists ceased to be very pro-Irish when they discovered what Mr. De Valera's Eire was doing with its freedom, so they may cease to be very pro-Indian as that unhappy sub-

continent goes its way—which is highly unlikely to be a nice
Leftist Jefferson-and-Tom-Paine way. No doubt the American
Leftists can always find some group under the British flag for
whom they can lunch. American Leftist criticisms of the British Empire may be considered a constant but minor factor in
Anglo-American relations. They are balanced by the British
Leftist criticisms of the way we treat the Negroes, of the
wickedness of our moneyed classes, of the crassness of our
Hollywood civilization. What is vastly more important is the
fact, brought out clearly in the press, in public opinion polls,
and most evident to anyone who had anything to do with the
American soldier in Britain, that ordinary Americans, normally
no friends of radical causes, felt that India had had a raw deal
from the British. They thought that India had the same sort
of right to independence that we had in 1776. And they were
distrustful of the mildest arguments in favor of British policy
in India. Indeed, the most skillful propaganda in defense of
the British position in India tended to defeat itself in this
country and give rise to the remark—which is not usually
made of propaganda by Indians, a propaganda among intellectuals in this country very active indeed—that if the British
cause were really just it wouldn't need all this propaganda.

Even now that the British have allowed the Indians to do
the best they can for themselves, even now that the two self-
governing Dominions of India and Pakistan are a reality,
American opinion tends to blame the British for what has
gone on in India. Early in 1948, India's prospects look bad,
at least in the short run. Communal sentiment shows few signs
of diminishing, and already Hindu-Moslem warfare has made
civilian victims on quite the scale of the last war in Europe
and the Far East. Gandhi has come to a tragic, and most
Western, end. It is risky to attempt to guess whether either
or both India and Pakistan will vote themselves out of the
Commonwealth entirely in August, 1948, as by the treaty
setting them up they have a perfect right to do.

In this state of uncertainty, no clear-cut American policy

in India is possible. We ordinary Americans should do what we can to inform ourselves about what is going on in India, and above all learn more about the grave complexities of the accumulated ills of the subcontinent. With more knowledge, we should be more tolerant of the British position, and, above all, should not be astounded if Britain cannot completely cut all the ties that bind her to India. After all, the British have lived up to the pledge they gave in an act of parliament passed in 1942 in the midst of war: to grant the people of India dominion status following the war, with the right to secede from the Crown. Though the most stupid of American Anglo-phobes will not of course believe it, British policy by no means encouraged partition. Long before 1942, the British were be-yond the superficial Machiavellianism of "divide and rule." A strong united India, even hostile to Britain, would clearly be better than a torn and divided India, open to—indeed almost inviting—intervention from the outside. To be very frank: the British do not want to go back into India, but they cer-tainly don't want the Russians to go in. No one else could go in, nowadays—unless perhaps ourselves. And surely even Colonel McCormick doesn't want that?

India, then, is still a most uncertain and disturbed element in the world. We cannot be sure what will happen there. Meanwhile, Americans should note three things. First, with the best British will in the world, there will be some delay; you cannot peacefully liquidate a partnership—even a partner-ship unwilling on one side—of two centuries' standing at a single stroke. Second, we cannot expect that the British will cut themselves absolutely off from an independent India any more than we shall cut ourselves off from an independent Phil-ippine Commonwealth. We cannot let a hostile power get a hold in the Philippines, and we cannot entirely cut our eco-nomic ties with the Philippines. As long as Britain is a great power, she has to try to defend strategic and economic interests in India. She will for obvious reasons have a much harder task doing this in India than we shall have with a similar task in the

Philippines, but we ought not to blame her for making the attempt. Third, we should accept British touchiness over American "interference" in the Indian Question as wholly natural. Not so long ago we had, in the epoch of intervention and the marines, our own troubles in the Caribbean basin. To those troubles the "good neighbor" policy has happily put an end. But while they were going on we should certainly have resented the best British advice, let alone British criticism.

What holds true for India holds true in general of the place of the Empire proper in Anglo-American relations. Our Left we have always with us. Should India gain its freedom from Britain, the sympathies of our Leftist groups could readily find an outlet in the wrongs of other peoples under the Crown— perhaps in South Africa, where the Negro Question is at least as acute as it is in Alabama. The ordinary American's feeling that the British Empire is not A Good Thing is probably a constant of Anglo-American relations, but under normal conditions does not stand in the way of effective coöperation between the two countries. Britain, under either a Conservative or a Labour government, will try to hold the Empire together, because without the Empire she cannot be in the contemporary world a great power.

Finally, there are the Dominions. Just as most Americans have trouble understanding the real position of the King in the British Commonwealth and Empire, so they have trouble understanding the real position of the Dominions. The story of the American who asked his taxi driver in Toronto "When are the British going to stop oppressing you people?" is no doubt a bit of American humor. And Mr. Allan Nevins' American sergeant in Australia who remarked to him, "What a country this would be if the British would get off their necks!" may be unrepresentative of American opinion. But the American does have a hard time understanding the fact that, though he sees the face of George VI on Canadian postage stamps, and hears of Canadians as "subjects" of the King, by the Statute of Westminster of 1931, Canada is an independent nation, with the right, if she wishes, to secede from the Crown. He will continue to believe that Canada's vote in an international assembly is in fact a British vote, and will not be impressed when a crude Russian or an inconsiderate Britisher announces his belief that Cuba's vote in an international assembly is in fact a United States vote.

But the Dominions—Eire, Canada, Australia, New Zealand, and South Africa—do have the full diplomatic apparatus of independent nations, and we can and do deal with them in the usual way of diplomatic negotiations. The really important political problem of our relations with the Dominions is whether or not we shall be tempted—or they be tempted—to actions that do in fact break up the apparently tenuous bonds that hold them together among themselves and with the mother country. That they are now in fact strong bonds this war has shown; but they certainly are not conventional bonds of "sovereignty" and they cannot be strengthened by British use of force. If the United States and Great Britain should fall into outright rivalry in a world of blocs and balance-of-power politics, we should certainly be driven to attempt the capture of some of the Dominions—not necessarily, of course, their annexation—but their assimilation into a power bloc dominated by the United States. Canada is so near us that, though the attempt would be bitterly resisted in some quarters there, it could hardly fail. South Africa is at present so far outside our orbit that we should hardly make the attempt. Australia and New Zealand, however, though distant, are key countries of a Pacific area in which, no matter how successful we may be in creating international authority in place of the international anarchy of the 1930's, we cannot entirely give up some reliance on separate negotiations and old-fashioned diplomacy. The normal expectation is surely that we can protect our strategic and economic interests in the Pacific without political interference in the affairs of Australia and New Zealand, and without affecting relations between those commonwealths and the United Kingdom. New Zealand is intensely loyal to the Home Country most New Zealanders have never seen. Australia, however, if by no means disaffected, is at least a more restive dominion. In the midst of the invasion scare of 1942, there was some talk among Australians to the effect that the United States could give the protection Britain was not giving, and that Australia might well in the future come under some American "system." Such talk appears to have died down, and though we must work closely with Australia in the task of preserving peace in the Pacific area, we should be unwise to encourage the revival of such talk.

Politically, then, the immediate problems of Anglo-American relations are not of the threatening sort. Neither covets lands of the other. Neither differs radically with the other over the treatment of the defeated Axis powers. There are all sorts of detailed problems—trusteeship of backward peoples, restoration in liberated Europe, the future of India and many others —on which they differ, and about which there will have to be the give-and-take of negotiation. Americans, in particular, have long shown a concern over British imperial problems which irritates many Britishers. But the governments and peoples of both nations wish to build out of the present disasters, not a joint Anglo-American hegemony over the world—that, as we shall see, is hardly more than a crank's dream in either country—but an efficient international organization in which all nations, great and small, will find order and justice. They feel, and quite rightly, that although Anglo-American coöperation cannot by itself alone build such an organization, *without* a degree of Anglo-American coöperation no effective international organization can possibly be built. The possibility of such coöperation depends on the solution of economic and political problems of Anglo-American relations we have been discussing in the last two chapters; their successful solution depends in the long run and most fundamentally on the ability of Americans and Britishers, in private life as well as in positions of government responsibility, to understand one another and to get along with one another. To this psychological problem we now turn.

10. Psychological Problems

There are, then, grave economic, less grave political, issues between the United States and Great Britain. Perhaps, in this time of troubles, the mind is tempted to dwell too much on the possibilities of conflict which the history of our modern system of nation-states shows clearly to exist between *any* two members of that system. It is certainly unwise to bend over Anglo-American relations as if they were on a sickbed, but it is equally unwise to assume that they are in a state of perfect health which can be maintained if we repeat a few formulas like "hands across the sea." Statesmen and experts of both countries in the last few years have formed the habit of close mutual study of the issues between us. They differ, not always on national lines; but up to this time they have managed to come through discussion and compromise to tentative agreements, which will become binding only after the elected representatives of each people approve them. The sum total of agreements actually approved since 1945 is very great— from Bretton Woods to the Marshall Plan. In neither country has press or legislative body been muzzled. Some of us have certainly said all sorts of nasty things about the British; and some of the British have said cutting things about us. Indeed, at the height of British agitation over the loan of 1946, many Britishers announced firmly that they did not want help under the terms some Americans were insisting on. But the process is never ended. The working out of the plans sets up new problems, and these problems, though they can sometimes be settled in specific details by the administrators, sooner or later pile up into what we call a "political" issue. And, skeptics of the democratic process not withstanding, political issues are ultimately decided by people like you and me.

We have formed the habit of accepting at any given stage in this endless political process what we call the "verdict of the ballot"—on domestic issues. We have not formed such a habit, indeed we have no voting machinery to get habituated to, when it comes to joint consultation of two peoples on international issues. Britain and the United States are separate nation-states, and decisions on matters at issue between them must be registered separately. This will certainly not be changed in our time; the dream of a legislative federal union between the two countries is no more than the dream of a few enthusiasts. But when we vote as a nation we inevitably vote in some senses as nationalists, or at least as patriots. There are crusaders who tell us that we shouldn't be patriots at all, but citizens of the world and lovers of the human race. We do not commonly pay them much attention. There are other crusaders who tell us that we should be patriots unlimited, superpatriots, and these we find it more natural to listen to. For it is fatally easy to assume that conduct which in the individual would be shortsighted, selfish, and indeed obviously against his own interests is conduct fitting and proper for the nation. We pool our nobler as well as our baser feelings in our loyalty to any group of which we are a part, from family and school to nation; but in a quarrel the baser often come to the fore. It is commonly respectable to quarrel with a foreigner as it is not commonly respectable to quarrel with a fellow countryman.

If we are not to quarrel as a nation with Britain as a nation, ordinary people in both countries have got to show that they can get along with one another, not indeed perfectly, for human beings can't do that even within family, club, or neighborhood, but at any rate rather better than the record shows that they or any other peoples of great nation-states have been in the habit of getting along together. This is the challenge of our time: we have got to do better as *human beings*, we have got to exercise harder virtues than patriotism —which does not mean that we cease to be patriots—or the best international plans and organizations will fail. We have got to find a halfway house between an impossible world-state based on a world-patriotism and an impossible world of sixty-odd sovereign states inhabited by men and women brought up to believe in, *to feel in*, formulas like "my country, right or wrong."

Once more, it will by no means be enough if Britishers and Americans alone find such a halfway house in their own relations. But again once more, if it cannot be found by Britishers and Americans, it is not likely to be found by the rest of the world. The chances that it will be found by the two peoples are good. They have, indeed, already found it during this war. They have, quite humanly and therefore very imperfectly, been able to get along together in the war against the Axis. In any estimate of their chances of continuing to get along together, their attitudes towards each other, not only as they have been affected by this war but as they have grown up through long years must be reviewed. In a brief survey of psychological elements involved in relations between British and Americans, we may well begin with an extreme—the extreme for which our common language has adopted the sometimes awkward Greek suffix "-phile," as if to mark the thing signified as foreign and abnormal.

1. AMERICAN ATTITUDES TOWARDS BRITAIN

Anglophiles, lovers of England, we have had in the United States from the very start of our national existence. They have been commonly misunderstood by the mass of their fellow countrymen, who usually assume social snobbery to be the prime motive of their love of England. It would be foolish to deny that there have been, and perhaps still are, Americans who think of England as a land where, among many things that are right, is the fact that one can be a gentleman there, and of the United States as a land where, among many things that are wrong, is the fact that one cannot be a gentleman there. But such simple snobbery has never been the mainspring of the American Anglophile's attachment to the old country. It is a sentiment compounded of many ingredients—longing for traditional, well-established ways of life consecrated by the centuries, admiration for the ripeness of English culture, desire for the leisureliness and assurance of an England assumed to be free from our American hurly-burly, above all, perhaps, respect for Britain as possessor of the civic virtues, law-abidingness, tolerance, love of fair play. In its more extreme forms, such affection could find satisfaction even in British weather and in British cooking.

Some of the elements in the Anglophile's love are elements in the milder affection which most Americans not actively hostile to Britain feel for that country. What marks off the Anglophile is the strength, intensity, and uncritical nature of his feelings toward Britain. At the extreme, he seems to feel that everything is right in Britain and everything is wrong in America. He is not, of course, liked by the British, whose strong sense of fitness is deeply shocked by his disloyal behavior and whose sense of self-esteem is so well-rooted as to be proof against ordinary flattery. Indeed, a bright young Englishman once remarked to an American admirer of things British that he had been much happier traveling in the Middle West than among certain circles in New York and Boston, "because, you know, in America as elsewhere the Englishman prefers the native to the half-breed." As for the average American, he has been in the past infuriated by the behavior of his Anglophile fellow countrymen, and has somewhat irrationally blamed the British themselves for the existence of the Anglophiles. Naturally, too, the average American has been inclined to believe the British reality all the more wicked by contrast with the perfection the Anglophile saw.

Thus the more extreme American lovers of Britain are a

handicap to good relations between the United States and Britain. Many of them are incurable, but they are no more than a small minority of Americans. The more sensible American Anglophiles should, if only for reasons of policy, moderate their enthusiasm and admit a few imperfections in the object of their affections. They might thus have more influence over their fellow countrymen, who are by no means unfavorably disposed towards Britain.

Indeed, it is clear that good solid patriotic Americans of all classes in the balance admire and respect the British. One people probably never really "likes" another. The psychologist Dr. A. Roback has made an interesting study of the nicknames peoples have for other peoples. We are familiar with many of our own—limeys, squareheads, wops, bohunks, and the like. We know the British call the French frogs, and the French call the Germans boches. (This last, by the way, seems to come from *caboche*, a square-headed nail.) These are all bad names; there simply are no good names in the list. Yet we do not often nowadays call the British "limeys," and insofar as a people can have generally favorable sentiments towards another, it is fair to say that we have such sentiments towards the British. A curious and important piece of evidence of this, since it springs from levels of the American people who are not so articulate as the rest, comes from a study of the pulps, the cheap magazines of fiction of horror, mystery, adventure, miraculous pseudo-science. In this fiction the Englishman and the Scot come out very well. They are almost never villains, and are often heroes. At the worst, the Englishman is the butler type, or slow to see a joke, and the Scot penurious. The favorite type is the clever, daring, urbane Englishman, straight from the pages of Ouida or Christopher Wren. The ardent internationalist should not be unduly encouraged by this pulp fiction; Latins, Slavs, and of recent years Germans and Japs, come out very badly, and provide more than their share of villains.

We have, of course, better evidence than the pulps that

Americans are predisposed in favor of the British. Americans were, especially after Dunkirk, wholeheartedly unneutral in favor of the British. The British gained American esteem during the Battle of Britain much as the French lost it during the Battle of France. Moreover, there is a deeper layer of sentiment favorable towards the British than this one born of their courageous resistance to the victorious Germans. This is a feeling, less intense among the masses of Americans than among our Anglophiles, but recognizably the same sentiment, that on the whole and in spite of dukes, butlers, diplomatists, and India, the Britisher is a decent fellow—reliable, orderly, politically and morally on the right side. Admiration for the Britisher as a political animal, as a man who has been able to reconcile freedom and authority, goes in America far beyond narrow Anglophile circles.

Not that the average American's feeling towards the British are unmixed; far from it. Most of his doubts and dislikes we have already encountered. There is a widespread distrust of British doings in India, and throughout the Empire. There is puzzlement over the Britisher's retention of so much that is apparently undemocratic. There is the suspicion that the Britisher, above all when he is being unusually cordial, still feels patronizingly towards us as colonials and is really trying to use us for his own purposes. There is the folk legend of the wily British diplomatist, polished and unscrupulous, who, if given any chance at all, can do what he likes with our honest, unskilled American negotiators, and has wholly corrupted the shallow snobbish Anglophiles so numerous in the State Department. That this folk legend is almost wholly at variance with the facts of our diplomatic history does not seem to have lessened its hold over the American people.

What are to most Americans mere doubts and qualifications of their generally favorable sentiments towards the British are articles of faith among our Anglophobes. Haters of Britain are like lovers of Britain, a small minority of the American people. But both groups are noisy and active, and both are factors in the complex equation of our relations with Britain. The British public tends to exaggerate the strength and importance of Anglophobia in the United States. The normal is not news. Inevitably the British hear more about Mr. Hearst and Colonel McCormick than they do about John Doe. Their own newspapers are not altogether guiltless in this matter, for they tend to play up unduly the antics of our twisters of the lion's tail. Like the extreme Anglophiles, the extreme Anglophobes are incurable. They are by no means wholly recruited from Americans of Irish or German stock. There is a long-established native tradition of distrust of Britain, which can easily ripen into dislike in troubled times. Even in Boston, which most Americans believe is, save for the Irish, rather more than half British, there is a strong Yankee heritage of mingled admiration and dislike for the British, which comes out neatly in the history of the Adams family. Native American populism or progressivism has in it a definite strain of hostility towards rich and monarchical Britain, the inevitable ally of Wall Street. In our own time, a good many less clearly homespun American Leftists, though they may have some hopes of the Labour Party, are so impressed with Tory wickedness in India, the Middle East, and indeed throughout the world, that they act like outright Anglophobes. If the difficulties of setting up an effective international order in the next few years can be overcome, our violent Anglophobes can hardly do much damage. The danger is that in a time of troubles their hatreds may spread and infect the whole country. The best specific is for ordinary sober citizens to recognize Anglophobia for what the psychiatric origins of the term imply—a diseased state of mind. Any form of xenophobia—obsessive hatred of foreigners—is a disease, all the more dangerous because it is at least as contagious as typhoid. Some day we may treat xenophobes as we treat typhoid carriers—instead of rewarding them with handsome salaries as columnists.

2. BRITISH ATTITUDES TOWARDS THE UNITED STATES

Our analysis of American feelings towards Britain, into the loves and hatreds of the extremist few and the more mixed and much less intense feelings of the many, will hold conversely of British feelings towards the United States. Though most Americans hear little about them, there are British lovers of the United States (the word Americanophile seems somehow a bit too awkward for regular use). Historically, British liking for the United States stems from the little group of eighteenth-century rationalists and whigs who sympathized with the rebellious American colonists. Throughout the nineteenth century, British radicals, often republicans at heart, mildly anticlerical, firm believers in evolutionary progress, were attracted to the great republic of the West. The Benthamite tradition of philosophical radicalism was on the whole pro-American. Such people held firmly for the North in our Civil War. Their admiration usually stopped well short of idolatry; they did not like what they heard about our frontier lawlessness, they were disturbed by our treatment of the Negroes, and they were alarmed by the growth of our great fortunes. Today the British Left is inclined to economic collectivism, and has come to distrust the United States as the last great embodiment of laissez-faire individualism. Just as the American Left today sees Britain as a Tory and Imperialist power, so the British Left sees the United States as a conservative Republican power masking its imperialism as isolationism. Yet there remains a residual admiration for the United States even among British Leftists; and there are other Britishers who admire us for our energy, our willingness to experiment, our love of gadgets, our lively slang, our very lack of what the Victorian Bagehot held to be the most marked of British traits—a "deferential character." In short, there *are* Britishers who like us; and they like in Americans exactly those things that the American Anglophile dislikes.

The mass of Britishers are certainly favorably disposed towards the United States. They are grateful to us for the aid we have afforded them in two wars. Some oversensitive Americans who were in Britain during the late war believe they are insufficiently grateful. But the British—like the Normans, whose attitude many Americans also misunderstood—are a most undemonstrative people, schooled not to display their emotions. They are, furthermore, unused to being in debt, literally or figuratively, to another nation. Some Americans thought that the British in public gatherings responded more warmly to the mention of Russia than to the mention of the United States. This may have been so, and was not at all surprising in 1943, when Russian successes seemed a miraculous gift of the gods. Britishers expected us to succeed eventually; but they were astonished when the Russians succeeded. Moreover, Britishers were in daily contact with American troops almost everywhere in the islands; and though familiarity need not breed contempt—the best observers are convinced that here it did not—it does take the shine off the miraculous.

The British are also convinced that, for all the differences of accent and behavior they know distinguish the two peoples, we and they share political and moral habits which make collaboration easier than it commonly is between separate nationalities. They have been told often enough recently that the United States is a great melting pot, by no means "Anglo-Saxon" in the sense that New Zealand, save for the Maoris, is Anglo-Saxon. Pamphlets, books, and newspaper articles during this war have cautioned them not to expect from Americans the kind of reactions they would expect from themselves. Intellectually no doubt a good deal of this has sunk in. A few Britishers have learned the lesson too well, and are habitually on the lookout for new and startling differences between our behavior and theirs. But most of them continue to feel that after all, we're still members of the family, and that they can expect from us a lot more in the way of wordless, habitual understanding than they could from Frenchmen or

Russians. This attitude, which is not reciprocally shared by most Americans, is one of the serious psychological difficulties of Anglo-American relations. Even Britishers wise in American ways expect—not in their conscious thinking, but deep down in their subconscious—that we will want to do what they want us to do, because we do naturally what they do. They have no such illusions about the French or the Russians.

There is also among the British common people a milder form of the admiration for American wealth and American ways, for the American "standard of living," which marks off the more extreme British lovers of the United States. They admire our educational system, which they commonly think is more nearly perfect than it is. They admire our absence of class distinctions, which they commonly believe is a total absence. They are not really afraid of the prospective Americanization of Great Britain. They very much want their economy modernized, and they are still strong enough in self-esteem to believe that they can adapt American ways to their own rather than be submerged by Americanization.

The average Britisher has his doubts about us. He has at moments uneasy feelings that perhaps after all we are as different beneath as we seem to be on the surface, that perhaps we aren't really members of the family. But at the moment these doubts are overwhelmingly concentrated on the possibility that the United States will revert to an isolationist policy in international affairs. The Britisher is quite familiar with isolationism. His own Lord Salisbury popularized the term "splendid isolation" to describe Britain's policy towards Europe in late Victorian times, and he knows the temptations of the policy. He is usually, either because he has a bad conscience in the matter or merely because that is his way, very fair-minded about prospective American isolationism. You will not find Britishers, as you will find Frenchmen, querulous, injured, and wholly without understanding when they discuss the matter with Americans. They will often tell you, "after all, why shouldn't you people want to keep out of this mess

—it's perfectly natural." They very much want us in, however. They cannot quite persuade themselves that we shall really stay with the United Nations, that we shall continue to take seriously our duties as a world power. They fear that our idealism won't hold up much longer, and that we shall leave them to their fate. Their fears have made them—for Britishers—almost sensitive and jumpy. Notably, they feel they must reinsure elsewhere, that they cannot afford to put all their faith in the United States.

Illogically but quite humanly many of the same Britishers who are afraid that we will withdraw from our international commitments are also afraid that we will turn imperialist and try to run the world—and them. Most of those who protest loudest against American imperialism are Leftists, but the ordinary Britisher is beginning to have some doubts about the American Century, and the American Way. He would like to have just the right dosage of America, but he isn't quite sure how to measure this dosage.

We Americans naturally hear about British Americanophobes, just as the British hear about our Anglophobes. The minority of Britishers who really hate us—and it is a minority —are mostly upper-class people, or at least intellectuals, and they are likely to place great emphasis on the horrors of a possible Americanization of Britain. They have all read Mr. Lewis's *Babbitt*, and they see a George Babbitt, or worse, in every American. We are to them Hollywood incarnate, out to make Britain, and then the world, into one vast Hollywood. They are mostly nervous and complaining souls, and they do not trust the mass of their own fellow countrymen, whom they suspect of being quite willing to turn Lyme Regis or Lichfield into one of those horrible places they have read about in our novelists. Most British extreme Tories have of course always disliked us, because along with France we stood for those democratic "principles of 1776 and 1789" they regard as the ruination of the world. They are joined in their dislike of the United States, though outwardly in little else, by a very few doctrinaire intellectuals of the extreme Left, who regard the United States as a bulwark of anticommunism and reactionary economic and social policy. Yet if you scratch beneath the surface of most of these Leftists, you will find that what they really dislike in Americans is substantially what their Tory opponents dislike—what is to them American vulgarity, brass, and all-too-evident worldly success. Political extremes really do meet in this world, in the simple, systematic conviction that whatever is, is wrong.

3. WARTIME COLLABORATION

This war was a working experiment in direct Anglo-American coöperation, in which several million people took part. But it was in many ways an experiment carried out under abnormal conditions, and should not be taken as final evidence of the nature of peacetime relations between the two peoples. Most obviously, the need to stick together to win the war worked to curb national selfishness and intransigeance; and this need was greater for the British, or at any rate was felt by them to be greater, and made them more conciliatory than they can be expected to be now that the pressure of war is removed. And then, the experiment has been one-sided in that millions of Americans have lived in the British Isles and the Dominions or fought beside the British in many parts of the world, while only a few British air cadets, other specialists, and refugee women and children, have lived in the United States.

There have been alarmist reports of how badly our boys in the "American army of occupation" in Britain got on with the British people, and there have been soothing reports of how well they got along. Human nature being what it is, striking and painful incidents are more likely to make headlines than the routine of day-to-day relations. A case of rape involving an American soldier is news. It is of course also news when an English village puts up a plaque to honor an American flier who crashed to his death rather than risk killing civilians by a forced landing on the village green. But it is not news when a Britisher entertains American soldiers on leave, or stands them a drink in a pub. Our social statistics, in spite of Gallup polls, Mass Observation, and the like, are still imperfect. We record the thunderstorms and the rainbows, but have only rough and subjective estimates of the general course of the weather, the "climate" of Anglo-American relations in Britain during this war.

It is true that a great many American soldiers were unhappy in Britain. They complained about the weather, the "coldness" of the British, the thinness of British beer, the lack of soda fountains, the glumness of the British village or town shut down for Sunday. Their complaints were endless. But what most of us forget is that they would undoubtedly have complained had they been stationed in a Garden of Eden. A conscript army, unlike a professional army, is not composed of adventurers. It uproots men whom nature meant not to be transplanted. This is not a reflection against the courage or competence of our armies; the record of what they have done puts these qualities beyond a doubt. But the experience of the war makes it clear that, for all our reputation as a people of rolling stones, a very great number of Americans are really well-rooted, fond of home, set in their ways—in short, quite like the rest of the human race. The Army and Navy, the Red Cross and the USO, did an extraordinary job in surrounding the transplanted American fighting man with as much of his home soil as could possibly be moved. Britishers commented on how successfully we moved American folkways, from Coca-Cola to rebroadcasts of *real* (American) radio entertainment, wherever we went. But we couldn't move everything. So American boys, in their leisure moments, took to lounging most unmilitarily on street corners in once-smart Mayfair, commenting on the girls who passed by, and otherwise behaving as if they were on the corner of Main and Elm in the home town.

The British were a bit surprised, and a bit hurt. They

found it hard to understand the depth of American homesickness. They did their best. They organized all sorts of committees to provide entertainment for the Americans, and all told, as individuals, they did a good deal to make our men feel as much at home as possible. But they are not an unreserved and openhearted people, and many of their folkways clashed with ours. A single concrete example: you don't thumb rides and hitch-hike in the British Isles. There were, of course, very few civilian motorists left, and these were mostly doctors, nurses, clergymen and truckdrivers on their regular business. They were not in the habit of picking up strangers, and to most of them it never occurred that the American soldier they passed would like a two-mile lift to the movie in the next town. They didn't offer a lift, and very often the American didn't make a gesture to show that he wanted one. Indeed, the average American in the British Isles displayed a rather surprising reticence in such matters, so much so that many Britishers commented on how shy Americans were! This may have been due partly to the warnings given by the American Army in pamphlets and talks to prepare our men for life in Britain. They were good pamphlets and talks, but they may have overemphasized British dislike of backslapping, and made the Americans a bit too self-conscious about getting on with the British. But that Americans should be regarded as shy would also seem to be further evidence that we have got well past our frontier boisterousness.

By 1944, the British Isles were pretty crowded. American men, ships, planes, and supply dumps were everywhere. No sensible Britisher was ever anything but delighted at our presence, but one could hardly expect them all to take us in stride, on top of the hardships and inconveniences they had had to put up with since the beginning of the war. A good deal depends on how much you expect of human nature. If you are not a perfectionist, you will conclude that the American occupation of Britain passed off as well as could be expected. There seems to be no reason to believe that it has left any permanent scars on either people, and it has undoubtedly given both British and Americans more first-hand knowledge of the other people than they have ever had before. That knowledge is still imperfect, but it is better than ignorance, or the illusions of second-hand experience.

More serious is the kind of rivalry that developed once we were both in action on the continent. There was tendency, reflected in the press of both countries, for nationals of each to criticize the military effort and achievement of the other. The Britishers were holding us back; Montgomery was too cautious at Caen; we were doing the really bloody work. Or the Americans were hogging the limelight, taking all the credit, keeping the British out of Paris; they were careless in December 1944 at the time of the German break-through in the Ardennes. And so on. There was certainly a lot of such talk, stemming from that aspect of nationalism Clutton-Brock called "pooled self-esteem," heightened by the irritations of wartime. It has certainly not died out with the coming of peace, and sensational journalists like Mr. Ralph Ingersoll are probably setting the pattern for soberer, duller, and no less partisan historians to come. And yet this nationalistic back-biting (at which all nations are good) can, we must hope, be appreciably reduced by another kind of talk directed at the eternal task of the moral education of the race. It may yet be in our own times at least in part sublimated into something like what William James called the "moral equivalent of war." And, as the experience of British and Americans working together in this war also shows, national feeling may be in part subordinated to the practical needs of a given task.

For, in spite of national jealousies, British and Americans, soldiers and civilians alike, during this war worked together in hundreds of effective teams. Not all the talk about "here there are neither British nor Americans, but only Allies" was bunk—far from it. The tale that General Eisenhower sent an American officer back home, not because he called a superior a son-of-a-bitch, but because he called him a *British* son-of-a-bitch, may well be apocryphal, but like most such stories it is symbolically true enough. So strong indeed is the old Adam in men that these joint Anglo-American teams sometimes developed a team-spirit that found an outlet in rivalries with other Anglo-American teams. At the height of one of these jurisdictional disputes, anyone listening to the participants could have no doubt that nationalism *can* be transcended. The cynic might reflect that this really was the Jamesian moral equivalent of war. But the transcending, the fruits of which we all now enjoy in victory, was a positive as well as a negative thing, or there would have been no victory.

The jealousies and the quarrels between Britishers and Americans which marred their wartime collaboration must seem to all but the obsessed idealist insignificant in comparison with the closeness and effectiveness of that collaboration measured in terms of actual achievement. The extraordinary experiment of completely interleaved staffs called for superhuman efforts from officers and men trained in very different routines and etiquettes, soldiers—and this is said in explanation, not condemnation—inevitably at least as devoted to set forms as any civilian bureaucrat. A certain surface efficiency was undoubtedly lost in this joint staffing, but it seems likely that historians will conclude that on the whole we fought this war more effectively than the last, when a supreme allied command under Foch was established only very late in the war, and was never really a joint staffing.

4. FUNDAMENTAL PSYCHOLOGICAL DIFFICULTIES

If there is to be a real chance for world peace, Britain and America must at least "get on" together. In terms of very broad psychological generalizations, the main prospective difficulties of such getting on together would seem to be, on the British side, adjustment to a new and still, perhaps, insufficiently felt weakness, and, on the American side, adjustment to a new and still, perhaps, insufficiently felt responsibility for strength.

The British need us more than we need them. Autarky is in the long run an utter impossibility for the United States, but something like autarky is by no means impossible, however undesirable, in the short run. But even in the short run, autarky is impossible for Britain. Some Britishers, as we have seen, believe that, in a world as near international anarchy as the world we have all grown up in, a self-sufficient Empire and Commonwealth can be built with the direct or indirect aid of Western Europe, and will in our time enable Britain to keep her status as a great power. In terms of pure economics, such an Empire and Commonwealth is by no means impossible. What makes it a mere dream is its *strategic* impossibility. We can almost rule out the fantastic prospect of a modernized, efficient India thoroughly loyal to the Crown. Without India, the Empire and Commonwealth simply has not got the manpower or the material resources necessary to defend alone in a warring world hundreds of bits of territory scattered all over the globe. The United States is by no means as strong in sheer manpower nor as self-sufficient in all the materials necessary to modern war as our unthinking jingoes assume; and more scientific progress (which seems inevitable unless we are really entering the new Dark Ages prophets of doom threaten us with) is likely to expose even continental United States to hostile attack in a way our unthinking isolationists refuse to admit. But in comparison with the British Commonwealth and Empire the United States is a compact and yet extensive unit, economically and strategically capable of effective defense.

Britain, then, cannot stand alone. It is true enough historically that she has not stood alone in the past. All her major wars from the sixteenth century on have been wars of coalition. But she has usually been the dominating, and certainly the richest, ally in the coalition, and the coalitions have furthermore always been patched-up affairs, put together hastily according to the need of the moment. Once the war was over, Britain resumed her "independence"—an illusory one, like our own present one, but none the less real and important in British minds. It must constantly be kept in mind that Britain, and especially in those Victorian days still so fresh in British memories, thought of herself as in "splendid isolation." Only yesterday—this simple, concrete fact should fix the matter clearly—Britishers could take as a norm of their strength the "two-power" standard for their navy. This meant that the British navy alone should be at least equal in strength to the combined naval forces of the two powers next in strength. Not all the shipyards of the Commonwealth and Empire could today restore the Royal Navy to its lost supremacy and the two-power standard.

Britain cannot stand alone, but her people are used to thinking of her as standing alone, or at any rate, as standing on top of the heap. They have not the habit of dependency. They, and in particular their statesmen, diplomatists, publicists, and business leaders—their "ruling class"—are not used to wooing other peoples. And they have got to woo somebody. They might woo Russians, French, even Germans, and this they may well do. But right now it is pretty clear that they have got to do a certain amount of wooing of Americans. Let there be no misunderstanding. The British are, as peoples go, realistic and adaptable, and they have shown signs of plenty of ability to make in international affairs the kind of sensible and necessary compromise they have learned so well to make in their own domestic politics. But in that admittedly vague and ill-explored, but very real and important aspect of human life, the unconscious and the sub-conscious, there is still a good bit of Kipling in the Britisher. He is used to running things, used to leading the league. His intelligence and common sense tell him that in an unregulated free-for-all among "sovereign" nations Britain cannot survive without powerful friends. He sees clearly therefore that it is in his own interest to regulate the struggle, to make it something better than a free-for-all. All things considered, the British are probably more sincerely "internationalist" than any of the great people of the world today. But they cannot be expected to slough off old habits overnight; they cannot get rid of their history. When that bugaboo of the internationalist, "national prestige," comes into play—as it must constantly come into play in our time, for none of us can get rid of our history—*Rule Britannia,* and a lot else, come flooding into British minds, and they are tempted to behave as if Britannia still did rule the waves.

They do not like being dependent on us for material aid. Here we are dealing with attitudes which require for their understanding a touch of something—cynicism isn't quite the word—most distasteful to many upright and intelligent men. The British should be grateful to us for Lend-Lease, the loan of 1946, the continuing aid under the Marshall Plan. And they are grateful. But they are also ashamed of needing help, even though intellectually they can satisfy themselves that they need it through no weaknesses of their own, and even though they tell themselves that they are not accepting charity and are in fact giving us the opportunity to make good investments. They are tempted to take some of their feelings out on us, and may therefore seem to some Americans ungrateful. But after all no people can really be expected to be Christian enough to forgive their creditors. The British are still, be it repeated, a proud people.

We have been brutally frank about the British position; to equalize matters, let us be equally frank about the American position. We now are stronger than they. We face the dangers all parvenus in this world face. Folk wisdom has plenty of words for it: we may "feel our oats," our new power may "go to our heads," we may try to "rule the roost." To use highbrow instead of lowbrow terms, equally threadbare and equally true; we may take over the privileges of greatness without taking over the responsibilities of greatness. Towards the British in particular, though to a certain extent towards "old" Europe in general, many Americans have long had a certain feeling of inferiority. In matters of culture this feeling has not yet entirely died out. We did a lot of obvious compensating for such feelings. One whole aspect of our isolationism was such a compensation. Some, perhaps most, isolationist feeling in the United States springs from the simple human desire not to go through the hell of war; it is of a piece with the isolationism of Eire and Quebec. But some of it had less simple origins in the belief that we were "above" old-world intrigues and wars —an honest belief, but one not wholly unmixed with the feeling that we should come out second-best in any such encounters. The notion of American diplomatic innocence and incompetence face to face with the suave British devils in frock coats betrays the fact that some of our past isolationism sprang from a sense of inferiority.

Such isolationism can easily turn into jingoism, for it has the same psychological origins. Americans may be as overbearing towards the British as we have been in the habit of thinking they have been towards us. We shall have to learn tact, moderation, ability to put ourselves imaginatively in the other fellow's place, and see ourselves as others see us—none of them virtues natural to the parvenu. We shall have to practice as much as we can of genuine humility, the Christian virtue most difficult to reconcile even with the purest patriotism. The task will be the harder, since, as has been pointed out already in this essay, we Americans share with the British to a high degree an intensification of the universal human tendency to believe that our national policy always coincides with the highest morality. Were we as a nation to pursue a course of selfish imperialism, we should never do so in the name of crude concepts like that of the Germanic "master-race," or "Might makes Right," or anything of the sort. Nor should we, like the French, do so in the name of the universality of our culture. We should simply take over from the British the White Man's Burden. The ironic spirit might then have the satisfaction of recording the fact that the British called us hypocrites, and the French called us *perfide Amérique*.

The years since the end of the war of 1939–1945 have seen the growth of an American attitude towards Britain already evident after the war 1914–1918—the attitude that Britain

is finished. Much since 1945 has gone to strengthen this attitude: the obvious economic difficulties of the British homeland, the British withdrawal from Greece, the concessions in
India, Burma, and elsewhere in the Empire, the complaints of
the British themselves, the harrowing tales of American travelers—some of them trained social scientists—in Britain. Now,
as we pointed out in our first chapter, it is quite impossible
to make accurate quantitative measurements of the "strength"
or "capacity," physical, intellectual, and spiritual, of a nation.
Even if you look at international life as a competition pure
and simple, ultimately tested in war, it is not the kind of
neatly organized and measurable competition you get in a
baseball league, for instance. Yes, Britain probably led the
league in 1870, and no longer leads; but you can't say she's
in third, or fourth place, nor by how much. At any rate she's
clearly still in the league.

There is, of course, no use telling Anglophobes that Britain
is not finished. As unreasonable people, they have no trouble
maintaining in the same breath that Britain is both powerless
and a world menace because of her power. For the rest of us,
the facts and figures brought forth in this book should at the
very least show that Britain and the Commonwealth—the British complex—is still a major factor in international relations.
The historian of Europe, familiar with the ups and downs of
nations, and with the extraordinary ability to come back after
serious economic and military disaster shown in the past by
France, Germany, Russia—and by England herself in 1640–
1690—will be very hesitant to decide that even in terms of the
long run Britain is irrevocably declining. In times like these,
every voice is Cassandra's. But we shall never in our lifetime
know the answer in terms of the long run. We do know that,
at least in modern times, nations do not die with melodramatic
finality. Even Spain has not died that way. The Britain we
Americans are going to have to deal with in our lifetime is
and will be very much a going concern, and we shall not help
ourselves, the British, or the cause of world peace by bemoan-

ing, or gloating over, Britain's dismal prospects. To the internationalist, of course, we share Britain's fate. If the bell is tolling, it tolls for us, too.

There has long been great debate as to whether we Americans are more like or more unlike the British. The debate is endless, for national traits can never be fixed in any formula. But the mere fact that there is a debate points up the inescapable truth that the two peoples are tied by their history in no ordinary relationship. We do not often debate whether Americans are more like or more unlike the Turks. The concept of a parent-child relationship between Britain and the United States is admittedly a figure of speech. Such figures are fine for rhetoric, and dangerous for analytical thought. But, though the narrowly rationalist intellect may try to get along without them, only by the use of such figures of speech can we begin to fathom our way through the complexities of human relationships.

If we are willing to use it as guide, in full awareness that it is no full description of reality, not even of psychological reality, the figure of the parent-child relationship between Great Britain and the United States may help us in the difficult adjustments we must make in our dealings with the British. The child has outgrown the parent. It has set up its own household, and is fully independent. All this the parent knows, and accepts. But the tie exists, not altogether without Freudian touches. The child must have its moments of wanting to assert dramatically, conspicuously, and often unnecessarily, its independence; it must be tempted to remind the parent that he is beginning to show some of the weaknesses of old age; it must feel some fears that it will have to take care of the parent, fears not made more generous by a not-so-secret satisfaction that the role of the dependent is being reversed. On the other side of the relationship, the parent cannot help feeling himself wiser than the child; he can never entirely forgive the child for growing up; he must have even less generous fears than the child about the prospects of a

reversal of dependency. Happily, both convention and morality intervene against these Freudian undercurrents—a fact that
Freud himself fully acknowledged. Parents and their grown-up
children can and do get along together in this world. And
we should not forget that our figure of speech breaks down at
a most important point. There is no prospect that in any
span of years that need concern us Britain will "grow old" to
the point of helpless invalidism, utter senility. Britain need
not be, economically or in any other way, a charge upon
us. She is quite able to take care of herself—in a world in
which Anglo-American coöperation supports genuine international order. In a world of international disorder like that
of the last few decades, we are both likely to be caught up in
destructive passions for which even the popular conception of
Freudianism has not colors black enough.

11. The United States, Britain and World Order

There are almost as many prospective permutations and combinations among the nation-states of the world as there are writers—and talkers—on the subject of international relations. For the sake of clarity in analysis, we may state the two polar extremes, noting again that they cannot be lived in by human beings. At one extreme is a single sovereign world-state, towards which each present-day sovereign state would stand as each of the forty-eight states of the United States stands towards our federal government. No such world-state can possibly emerge from the present crisis. At the other extreme is complete international anarchy, no sovereign state admitting any limitation but that of force on its freedom to conduct as it likes its relations with other states. It will perhaps not be clear to the confirmed pessimist that this concept too is utterly unreal. But bad as international relations among nations have been since the modern system of states emerged out of the Middle Ages, they have never been wholly anarchical. Treaties have been violated, but there have always been treaties. Concepts like that of the brotherhood of man, natural law, and international law have been denied in principle and in practice, but they have always guided the actions of some men somewhere; they have never wholly given way, as a description of reality, to the Hobbesian formula, "man is a wolf to other men."

In between these two impossible extremes lies the region in

which international relations in our time will develop. The world may draw nearer to the pole of international organization, or it may draw nearer to the pole of international anarchy. All the signs of the times show that the great majority of the peoples of the world are desirous of drawing closer together in some form of world organization that will not, however, be a sovereign world-state. But it would be folly to neglect the possibility that these desires may be cheated, and that mankind may fall back even further towards the pole of international anarchy—or what would to us Westerners, children of the idea of progress, be quite as bad, continue more or less in its present condition. There are, broadly speaking, two real possibilities each presenting in practice an almost infinite number of concrete combinations impossible to forecast in detail: first, that even under the new international organization the United States and Britain will have to adjust themselves to the realities of a world of competing and almost unbridled nation-states, held together by nothing stronger than the old rules of "balance of power"—that is, to a world in which international relations are essentially what they have recently been; and second, that the new international organization *really does work*, and thus makes it necessary for the United States and Britain to adjust themselves to an international situation in part *new*.

1. THE POSTULATE OF INTERNATIONAL ANARCHY

Under the postulate of continued—or increased—international anarchy, there will come to the minds of some Americans the old, consoling formula of American isolationism. The formula ought not to console anybody, for in the three centuries of our history as a colony of Britain and as an independent nation, we have never been able to hold to it—though we have tried hard enough at times—in any of the great crises known as world wars. Historians may differ a bit as to the numbering of these crises, but they would agree that since the discoveries of Columbus rounded out the world, there have been at least half a dozen world wars. We Americans have taken part in all we possibly could, beginning with "World War II" (the war against the then current Hitler, Louis XIV of France), at the end of the seventeenth century. In our tiny contemporary world of miracles of transportation and communication, it would seem a truism that we cannot hope to escape involvements we could not escape in 1689 or 1812. But you cannot effectively argue with the convinced American isolationist, and we shall not attempt to do so here. The desire not to undergo the horrors of war seems normal among all civilized peoples, among Americans and Britishers as well as among Swiss, Swedes, and Irish, and a flare-up of isolationist sentiment in the United States is perhaps even likely if the world swings again towards a general war. But nowadays, all the indices of public opinion in the United States show that the kind of isolationism that produced the ineffective neutrality legislation of the 1930's is as dead as the kind of teetotalism that produced the ineffective prohibition legislation of the 1920's. The American people still undoubtedly regard alcoholism as an evil, just as they regard war as an evil, and they would like to cure both. But, in spite of the pessimists who maintain that in such matters we human beings never learn from experience, the American people does seem to have learned that great social evils cannot be cured merely by comprehensive legislation or agreements abolishing them on statute books or in treaties.

There exists in some American minds a variant of the simple formula of isolationism for the United States. This is hemisphere isolationism, the establishment of some sort of self-sufficient bloc or union among the states of North and South America which could stay out of the wars of the old world. We need not linger long over this unrealistic proposal, which is a perversion of the Monroe Doctrine. The economic, political, and cultural ties which bind Canada and Latin America to the old world are in some ways closer than those which make it impossible for the United States to quarantine itself against the infection of world wars. There is already an effective regional agreement among the states of the Western hemisphere which can and does do its work *within* the framework of world relations. There are no good grounds for believing that any such agreement could be transformed into a union *outside* this framework. In cold fact, a self-sufficient Pan American Union in the kind of international anarchy we are postulating would have to be, not just a "sphere of influence" of the United States (which is how anti-Americans even now translate the Monroe Doctrine) but an Empire of the United States. We could hardly build up such an Empire peacefully in a world of competing nation-states, even if we wished to try. But we clearly do not wish to try.

Another proposal for something less than world-wide international organization may be considered at this point—that for a full federal union between the United States and the British Commonwealth and Empire. In fairness to the small but enthusiastic groups which, under the impetus of Mr. Streit, have been formed in this country, in the United Kingdom, and in the Dominions to work for this union, we must admit that they sincerely believe that it would not be a union *against* the rest of the world, but for the ultimate benefit of the rest of the world. Most of its proponents are not Anglo-Saxon imperialists, but well-meaning internationalists, for whom the union of the Anglo-Saxon peoples would not be a closed union, but rather the nucleus of a world-state which other peoples could, as they became fit, voluntarily join. It should not be forgotten that Mr. Streit's original concept, before the fall of France, was a union of the democratic states of the Western World and that he has, since the defeat of Germany, reverted to something like his original idea of a union of the virtuous democracies.

As an immediate possibility, Anglo-American federal union

is simply not worth discussing. No sensible person believes that any concrete measure for such a union could pass today or tomorrow in the American Congress, the British Parliament, or in a Dominion Parliament; and it could not pass, not by any means because of the blindness or contrariness of the politicians, but because their constituents, the people of the United States, Britain, and the Dominions, do not want it to pass. The cliché will infuriate the enthusiasts for "Union Now," all the more because as enthusiasts they hate and reject the reality of which clichés are a reflection: but the English-speaking peoples simply are not "ready" for "Union Now."

Whether such a union among English-speaking peoples is, however, in the long run possible and desirable, and therefore worth our working for now, as devoted men and women worked against great odds in the eighteenth and nineteenth centuries to prepare the way for the ultimate abolition of human slavery, is a different and much more serious question. The reader owes it to himself and his children to examine the question carefully, for a successful Anglo-American federal union would be big with consequences.

It is tempting, in a world of sixty-odd "sovereign" states, quarrels between any two of which may spread to the whole lot, to hold that almost any reduction in their number would reduce the hazards of conflict. It is tempting to believe that, since history records that the hundreds of potentially and actually warring units of medieval Europe were actually integrated into the internal peace of the modern nation-state, there is something "natural" and even inevitable in the continuation of the process by integration of certain existing states into still larger units based on something common and traditional—language, institutions, or even that now somewhat discredited concept, "race." Advocates of Anglo-American federal union ought logically, as indeed some of them do, also to advocate similar federal unions among Latins, Slavs, Germans and other peoples with at least something partly "national" in common.

There is, of course, a fallacy in the assumption that a mere mathematical reduction in the number of sovereign states would diminish the likelihood of war. If the newer and fewer states were no more than the present nation-states enlarged, but still essentially unchanged in their nationalist habits, there would be no progress towards lasting peace. Anglo-American union would not in itself diminish the possibilities of world war. A minority of those who advocate such a union are, of course, at heart Anglo-Saxon imperialists in the tradition of Cecil Rhodes and Rudyard Kipling; what they really want is for the English-speaking peoples to get together and set up, by means of war if necessary, some sort of modern equivalent of the old Roman Empire. The majority of the advocates of Anglo-American federal union, be it repeated, think of their proposals as part of the whole complex of plans to outlaw war, as essentially part of what we have called the postulate of international organization. Yet there are grave reasons to believe that in fact proposals for Anglo-American union should rather be considered as leading in the direction of international anarchy.

To the rest of the two billion human beings who are not Anglo-Saxons—that is, to 90 per cent of the human race—proposals for an Anglo-Saxon federal union already look like proposals for Anglo-Saxon world domination. Such an attitude on the part of the rest of the world is natural, not to be reasoned away, and by no means unreasonable. Were the grave and perhaps insuperable obstacles to the construction of such an Anglo-Saxon union overcome, and the thing created, the temptation to use it as an instrument of imperialistic power in world politics would be very strong indeed for the men who ran it. And these men would not—the lessons of history are crystal clear in this respect—be kindly and idealistic pamphleteers and propagandists like Mr. Streit and his followers. They would be successful politicians.

Anglo-American federal union is not enough. It is not even a first step towards the transcending of the sovereign nation-state in a genuine international order. It is *the wrong kind of step*. We should not prepare to take it.

Neither American isolationism, either simply within the present limits of the United States or more complexly within a tight North and South American bloc, nor Anglo-American federal union, is a satisfactory solution of the problems of the international relations of the United States even in a world no better organized than the present one. They are not really *possible* solutions in terms of current conditions. We are, however, still postulating a world of competing nation-states not so very different from the one we have been brought up in. The very existence of the United Nations is going to change that world somewhat—we may hope, a great deal. But there will be sovereign nations within the United Nations, and those nations, short of an almost inconceivable spiritual revolution in human nature, will pursue policies not altogether unlike those they have pursued in the past. Let us, for purposes of clarity, assume that in some senses the phenomena we are used to under names like "balance of power," "spheres of influence," "alliances and alignments," and the rest are going to continue.

There are those who are so horrified at the thing itself that they refuse to use the names, even for purposes of study. And there are also those who seem so fascinated by the thing that under the cloak of studying it they indulge themselves in a good deal of vicarious satisfaction. Many of our numerous prophets in international relations, working out in detail the "inevitable" permutations and combinations among the powers, appear to be yielding to an unprofitable and unsound fascination. They are too clever, and the worlds they spin out of their minds are at least as unreal as the world of the innocent internationalist.

A favorite game of these prognosticators in international relations is to announce the probable line-up and the approximate date of outbreak of the "next world war." History, economics, psychology, strategy, geography, demography—even discredited pseudo-sciences like geopolitics—are all appealed to for support. The still imperfect social sciences, as their more modest practitioners well know, give no such exact forecasts. But this does not deter the crystal gazers, who are in no sort of agreement about what they see in their crystals. Were all this mere private speculation, we might dismiss it as unimportant. But most of these crystal gazers are also publicists and propagandists. Each is convinced that he really knows the line-up of the next war, and each is determined that his own country shall be on the winning side—which, of course, he also knows in advance. And so, if we are Americans, we are told that we have got to beat Russia, and therefore that we ought to have at least Britain and China on our side, or that we cannot beat Russia, and that therefore we must have Russia on our side even if we quarrel with Britain, or . . . but the thing can, and does, go on indefinitely.

If you will examine the arguments of such people, you will find that all but the few very cleverest of them are obsessed by some one single factor they have fastened upon out of the many factors that influence the interactions of human beings. Some think that sea power must fight land power; others think that sea power can't fight land power. Some hold that a showdown must come between capitalist societies and collectivist societies. Others predict that the next Armageddon will be a struggle between the white race and the yellow race. Right now the simple polar dualism of the United States *versus* Russia seems to sum up the inevitable antagonisms of international politics. But international politics sometimes makes even stranger bedfellows than domestic politics. No one should assume that the opposition of the United States and Russia is permanent, or even that it will endure until another war.

For it is, of course, impossible to predict future combinations of powers. War is a very complicated disease, in which diagnosis is difficult and prognosis almost impossible, at least in detail.

Nevertheless, the history of the five-hundred-year-old system of nation-states permits a few first approximations, a few very rough generalizations which seem sound, and have at least the negative value of being effective checks against the wilder prophets. This system of nation-states grew up in Europe, and with the development of the United States, the British dominions, Latin America, Japan, and China, and with India and the Arab states becoming nation-states in our own day, has now spread throughout the world. Its extension from Europe to the whole world has brought new complexities, especially those involving very "backward" peoples, but has by no means invalidated what we can learn from its earlier history in Europe.

First, it is clear that the members of the system will, though usually with great difficulty, coalesce against any member who seeks to destroy the system by absorbing any considerable number of its constituent members. Attempts to "dominate" Europe and then the world by the Spain of Charles V, the France of Louis XIV and Napoleon, and the Germany of William II and Hitler have all been defeated by coalitions of threatened states, big and little. If you approve the process, you will say that eventually mankind unites against the bully; if you do not approve it, you will say that mankind is jealous of the strong and efficient, and has in modern times ganged up against powers which might have brought to a divided Europe and a divided world a new unity like that of the old Roman Empire. Most Americans will feel that fortunately mankind unites against the bully, that whatever makes nation-states want to be "free" is at bottom good, that if the system of nation-states is to be transcended, it must be transcended by the method of consent (federalism), not by the method of force and guile (imperialism).

But what about the record of Britain in this process? Hasn't she put together an Empire greater than anything Charles V, Louis XIV, Napoleon, William II, or Hitler ever succeeded in grabbing? Hasn't Britain merely been a *successful* bully? The answer is yes, in the same sense that the United States has been a successful bully towards the Red Indians. Ever since the days of Joan of Arc, Britain has renounced the attempt to make conquests in Europe, and has intervened in Europe only to preserve the "balance of power"—that is, to prevent the destruction of the system of nation-states. She has expanded only at the expense of backward peoples outside the system, as have France, Holland, and the other colonial powers— as we have in our West. But nowadays *there is nothing outside the system.* Any attempt by Britain, or indeed by any great power, to make further considerable acquisitions of territory would produce a coalition against her. This really is a "lesson of history."

Second, the record shows a persistence, a vitality, among the constituent nation-states in the system which ought to give pause to the prophets who tell us that nowadays only the great powers, indeed, only the "super-powers," count. It is very hard to kill a nation-state. Eire has emerged into independence after six hundred years of dependence on England or Great Britain. Poland has stood four partitions in a century and a half, has disappeared from the map, and has been twice reborn. Korea, a very late-comer to the system, is about to be born again. It may be that only the rivalry of the great powers has enabled the small and middle-sized powers to survive. But it is precisely the continuation of rivalry among the great powers that we are postulating in this section of our study. The burden of proof is on those who maintain that under modern conditions the smaller powers cannot survive, and therefore can be neg- lected in our thinking. They can point to economic and tech- nological changes which make the small state an anomaly; but they cannot point to changes in human nature which make a Dutchman want to cease being a free Dutchman.

In a contest between economics and technology and human nature, human nature wins oftener than our more naive prophets will admit. These same prophets announced in 1940 that under modern conditions guerilla warfare was impossible, that none of the lands Hitler had conquered could repeat the effective role of Spain in rising against Napoleon in 1807– 1814. Jugoslavia, and even "effete" France, gave them the lie.

Tanks, airplanes, speedy communications, all the most efficient weapons for keeping conquered peoples down, still need to be handled by human beings. It is probably easier to control conquered populations than it was in the days of Napoleon. All things considered, Hitler perhaps came closer to success than any other would-be world-conqueror. To use the glib phrase of the prophets, "next time" a world-conqueror may succeed.

Very few Americans indeed want that always possible world-conqueror to be an American. They do not want a world put together by force, even though it is they who do the putting together. Our brief review of the growth of the present system of nation-states shows that the system does have a tendency to persistence, a rough and always precarious equilibrium, for which the cant term is "balance of power." Most Americans probably believe that even balance of power is better than an authoritarian world-state put together by force, and held together only by force and the deadening hand of force hardened into custom. If we cannot do better—and perhaps we cannot—we should do well to guard the good elements of the present state-system by an intelligent and farsighted pursuit of a policy of balance of power.

There is, however, no such simplifying formula for the pursuit of such a policy as some of our publicists discern. This is the field of speculation above all dear to the prophets and prognosticators, and they have come up with some extraordinary suggestions. There are only two prominent two-power combinations commonly brought forward, at least for the present: Anglo-American or Russo-American joint domination—for the good of the world, of course. We have already examined and rejected *Anglo-American* federal union, in part because such a union would in fact be very likely to turn into an attempted Anglo-American domination. Without a formal union, such an attempt would be just as unfortunate, and perhaps even less likely to achieve temporary success. Advocates of *Russo-American* world-rule have in these days to be rather on the lunatic fringe. There is the old Marxist dream of a world revolution, but in terms of this dream nothing so bourgeois as world hegemony enters. The realists are quite unable to conceive of Russo-American collaboration in anything. Nevertheless, there are a few who, influenced by what is called geopolitics, think that if only Russia and America can come to speaking terms, all will be well. Their favorite argument is that these two great powers cannot fight each other, any more than a whale can fight an elephant; that they have hardly any more real field of competition than have those two animals; that therefore peace between them is "natural"; that each is so strong that it can prevent any third power, or group of powers, from disturbing the peace. The advocates of joint Russo-American domination commonly dismiss the British Commonwealth and Empire as so weak strategically, and even as so weak economically and politically, in spite of the imposing statistical strength of the whole agglomeration under the British Crown, that it can be more or less disregarded, equated with the lesser states. This risky assumption alone should make us suspicious of their arguments. But history—not just modern history, but history way back to the days of the ancient empires of the Nile and the Tigris-Euphrates basins—shows that their basic metaphor of the whale and the elephant does not hold. Sooner or later, two great nations left alone in competition seem bound to fight. No ocean is today as wide or as hard to cross as were once the few hundred miles of desert that separated the Nile and the Euphrates—and which organized armies crossed nearly four thousand years ago.

At the end of the war, there were those who argued that if only the three superpowers, the U.S.A., the U.S.S.R., and the British Commonwealth and Empire, would stand together, there need be no worry about the rest of the world. They have not stood together, and there are no signs that they will do so in the near future. But the whole notion that a balance of power among superpowers is possible, or easier than a balance of power among sixty-odd nations, is clearly false. The very mentality that produced a phrase like "superpower" is an indication of the impossibility of an international order through conventional balance of power. British, Americans, and Russians taken together make up considerably less than half mankind, condemned to be "minor powers." But they are not necessarily so in fact. Alarmists already are worried over what could be done by a small, well-disciplined, and well-organized state that deliberately set out to exploit in a Spartan manner the possibilities of ultra-modern warfare. After all, it took a huge coalition to beat Germany, which was by no means a superpower.

The truth is that as long as nation-states exist and as long as they feel they are and should be independent, no kind of international stability can last very long if *any one* of these nation-states is badly maladjusted. Those who think they are simplifying the problems of world peace by talking about superpowers are in fact falsifying them. A bitterly angry and balked Eire, an Argentine dissatisfied with what the world thinks of the Argentine, could disturb hopelessly a world (a quite impossible world, of course) which the three superpowers in concert had decided to run on their own. They could always break up, sooner or later, the concord among the Big Three. But speculation about the future in terms of superpowers is essentially naive; it is perhaps unduly prevalent in America, because of our natural tendency to equate size and importance. We should at least recollect that a very small microbe can upset the balance of a very big organism.

There is, then, no really effective simplification for the subtle and difficult task that confronts the United States if we *must* play the old game of balance of power. If we must play the game, we should play it well, and not rely on anything—not even on the miracles of modern science and technology—to make it easier than in the old days, for it will not be easier. Such a policy would in fact make us the heir of Britain in international politics. Like Britain in the nineteenth century, we should hold on to what we have got and perhaps add a few small bits of territory here and there; we should through our sea power, supplemented in this twentieth century by air power, act as a sort of international policeman of the seas, islands, and outlying parts of the world; we should in fact be the benevolent protector rather than merely the good neighbor of the peoples to the north and south of us in the *Western* hemisphere; we should normally abstain from anything like direct political intervention in the affairs of the *Eastern* hemisphere and use our influence indirectly to preserve the *status quo* there; but, just as Britain has historically had a particular concern for the independence of the rim-lands of Europe opposite her coasts, we should have a similar concern for the independence of those rim-lands, of which from our point of view the British Isles themselves would form a part; and, because of our geographical position, we should have to have a similar concern also for the Asiatic rim-lands opposite our Pacific Coast; finally, if some wicked continental power, Germany, Russia, China, or some other, should grow too strong, should show signs of wanting to follow in the footsteps of Napoleon and Hitler, should, that is, disturb the balance of power by grabbing some of these rim-lands, we should put together a coalition, and go to war against that wicked power. If we followed to the last the British parallel, as we clearly did in 1939, we should go to war almost, but not quite, too late.

Though he puts it more guardedly, and in much nicer words, this is the policy Mr. Walter Lippmann really is telling us we ought to pursue—within the framework of some sort of international organization, of course, but in full awareness that such an international organization isn't going to change much in international relations, isn't going to alter fundamentally the world-system of nation-states and the habits and feelings of men brought up in patriotic love for some one of sixty fatherlands. Now this is not, like some current schemes for the manipulation of balance of power politics, a fantastic policy. It may even be the best we can get. American internationalists

in 1919—and there were millions of them—were perhaps too
naive, too hopeful, aimed too high. A little skepticism, even a
little disillusionment about the working out of any plans for
international organization, is probably a good thing. But to
propose that the United States content itself with taking over
Britain's historic role as guardian of the balance of power is
to aim too low. All policy, from running a garden to running
international relations, is an attempt to close the eternal, painful, and stimulating gap between the ideal and the real. Last
time in international relations we tried too hard to close the
gap entirely; this time we may be in danger of not trying hard
enough.

An attempt on the part of the United States to take over
from Great Britain her traditional place in the politics of
balance of power would certainly sharpen the difficulties of
Anglo-American relations. Not even nice phrases about partnership could alter the fact that the United States was running
the show. And it could only be a successful show if we really
did run it. The United Kingdom, under such conditions, would
have to take something like dominion status in an *American*
Commonwealth and Empire. This might be a "good thing"
for the British, but the psychological difficulties, on their part
and on ours, of such a relationship would be almost insuperable.
They would be at least as great as those confronting a specific
legislative union of the kind desired by Mr. Streit and his
followers. They would involve in a singularly naked and un-
disguised form those adjustments to the reversal of the parent–
child relationship we discussed in the last chapter. We can get
on with the British, even though we are obviously much
stronger than they, and are at times a bit tactless about reminding them of that fact, as long as we are both fellow members of a world organization, a league of sovereign states; we
can work with them as equals—do not sneer at that word as
meaningless, because it is not meaningless—in close collaboration, in practical alliance, within such a world organization.
We *might* be able to work with them if we treated them

merely as our European agent to maintain balance of power; but they would certainly be sorely tempted under such conditions to try to set up in business for themselves. It is a business they have long been running on their own.

The telling argument against our practicing—or attempting to practice—balance of power in the traditional British manner is that, even though the British fitted themselves willingly and effectively to the role of our European agent or outpost, and even though we secured a good oriental agent, the last five centuries show that such a policy is no cure, and hardly even an effective palliative, for the evil of war. Again, as Mr. Lippmann and his fellows keep reminding us, perhaps we ought not to attempt to cure the evil of war, but only to palliate, by postponing, its outbreak in the form of total or world war. But surely we ought to get the best palliative possible? We should try to make the new international organization work, allowing for the inescapable realities behind phrases like "nationalism," "imperialism," "balance of power," but not accepting them as unchangeable, not basing our action upon them as norms, not conditioning ourselves to think and feel according to them. We must attempt a fundamental task of reconditioning ourselves; we must try to break the *habit* of nationalism. It makes all the difference in the world whether we approach the problem as one of minor adjustments to unalterable conditions or one of major alterations in the conditions themselves. It may be granted that we cannot at once altogether escape the balance of power; but, to have recourse again to a metaphor from human pathology, we can choose between accepting chronic invalidism, lightened though it may be by the best wheel chairs and the latest modern contrivances, and actively following a therapy that calls on us to strengthen our muscles, improve our diet, get out in the air, and above all, determine not to accept the limitations of old-fashioned chronic invalidism. Balance of power, even when touched up agreeably after the manner of Mr. Lippmann, is no more than a wheel

66 *The United States and Britain*

chair; the cruder schemes of most of our geopolitical prophets
aren't even good sound crutches.

2. THE POSTULATE OF INTERNATIONAL
ORGANIZATION

We come, then, to the second postulate: that the international organization growing out of the work of the meetings
at Dumbarton Oaks and San Francisco, London and Lake Success—and out of a lot of hard and unpublicized work all over
the world—is not to be a mere cloak for old habits, but an
attempt to form new ones.

But before we come to the problems of Anglo-American
relations within the United Nations, we must say a word about
the possibility that a more genuine world government might
emerge directly from the present difficulties we are going
through. There are those who maintain that the atomic bomb
has brought something so new into every human relation that
all history, all previous planning, is invalidated. If these prophets are right, this whole book of ours is pretty pointless. We
cannot here agree with them. If the simple dichotomy is:
world government tomorrow or destruction of the work by
atomic warfare day-after-tomorrow, we frankly believe the
world will be destroyed. But we do not accept the dichotomy
in any of its implications—not even in the implication that
atomic warfare will wipe out the human race, and certainly
not in the implication that the threat of such warfare will
produce a United States of the World. The United Nations
may gradually become something more than the league, the
international forum, the complex center of balance of power
it now is. It may become something more like a true government. But not overnight. It remains an organization within
which peace-loving men and women can work realistically for
peace.

As members of such an organization, the United States and
the British Commonwealth and Empire will play leading parts.

Their own problems of mutual relationship will remain serious problems, by no means guaranteed automatic and easy solution by their membership in a genuine international league. But the solution of those problems should be facilitated by such membership, first because many of them, and notably those of Anglo-American trade, are in fact problems of multilateral world relations which cannot be settled by the two countries alone even in the closest mutual agreement; and second because the self-esteem, the pride, the vanity of both peoples—and remember that though the British will be harder tested in this respect than we, we shall both find ourselves touched in these very human ways—will be less vastly injured by concessions made in a world assembly than by concessions made in dual negotiations.

This last statement may be challenged by lovers of smallness, who will argue that the smaller the circle the more easily agreement is achieved, the more readily conflicting egos are reconciled. Town-meeting politics do not wholly bear them out, but at any rate, we cannot run world politics by the methods of town-meeting politics. Bigness is with us, and is not to be avoided. Anyone who has had experience of large-scale organizations knows that, once you get beyond the level of very small groups of intimates, authority is more readily accepted the more general and impersonal it appears to be. We shall have to accept some authority in some major matters above the authority even of Washington and Westminster— that indeed is merely another way of putting the necessity for transcending nationalism. Once we can make a habit of accepting the authority, in major affairs as in minor ones, of the organs of the United Nations, we shall have got over the hump. We shall not have landed in Utopia, but we shall at least have passed through the Time of Troubles which began in 1914.

It is sometimes said that the new international organization will have no authority, because it will have no police power, no power to *compel* a constituent nation-state to obey. It is true that the new organization will be, to use two very precise German words which English unfortunately lacks, a *Staatenbund* (league of states) and not a *Bundesstaat* (state composed of units enjoying local self-government). The new organization will have to *win* its authority by the slow, patient, and in detail quite unspectacular way of discussion and compromise; it cannot start its work endowed with such authority. An international organization might conceivably start endowed with compulsive powers, but the Axis has just signally failed in what was after all an attempt to found two international organizations, the Nazi "New Order" and the Japanese "Greater East Asia Co-prosperity Sphere," which would certainly have had a very generous endowment of compulsive powers over their constituent units.

Men are not governed, order is not maintained, by force alone. This statement is not woolly idealism, but the hardest kind of realism. Men are governed, order is maintained, by a delicate and constantly changing equilibrium into which enter as major factors men's notions of their self-interest, their fears ("force"), their loyalties ("consent"), their habits, their traditions. Of these, habits and traditions are probably the most important factors in the long run in maintaining law and order. But you cannot, as the advocates of World Federation now apparently wish, start with habit and tradition; you must either start with force and try to get the rest (let it be repeated, the rest *must* be got); or you must start with consent and try to get the rest. The Axis started with force, and failed. We are going to start with consent.

Now though the member-states of the United Nations vary greatly in economic, social, and political structure, we may believe that to a great extent the consent of their peoples has been won. Consent to what? Consent to try to settle problems of international relations by regular, open consultation among representatives of nation-states. The regularity is important, and so is the openness. But do not make a fetish of "open"—a lot goes on in the corridors of established national and local legislative bodies, in the famous smoke-filled rooms of party conventions, and indeed wherever groups of men work to-gether in going concerns, in board rooms, faculty rooms, yes, in vestry rooms, which is not "open" in the innocent sense we most of us gave in 1919 to the Wilsonian phrase "open cove-nants openly arrived at."

We are going, then, to try to build up by the democratic method of discussion, compromise, and consent an international world order—not, though some of these will persist as ele-ments of the complex whole, just regional agreements; not just two, three, four or five-power alliances, hegemonies, recognized spheres of influence; nor any of the other largely ineffective devices of the politics of balance of power. The habit of such devices, based on the way of life we call national-ism among peoples, is strong among the statesmen, diplomatists, bureaucrats, and experts who will have to run the new organ-ization. Such habits will not be broken in a day. To the pessi-mist, they seem not yet, after three years, to show the slightest signs of breaking. Yet neither we nor the Russians have yet left the United Nations.

The truth is that we ordinary American citizens, whatever our columnists and commentators tell us, do not really expect the kind of miracle in international relations we once expected in the days of Woodrow Wilson. We know better. We know, too, or should know, that it is only because of the "national-ism" of us ordinary citizens that our leaders could conduct international relations as they did. We have all got to break the old habits, and build up new ones. There is no other way.

It is in this task of building up international government by discussion and compromise, *and only in this task*, that Anglo-American coöperation can usefully continue the work it began during this war. Both Americans and British are used to gov-ernment by discussion and compromise within their own coun-tries. They both have, as we have seen, party systems which have carried compromise to a point which is the despair of their relatively few doctrinaire extremists. They are both used to accepting the apparently simple, but really most devious and difficult, method of settling disputes which we call the "rule of the majority." In both countries, forty-nine counted heads will actually do what fifty-one counted heads tell them to do. They will do it begrudgingly, sometimes, and not without a certain amount of sabotage; and they will try very hard to make themselves into fifty-one counted heads and the other fellows into forty-nine. But they will do it.

Moreover, both leaders and peoples in the two nations have during this war come nearer to a kind of government transcending national lines—a government by discussion—than any modern peoples have ever achieved. We and the British have made, as between ourselves, a beginning of international government. We have developed, in these matters, what it is now the fashion to call by the unlovely phrase "know-how." We should both bring to the workings of the new international organization invaluable aid.

We and the British have not, of course, a monopoly on democratic know-how, either in domestic or in international affairs. If you tried to rank peoples in a sort of order of political virtue and decency—which of course you can't really do in fairness, since so many variables are involved—you would probably come out with some of the smaller peoples of Europe, Latin America, and Australasia very high on your list. Each people can and must contribute to the success of the new international organization. Britain and the United States can and must play a leading part, but by no means a dominating part, certainly not a domineering part.

This consideration brings us to the first of two special cautions which must constantly be in the minds of Americans and Britishers in their daily, practical work of international collaboration. Let us admit we are both more highly developed, more civilized, than the Ethiopians. All right, we are going to "lead" the Ethiopians in the paths of domestic and international political virtue. But even with the Ethiopians, we might as well be as tactful as possible when we deal with them, and not rub our virtue into them. When it comes to other peoples—well, to be frank, to the Russians, and after them the French, the Chinese, and our present enemy-peoples—some rather extraordinary caution is necessary. A holier-than-thou attitude comes natural to both British and Americans, and indeed we have already begun to annoy each other by applying it in our own relations with each other. Americans especially, who buy millions of copies of a book entitled *How to Make Friends and Influence People*, should know better than to remark to Britishers, "Look at the mess you people made in Burma, and how the Burmese welcomed the Japs as liberators. Now the Japs never got to first-base with the Filipinos. . . ." And Britishers should know better than to expect to influence American opinion—favorably to their own cause, at least—by remarking to them, "You've no business criticizing us in India; we treat the Indians better than you treat your colored people." Yet these remarks, and others like them, were made in discussions among British and American troops in Britain —discussions which, it is fair to say, really were on the whole friendly ones.

Now some of this sort of thing is a normal part of the democratic process. It can go on at a great rate between Yankees and Southerners. It is probably, when unaccompanied by much alcoholic stimulation, a useful safety valve. We and the British will separately indulge in it a good deal, towards each other and towards other nations. But we had better not develop a *joint* sense of virtue, a combined holier-than-thou attitude towards the rest of the world. Of all forms of Anglo-American collaboration, this would certainly be one of the worst.

Second, and in the more serious matter of actual day-to-day work in the councils of the United Nations, it is to be hoped that the United States and Britain will not in fact form an Anglo-Saxon bloc. The Russians, of course, think we have already formed such a bloc, but apparently the Russians read neither the *Chicago Tribune* nor the London *Daily Herald*. No one who knows a little history or who realizes the seriousness of the differences and issues between the United States and Britain, can believe that the two are in 1948 inseparably united—even against Russia. But were such a bloc formed, it would inevitably produce another bloc or blocs against it, would have the same effect as an outright Anglo-American union or close alliance, which is an almost certain recipe for reviving the days of the Triple Entente and the Triple Alliance.

British and Americans must, then, try to settle between themselves such questions as those of the Atlantic and Pacific bases —though even here they would be wise to make the final settlement a genuinely international one, for the security of the whole world is at stake. They should try to settle multilaterally, and in the framework of the organization of the United Nations, such largely multilateral problems as those of international trade, money, and investment. They should try to avoid the obsession with the problem of Russia so obvious in the press of both countries, and yet not adopt towards Russia the policy usually described (if apparently somewhat unjustly towards the bird in question) as an ostrich policy. They should be more patient towards Russia than the more vocal, more extreme, more virtuous, and perhaps more intelligent British and American minorities want them to be. They should work together, *but not as one*, however agreeable that slogan may sound in Anglo-American gatherings, festive and otherwise.

Americans, and especially conservative Americans, should not assume that the victory of the Labour Party will make it harder for Britain and the United States to get along together. It is perhaps true that if Britain should go in for out-and-out state socialism or for any other form of complete economic collectivism, and if the United States should swing completely away from what the Democrats have done since 1932 into laissez-faire individualism, Anglo-American coöperation might be more difficult. But, though such political prognosis is always risky, we may guess that in neither country will these antagonistic extremes be followed. Britain, as we have pointed out throughout this study, has for at least a generation been turning gradually towards an increase of government intervention in economic and social life. The Tories themselves have led her in this path, along which Labour has led them as yet at no breakneck pace. Long ago Sir Walter Scott, himself an ardent Tory, wrote in a somewhat sentimental metaphor of the Left and Right of those days, the Whigs and the Tories, as the stayropes which, by pulling in opposite directions, kept the mast of the ship of state upright. Though this way of putting it may gloss over somewhat the antagonisms of contemporary British politics, it still seems fundamentally true. Labour and Conservatives still have more in common than in opposition. In particular, both are committed to a foreign policy in its broad foundations identical.

We and the British shall have to steer, not in the same boat but in the same fleet, through dangerous and largely uncharted waters. But two of the dangers are well charted. One is an Anglo-American collaboration so close as to seem to the rest of the world an Anglo-American bloc against the rest of the world; the other is outright, old-fashioned, Anglo-American rivalry and quarreling. There is a way between, and we have got to find it. If we do, the whole world will be helped on its way along a middle course between two dangers as great as any those old Homeric stand-bys, Scylla and Charybdis, have ever been used to symbolize; between a sovereign world-state, which in our own lifetime could only be achieved by successful violence of the kind that has only just failed in Axis hands, and a world of unbridled, competing, sovereign nation-states, combining only in the shifting and shiftless alliances of balance of power—or in the hell of war.

Appendix I.   Some Vital Facts about Britain

POPULATION AND AREA

	Area, Sq. Miles	Population	Density of Pop. per Sq. Mile
UNITED KINGDOM	94,153	46,212,308	490.9
England	51,356	37,794,003	735.9
Wales	7,469	2,158,374	289.0
Scotland	29,794	4,837,673	162.5
Northern Ireland	5,238	1,279,745*	244.3
Channel Islands	75	93,205	1,242.7
Isle of Man	221	49,308	223.1

URBAN AND RURAL POPULATION OF THE UNITED KINGDOM

Nearly half the population lives in urban centers of more than 250,000; over two-fifths of them are concentrated in seven great metropolitan centers each of which contains over one million inhabitants. England and Wales (1931)

Urban population	31,951,918	80.0%
Rural population	8,000,459	20.0%

The urban population in 1931 is defined as the population of localities containing over 1,000 persons, and are burghs, special scavenging districts, or special lighting districts.

* Census of 1937.

THE STATUS OF THE OCCUPIED POPULATION OF GREAT BRITAIN, 1931

	Males	%	Females	%	Total	%
Managerial	1,028,600	6.9	152,000	2.4	1,180,600	5.6
Operatives (including those unemployed)	12,850,800	86.9	5,770,800	92.0	18,621,600	88.4
Working on own account	922,000	6.2	350,600	5.6	1,272,600	6.0
Total Occupied (Aged 14 and over)	14,801,400	100.0	6,273,400	100.0	21,074,800	100.0

POPULATION OF CITIES OF OVER 100,000 IN THE
UNITED KINGDOM (1931 CENSUS)

Cities	Population	Cities	Population
Greater London *	8,202,818	Portsmouth	249,288
London proper	4,396,821	Leicester	239,111
Glasgow	1,088,417	Croyden	233,115
Birmingham	1,002,413	Cardiff	223,648
Liverpool	855,539	Salford	223,442
Manchester	766,333	Plymouth	208,166
Sheffield	511,742	Sunderland	185,870
Leeds	482,809	Bolton	177,253
Edinburgh	438,998	Southampton	176,025
Belfast (1936 Census)	415,151	Dundee	175,583
Bristol	396,918	Aberdeen	167,259
Hull	313,366	Coventry	167,046
Bradford	298,041	Swansea	164,825
Newcastle-on-Tyne	283,145	Birkenhead	147,946
Stoke-on-Trent	276,619	Brighton	147,427
Nottingham	268,801	Derby	142,406

* Includes East Ham, West Ham, Willesden, Tottenham, Walthamstow, Leyton, Ealing, and Hendon.

Some Vital Facts about Britain
Some Vital Facts about Britain # Some Vital Facts about Britain

Cities	Population	Cities	Population
Rhondda	141,344	Southend-on-Sea	120,093
Oldham	140,309	Preston	118,839
Middlesbrough	138,489	Bournemouth	116,780
Wolverhampton	133,190	Huddersfield	113,467
Ilford	131,046	South Shields	113,452
Norwich	126,207	St. Helen's	106,793
Stockport	125,505	Walsall	103,102
Blackburn	122,695	Blackpool	101,543
Gateshead	122,379		

TEMPERATURE AND PRECIPITATION

City	Mean Temp. January	Mean Temp. July	Mean Annual Temp.	Annual Precipitation
London	37.9° F.	64.4° F.	50.4° F.	24.00 inches
Liverpool	39.8°	61.4°	49.8°	30.32
Glasgow	42.0°	65.0°	47.5°	37.91
Dublin	40.2°	58.4°	49.9°	27.37

THE BRITISH COMMONWEALTH AND EMPIRE

	Area in Square Miles	Population*
UNITED KINGDOM †	94,153	46,212,308
EUROPE (other areas)		
Eire	27,137	2,989,700
Gibraltar	2	20,399
Malta	122	268,668
ASIA		
UNION OF INDIA	1,050,000	295,000,000
PAKISTAN	290,000	70,000,000
Native States ‡	241,410	24,549,617
Aden, Protectorate and Perim	112,000	600,000
Socotra	1,400	12,000

* From the 1931 Census or recent official estimates.

† The United Kingdom and Dominions are indicated by capital letters.

‡ In late 1947 the principal autonomous native states were Hyderabad and Kashmir.

THE BRITISH COMMONWEALTH AND EMPIRE (*continued*)

	Area in Square Miles		*Population*
Bahrein Islands		250	120,000
Cyprus		3,572	383,967
Ceylon		25,332	5,312,548
The Maldive Islands		115	79,000
British Malaya		50,966	3,839,444
Straits Settlements	1,356		1,435,895
Federated Malay States	27,540		2,212,052
Other Malay States	22,070		191,497
British North Borneo		29,500	270,223
Brunei		2,226	30,135
Sarawak		50,000	490,585
Hong Kong and Territory		391	1,071,893
Palestine (status undetermined)		10,429	1,568,664

AFRICA

UNION OF SOUTH AFRICA		472,550	9,979,000
Cape of Good Hope	277,169		3,635,100
Natal	35,284		2,018,000
Orange Free State	49,647		790,800
Transvaal	110,450		3,535,100
South West Africa (Mandate to U. of S. Africa)		317,725	314,194
British South Africa		734,074	3,913,343
Basutoland	11,716		660,650
Bechuanaland Protectorate	275,000		265,756
Northern Rhodesia	290,320		1,381,829
Southern Rhodesia	150,333		1,448,393
Swaziland	6,705		156,715
British East Africa		716,315	14,276,647
Kenya Colony and Protectorate	224,960		3,534,862

THE BRITISH COMMONWEALTH AND EMPIRE (*continued*)

	Area in Square Miles	*Population*
Uganda Protectorate	93,981	3,825,608
Tanganyika (Mandate)	360,000	5,231,983
Nyasaland Protectorate	37,374	1,684,194
Zanzibar Protectorate	1,020	250,000
Somaliland Protectorate	68,000	345,000
British West Africa	553,935	28,255,970
Nigeria	372,674	21,040,720
Cameroons (Mandate to Great Britain)	34,081	868,637
Gold Coast	99,902	3,962,520
Togoland (Mandate to Great Britain)	13,041	391,473
Sierra Leone and Protectorate	30,169	1,793,100
Gambia	4,068	199,520
Anglo-Egyptian Sudan (Condominium)	967,500	6,342,477
Ascension Island	34	169
St. Helena	47	4,710
Tristan da Cunha	12	165
Seychelles Island	156	32,150
Mauritius Island	720	420,861
Dependencies	89	12,144

NORTH AMERICA

CANADA	3,694,863	11,506,655
Newfoundland	42,734	300,006
Labrador	110,000	4,718

CENTRAL AMERICA

British Honduras	8,867	61,068

WEST INDIES

Bermuda	19	32,451
Bahamas	4,404	71,474

THE BRITISH COMMONWEALTH AND EMPIRE *(continued)*

	Area in Square Miles	Population
Barbadoes	166	197,956
Jamaica	4,450	1,241,420
Turks and Caicos Islands	226	5,300
Cayman Islands	104	6,182
Leeward Islands	727	97,644
Windward Islands	821	262,006
Trinidad	1,864	506,316
Tobago	116	25,358
SOUTH AMERICA		
British Guiana	89,480	354,219
Falkland Islands and Dependencies	5,618	2,793
AUSTRALASIA		
AUSTRALIA	2,974,581	7,177,590
Papua, Territory of	90,540	338,822
New Guinea (Mandate to Australia)	93,000	668,871
NEW ZEALAND	113,315	1,631,414
Western Samoa (Mandate to New Zealand)	1,133	62,391
Nauru (Mandate)	8	3,460
OCEANIA		
Fiji Colony	7,083	220,787
Tonga Island Protectorate	256	34,130
Gilbert and Ellice Islands	180	32,838
British Solomon Island Protectorate	11,700	94,105
New Hebrides	5,700	54,531
Other Pacific Islands	60	300
TOTAL BRITISH COMMONWEALTH AND EMPIRE	13,083,202	541,409,116

GOVERNMENT AND POLITICS

HOUSE OF COMMONS

Party	New House (1948)	Old House (1935–45)
Labour	395	165
Liberal	12	18
Independent Labour	0	3
Communist	2	1
Commonwealth	0	4
Independent	13	31
Irish Nationalist	2	0
Conservative	190	356
Liberal National	13	26
National	2	4
Ulster Unionist	9	0
Vacant	2	7
	640	615

THE BRITISH CABINET

Prime Minister	Mr. Clement Attlee
Lord President of the Council	Mr. Herbert Morrison
Secretary of State for Foreign Affairs	Mr. Ernest Bevin
Lord Privy Seal	Viscount Addison
Chancellor of the Exchequer and Minister for Economic Affairs	Sir Stafford Cripps
Minister of Defense	Mr. A. V. Alexander
President of the Board of Trade	Mr. Harold Wilson
Lord Chancellor	Viscount Jowitt
Secretary of State for the Home Department	Mr. J. Chuter Ede
Secretary of State for the Colonies	Mr. A. Creech Jones
Secretary of State for Commonwealth Relations	Mr. Philip Noel-Baker
Secretary of State for Scotland	Mr. Arthur Woodburn
Minister of Labour and National Service	Mr. George Isaacs

THE BRITISH CABINET (*continued*)

Minister of Health	Mr. Aneurin Bevan
Minister of Agriculture	Mr. Tom Williams
Minister of Education	Mr. George Tomlinson

OTHER MINISTERS

Secretary of State for War	Mr. Emmanuel Shinwell
Secretary of State for Air	Mr. Arthur Henderson
First Lord of the Admiralty	Viscount Hall
Minister of Supply	Mr. George R. Strauss
Minister of Fuel and Power	Mr. Hugh Gaitskell
Minister of Pensions	Mr. George Buchanan
Minister of State	Mr. Hector McNeil
Minister of Transport	Mr. Alfred Barnes
Minister of Food	Mr. John Strachey
Minister of State for Colonial Affairs	Lord Listowel
Minister of Town and Country Planning	Mr. Lewis Silkin
Minister of National Insurance	Mr. James Griffiths
Minister of Civil Aviation	Lord Nathan
Minister of Works	Mr. Charles Key
Chancellor of the Duchy of Lancaster	Lord Parkenham
Paymaster-General	Mr. H. A. Marquand
Postmaster-General	Mr. Wilfred Paling

LAW OFFICERS

Attorney-General	Sir Hartley Shawcross
Solicitor-General	Sir Frank Soskice
Lord Advocate	Mr. John Wheatley

DIPLOMATIC REPRESENTATION

United Kingdom to the United States: The Right Honourable Sir Oliver Franks, *Ambassador Extraordinary and Plenipotentiary.*

United States to the United Kingdom: Lewis W. Douglas, *Ambassador Extraordinary and Plenipotentiary.*

United States to Australia: Robert Butler, *Ambassador Extraordinary and Plenipotentiary.*

United States to Canada: Ray Atherton, *Ambassador Extraordinary and Plenipotentiary.*

United States to Eire (Ireland): George A. Garrett, *Envoy Extraordinary and Minister Plenipotentiary.*

United States to New Zealand: Avra M. Warren, *Envoy Extraordinary and Minister Plenipotentiary.*

United States to the Union of South Africa: Gen. Thomas Holcomb, *Envoy Extraordinary and Minister Plenipotentiary.*

RELIGION AND EDUCATION IN BRITAIN

UNITED KINGDOM EDUCATION STATISTICS, 1946

Number of Students

Public elementary and secondary schools: England and Wales, 5,039,734; Scotland, 742,660; Northern Ireland, 205,469.

Special schools for mentally or physically handicapped children: England and Wales, 38,499.

Specialized education for industry and commerce and other technical education such as agricultural education, adult education, etc.: England and Wales, 33,358; part time, 1,265,054; Scotland, 10,126; Northern Ireland, 27,811.

Combined expenditures for education: England and Wales, £184,835,000; Scotland, £23,714,424.

UNIVERSITIES: ENROLLMENTS, 1946–1947

England
Oxford	6,446
Cambridge	6,265
Durham	3,121
London	14,993
Manchester	4,790
Birmingham	2,486
Liverpool	3,086
Leeds	2,895
Sheffield	2,906

UNIVERSITIES: ENROLLMENTS, 1946–1947 *(continued)*

Bristol	1,630
Reading	1,507
Scotland	
St. Andrews	1,600
Glasgow	5,453
Aberdeen	1,790
Edinburgh	5,439
Wales	
University of Wales	3,394
North Ireland	
Queen's, Belfast*	2,116
	69,917

CHURCH MEMBERSHIP

(Recent estimates for the main churches in England and Wales)

Denomination	*Full Members*
Anglican (communicants at Easter)	2,294,000
Roman Catholic	2,361,504
Methodist	1,262,596
Independent Methodist	10,388
Wesleyan Reform Union	13,198
Congregational	494,199
Baptist	382,337
Presbyterian	81,715
Calvinistic Methodist	243,593
Moravian	3,210
Church of Christ	14,000
Society of Friends	19,200

CIRCULATION OF NATIONAL DAILY AND SUNDAY NEWSPAPERS, 1947

National Morning Newspapers	*Circulation*
Daily Express	3,856,963
Daily Mirror	over 3,600,000

* 1945–1946.

CIRCULATION OF NATIONAL DAILY AND SUNDAY
NEWSPAPERS, 1947 (*continued*)

Daily Herald	2,143,556*
Daily Mail	2,007,542
News Chronicle	1,623,475
Daily Telegraph and Morning Post	1,015,940
Daily Graphic and Daily Sketch	761,668
The Times	269,779*
TOTAL	over 15,278,923

National Sunday Newspapers	*Circulation*
News of the World	7,548,061*
People	4,613,957*
Empire News (Manchester)	2,033,177
Reynolds News	675,877*
Observer	361,367*
Sunday Pictorial	over 3,800,000
Sunday Express	2,574,766
Sunday Dispatch	2,059,808
Sunday Chronicle (Manchester)	1,163,670
Sunday Graphic	1,154,238
Sunday Times	556,703
TOTAL	over 26,541,624

BOOKS AND LIBRARIES: UNITED KINGDOM

Books published in 1947: 13,046, of which 2,441 were reprints and new
editions.

Libraries

In 1947 there were 599 Municipal Library Authorities.

Circulations (issues)

In 1947 there were (according to 545 library authorities making returns)
285,007,258 issues of books, etc., an average of 6.13 issues per head
of population.

* 1946.

ECONOMIC STATISTICS

Normal pre-war value of the pound sterling: £1 = $4.86
Present value £1 = $4.03

UNITED KINGDOM MAJOR MANUFACTURES, 1935

Products	Value in £
Beverages, Food and Tobacco	669,451,736
Building	85,655,425
Chemical	196,231,359
Clothing	180,656,545
Engineering and Transportation	495,644,599
Leather	34,655,524
Metal	391,848,480
Textile	449,802,683
Wood and Paper	265,225,707
Miscellaneous	92,403,973
TOTAL	2,861,576,031

ENGLAND AND WALES MAJOR AGRICULTURAL PRODUCE, 1935

Produce	Value in £
Livestock	138,650,000
Farm Crops	35,900,000
Fruit	10,510,000
Vegetables	13,340,000
Greenhouse Produce, etc.	8,075,000
TOTAL	206,475,000

THE ESTIMATED DISTRIBUTION OF TOTAL MANPOWER* AT THE END OF APRIL, 1947

Industry	('000's)
Coal Industry	750
Public Utilities	262
Transport	1,381
Agriculture and Fishing	1,077

* Men 14 to 64, women 14 to 59.

THE ESTIMATED DISTRIBUTION OF MANPOWER (*continued*)

Building and Civil Engineering	1,280
Building Materials and Equipment	632
Metals and Engineering	2,817
Textiles and Clothing	1,443
Food, Drink, and Tobacco	603
Chemicals	327
Other Manufacturing Industries	1,286
Distribution	2,312
Other Consumers' Services	2,024
Public Service	2,145
Total in Civil Employment	18,339
Armed Forces and Auxiliary Services	1,371
Total in Employment	19,710
Demobilized men and women not yet in employment	115
Insured unemployed	385
Total working population	20,210

DISTRIBUTION OF PERSONAL INCOMES, 1937

Annual Income	Number of Incomes	% of Incomes	Amount of Incomes £	% of Total Incomes
Above £2,000	95,000	0.4	500,000,000	10.4
£1,000–£2,000	170,000	0.7	250,000,000	5.2
£800–£1,000	100,000	0.4	85,000,000	1.8
£500–£800	385,000	1.6	240,000,000	5.0
£250–£500	2,450,000	10.3	800,000,000	16.7
£150–£250	4,925,000	20.8	860,000,000	17.9
Below £150	15,600,000	65.8	2,065,000,000	43.0
TOTAL	23,725,000	100.0	4,800,000,000	100.0

Estimate of national income for United Kingdom in 1937, £4,800,-000,000. Number of income-receivers, 23,725,000. Average income, £200.

Two-thirds of all incomes were below £3 per week and amounted to only two-fifths of the national income. On the other hand, 3.1% of all income-receivers (those above £500 per annum) enjoyed 22.4% of the national income.

DISTRIBUTION OF WEALTH (1924–1930)

Estimate of the National Wealth of the United Kingdom, £14,420,-
000,000

Amount of Capital	Number of Persons *	% of All Persons *	Amount of Capital (£)	% of All Capital
Above £25,000	66,000	0.3	6,105,000,000	42.3
£10,000–£25,000	120,000	0.5	2,100,000,000	14.6
£5,000–£10,000	185,000	0.8	1,465,000,000	10.2
£1,000–£5,000	992,000	4.5	2,500,000,000	17.3
£100–£1,000	3,665,000	16.4	1,550,000,000	10.7
Below £100	17,307,000	77.5	700,000,000	4.9
TOTAL	22,335,000	100.0	14,420,000,000	100.0

* Aged 25 and over.

Over two-thirds of all the wealth in the country was owned by 1.6% of
the adult population; these 370,000 people had an average holding of
£26,000. At the other end of the scale 5% of the national wealth was
divided among 78% of the adult population; these 17,300,000 had an
average of £40 each. 0.3% of all persons of 25 and over possessed 42%
of all wealth in the country, or an average of £93,000 each. 99.7% of all
persons of 25 and over possessed 58% of all wealth in the country, or an
average of £375 each.

NUMBER OF INDIVIDUALS * IN DIFFERENT RANGES OF
NET INCOME ASSESSED IN 1938–1939 AND 1945–1946

Range of income after tax † £	1938–1939	1945–1946
150–250	4,500,000	7,950,000
250–500	1,820,000	5,225,000
500–1,000	450,000	652,000
1,000–2,000	155,000	137,500
2,000–4,000	56,000	34,615
4,000–6,000	12,000	840
6,000 and over	7,000	45
TOTAL	7,000,000	14,000,000

* A married couple is for income tax purposes counted as one individual.
† The tax deducted includes amounts repayable as postwar credits.

IMPORTS AND EXPORTS, 1947

(£ MILLIONS)

Imports from British Countries

	Monthly average, 1938	October, 1947
Eire	1.9	3.4
British West Africa	0.8	3.9
India	4.2	11.8
Australia	6.0	7.6
New Zealand	3.9	6.9
Canada	6.6	19.2
Total Imports from British Countries	31.0	74.0

Imports from Foreign Countries

	Monthly average, 1938	October, 1947
United States	9.8	27.1
Argentine Republic	3.2	10.3
Denmark	3.2	1.7
Sweden	2.0	4.2
France	2.0	3.0
Total Imports from Foreign Countries	45.6	87.4

Exports to British Countries

	Monthly average, 1938	October, 1947
Eire	1.7	5.9
British South Africa	3.3	9.1
India	2.8	9.3
Australia	3.2	6.7
New Zealand	1.6	4.1
Canada	1.9	4.2
Total Exports to British Countries	19.5	58.1

Exports to Foreign Countries

	Monthly average, 1938	October, 1947
United States	1.7	4.4
Argentine Republic	1.6	4.0
Denmark	1.3	1.8
France	1.3	3.2
Netherlands	1.1	3.0
Belgium	0.7	3.5
Total Exports to Foreign Countries	19.7	50.1

Imports Classified

	Monthly average, 1938	October, 1947
I. Food, Drink, and Tobacco	35.8	68.5
II. Raw Materials and Articles mainly unmanufactured	20.7	48.9
III. Articles wholly or mainly manufactured	19.5	41.8
Total Imports (including other classes of merchandise)	76.6	161.4

Exports Classified

	Monthly average, 1938	October, 1947
I. Food, etc.	3.0	5.9
II. Raw Materials, etc.	4.7	2.2
III. Articles wholly or mainly manufactured	30.4	96.8
Total Exports (including other classes of merchandise)	39.2	108.2

THE UNITED KINGDOM'S BALANCE OF PAYMENTS

Current Account
(£ MILLIONS)

Payments	*1938*	*1946*	*1947* Provisional
1. Imports (f.o.b.)	835	1,092	1,574
2. Government expenditures:			
(a) Military (net)	—	230	80
(b) Relief and rehabilitation	—	110	62
(c) Cost of Germany (net)	—	40	79
(d) Other (net)	—	− 90	− 10
Total Government expenditure	16	290	211
3. Shipping	80	140	163
4. Interest, profits and dividends	30	77	94
5. Film remittances (net)	7	17	13
6. Tourist payments	40	26	50
7. Total payments	1,008	1,642	2,105
Receipts			
8. Exports and reëxports (f.o.b.)	533	888	1,125
9. Shipping	100	149	180
10. Interest, profits and dividends	205	152	145
11. Other (net)	100	73	− 20
12. Total receipts	938	1,262	1,430
Surplus (+) *or Deficit* (−) *on* Current Account			
13. With Sterling Area	—	− 30	+ 80
14. With Western Hemisphere	—	− 360	− 680
15. With Rest of World	—	+ 10	− 75
16. Total	− 70	− 380	− 675

Britain's adverse balance of payments in 1947 was £675,000,000 (about $2,700,000,000) as compared with £380,000,000 in 1946, and £700,00,000 in 1938.

THE EFFECT OF THE WAR ON BRITAIN

BRITISH COMMONWEALTH CASUALTIES FROM
SEPTEMBER 3, 1939 TO AUGUST 14, 1945

United Kingdom	755,257	fighting force casualties
	146,760	civilians killed or wounded (hospitalized)
India	179,935	fighting force casualties
Canada	101,538	" " "
Australia	95,561	" " "
New Zealand	39,929	" " "
South Africa	37,633	" " "
Colonies	36,172	

Total casualties, military and civilian, were 1,438,196—444,426 dead, 96,108 missing, 565,647 wounded, and 332,015 prisoners of war. Of the United Kingdom civilian casualties, 60,585 were killed by Nazi bombs, buzz bombs, and rockets.

In the 5½ years that the United Kingdom was at war with Germany, air raids, buzz bombs, and rockets destroyed entirely over 200,000 houses, rendered uninhabitable more than 250,000, and damaged over 4,070,000 houses.

RÉSUMÉ OF FOOD RATIONING AS OF LATE 1947

The adult people of the United Kingdom were on small rations of meat, milk, eggs, butter, margarine, cooking fats, bacon, ham, sugar, tea, preserves, sweets, chocolate, and potatoes. Also on a "points" rationing system were canned meat, canned fish, canned fruit, dried fruit, breakfast cereals, and many other foodstuffs.

The only staple foodstuffs in Britain in unrestricted supply were fresh fruits and vegetables (except potatoes), fish, poultry, and game. Except during the home season, fresh fruit was very scarce. Ordinary consumers received an average of less than one egg a week during 1947.

Total consumption of meat per head in Britain in 1947 was twenty-two ounces per week—a fall of 27 per cent from the prewar average. Fresh fruit averaged twelve ounces a week—a fall of 56 per cent; butter, two and one-third ounces a week—a fall of 70 per cent. Special allowances of milk for children, pregnant women, nursing mothers, and invalids have helped to maintain minimum nutrition standards. Children have been given basic supplies of orange juice, and canteens have received special allowances of food for workers in heavy industries.

In late 1947 the calorie level was 2,700 a day. The 1946 calorie level was 2,870; the prewar level was 3,000.

Appendix II.   Suggested Reading

No one person, even though he worked during all his waking hours at the task, could possibly read the daily output of materials on Great Britain and on Anglo-American relations, let alone master the accumulated materials on the subject. The following list of suggested reading gives no more than a few soundings or samplings of this immense mass of materials. It is a rather long list, since its aim is to help the reader who has time for it to make a fairly wide and representative sampling, and to go on to a thorough study of the subject. The reader who has no time for such a study will find on page 298 a selection from this selection, a short list of half a dozen titles, which represents, not by any means the best of all the writings here cited, but rather an irreducible minimum of reading for an American who wants to be able to interpret for himself the daily—and confusing—outpourings from press, radio, and platform on Anglo-American relations.

1. BACKGROUND

L. D. Stamp and S. H. Beaver, *The British Isles; A Geographic and Economic Survey* (second edition; London and New York: Longmans, 1937) is an admirable book with which to begin the study of the United Kingdom. From innumerable histories, two fairly brief but comprehensive ones make a good sample: for an English point of view, G. M. Trevelyan, *History of England* (second edition; London and New York: Longmans, 1937), and for an American point of view, a very good textbook at the college level, W. F. Lunt, *History of England* (third edition; New York: Harpers, 1945). Incidentally, the identical title of these histories brings out the ambiguity of the word "England"; they are both in fact histories of the whole complex we have to call the "British Commonwealth and Empire." An interesting social and economic history of the British people, quite full on Scotland as well as England, is H. Hamilton, *England: A History of the Homeland* (New York: W. W. Norton, 1948). Ireland is worth a separate history; the handiest is S. Gwynn, *Student's History of Ireland* (New York: Macmillan, 1925).

On British government and constitutional history there is a great deal—including classics of political literature of the last two centuries: Locke, Montesquieu, Delolme, Bagehot, Dicey, Maitland, Lowell—but the modern reader will find a distillation in R. Muir, *How Britain Is Governed* (third edition, Boston: Houghton Mifflin, 1935). On the Commonwealth and Empire there may be mentioned first, W. Y. Elliott, *The New British Empire* (New York: McGraw-Hill, 1932); E. A. Walker, *The British Empire; Its Structure and Spirit* (London: Oxford University Press, 1944); Elton (Godfrey Elton, baron), *Imperial Commonwealth* (New York: Reynal and Hitchcock, 1946); and an excellent detailed study by an Australian scholar now at Oxford University, W. B. Hancock, *Survey of British Commonwealth Affairs* (three volumes; London: Oxford University Press, 1937–1942). Professor Hancock's short popular survey of the same subject in a Penguin book, *Empire in the Changing World* (Hammondsworth, England: 1943) is, in the best sense of the word, an apology for the Commonwealth and Empire, and one written with at least half an eye on American opinion. For a very fair-minded American view, there is A. Viton, *Great Britain: An Empire in Transition* (New York: John Day, 1940). To complete the survey of the British background in its broad lines there are two books on the strategic position of the Commonwealth

Page 296 — *The United States and Britain*

and Empire, Liddell Hart, *The Defence of Britain* (London: Faber and Faber, 1939) and Maj. Gen. J. F. C. Fuller, *Empire Unity and Defence* (London: Arrowsmith, 1934). A later survey is presented in *The British Commonwealth at War*, edited by W. Y. Elliott and H. D. Hall (New York: Knopf, 1943).

England's neighbors can often see her better than we Americans, who are both too near and too far from her. Here are three good books on the English national character and way of life, by a Spaniard, a Dutchman, and a Glasgow Irishman, all of whom have lived long in the British Isles: Salvador de Madariaga, *Englishmen, Frenchmen, Spaniards* (London: Oxford University Press, 1928); G. J. Renier, *The English: Are They Human?* (New York: J. Cape and H. Smith, 1931); D. W. Brogan, *The English People* (New York: Knopf, 1943). Do not expect textbook clarity and simplicity from books like the above. The subject tempts to allusiveness and epigram, and Professor Brogan in particular has yielded freely to temptation. Such books should be read following the more basic works on English life.

England has many firm friends on the continent, especially among the smaller nations; for a good example of this feeling towards England, see a Swedish symposium put out during this war by Swedish friends of Britain to counteract Nazi propaganda: G. Witting, editor, *Sweden Speaks*, translated by Edith M. Nielsen (London: Allen and Unwin, 1940). This book, apart from its value as an indication of the feeling of European Anglophiles, is an interesting, though uneven, survey of modern Britain. A recent collective work which covers most of British life is Sir E. Barker, editor, *The Character of England* (New York: Oxford University Press, 1947). The Germans are by no means wholly anti-British. A very good general book on modern Britain, from the Weimar period of German history, is W. Dibelius, *England*, translated from the German (New York: Harpers, 1931). A very pro-British book by a German Jew, H. Kantorowicz, *The Spirit of British*

Policy and the Myth of the Encirclement of Germany, translated from the German (London: Allen and Unwin, 1931), contains an excellent summary of British "humanitarian" movements.

To balance all this, outright anti-British propaganda should be sampled, in the full knowledge that it is propaganda. A good typical source is the publications of the German propaganda machine in the United States in the early part of this war. The following, all issued with the imprint of Flanders Hall, Scotch Plains, N. J., will do as samples: S. H. Hauck, *The Scarlet Fingers* (1939)—Britain's imperialist cruelties; A. van Werth, *It Happened Again* (1941)—Britain started this war, too; Jeanne LaTouche, *Inhumanity, Unlimited* (1940); N. Greene, *Doublecross in Palestine* (1940). One untranslated German book should be included, if only for the title: M. Everwien, *Bibel, Scheckbuch, und Canonen* (Berlin: Becker, 1939)—*Bible, Checkbook, and Cannon*, an Anglophobe's view of British achievements.

The reader can sample British propaganda in the United States, and at the same time get a very useful summary of what the war was like in Britain, from a forty-page pamphlet, *Whitechester, England: A Town at War* (New York: British Information Services, 1945). The pamphlet gives an account of the effects of the war on the life of an imaginary English town. It is buttressed with official statistics, and is written clearly and simply. It is now out of print, but can be consulted in major libraries.

There is hardly a better basis for understanding what is going on in Britain, what plans and hopes are moving the British, than four reports of typically British public commissions issued by the British Government as "Command Papers." The Beveridge report is world famous; but you will have a one-sided view unless you also realize what the Scott, Barlow, and Uthwatt committees, much less well known abroad, are getting at. The official titles of the four reports are: *Report of the Expert Committee on Compensation and*

Betterment (Uthwatt), London: H. M. Stationery Office, 1942, Command Paper 6386; *Report of the Royal Commission on the Distribution of the Industrial Population* (Barlow), 1940, Command Paper 6153; *Report of the Committee on Land Utilization in Rural Areas* (Scott), 1942, Command Paper 6378; *Report for the Committee on Social Insurance and Allied Services* (Beveridge), 1942, Command Paper 6404. To these four reports should be added Sir William Beveridge's book on employment, which has not the status of an official government report, W. H. Beveridge, *Full Employment in a Free Society* (New York: Norton, 1945). Note that Sir William's own original report was by him alone, and was not issued like the others by the committee as a whole. These five books are long and meaty, but well repay study. The reader who wants a brief summation of these reports can content himself with *Britain's Town and Country Pattern: A Summary of the Barlow, Scott, and Uthwatt Reports*, with an introduction by G. D. H. Cole (London: Faber and Faber, 1943) and *Social Security, Being a Digest of the Beveridge Plan* (London: Staples and Staples, 1943). Those who wish to dig further may consult *A Bibliography of Housing and Town and Country Planning in Britain* (second edition, with supplement; New York: British Information Services, 1946). A good semi-official report of experts on the Empire, dated just before the war, is *The British Empire: A Report on Its Structure and Problems by a Study-group of Members of the Royal Institute of International Affairs* (London: Oxford University Press, 1937).

To place Anglo-American relations in the frame of world politics, five books by contemporary Americans make an indispensable minimum of reading. They are Sumner Welles, *The Time for Decision* (New York: Harpers, 1944); Herbert Feis, *The Sinews of Peace* (New York: Harpers, 1944); Walter Lippmann, *U. S. War Aims* (Boston: Little, Brown, 1944); H. F. Armstrong, *The Calculated Risk* (New York: Macmillan, 1947); N. J. Spykman, *America's Strategy in World*

Politics (New York: Harcourt, Brace, 1942). These five books have a representative range. Mr. Welles and Mr. Feis, both of whom have had long practical experience in the Department of State, complement each other on the political and economic sides respectively, and both are sober and sensible writers, good Americans, and good internationalists. Mr. Lippmann in his present stage is the disillusioned liberal playing the realist, and edging towards the role of prophet. Mr. Armstrong, the editor of *Foreign Affairs*, is an expert with broad experience. The late N. J. Spykman, who was much influenced by the Haushofer school of geopolitics, is deliberately hard-boiled and rather far on the road to prophecy, but he should be read, if only as a corrective to easy optimism. To these four should be added, for an understanding of America's position, Seymour Harris, *The Economics of America at War* (New York: Norton, 1943).

Among recent books on Anglo-American relations are two brief, clear, and fair-minded treatments, George Soule, *America's Stake in Britain's Future* (New York: Viking Press, 1945) and Keith Hutchison, *Rival Partners; America and Britain in the Postwar World* (New York: Macmillan, 1946).

2. KEEPING UP WITH CURRENT DEVELOPMENTS

It is unwise to rely, for current information on Anglo-American relations, solely on ordinary newspapers, columnists, radio commentators, and weekly news magazines. By far the best way of keeping up with day-to-day developments in problems of Anglo-American relations and foreign affairs generally is to read *The New York Times*. For those who cannot afford this expenditure of time, and for all those with a serious interest in American foreign relations, the quarterly review of the Council on Foreign Relations, *Foreign Affairs*, is a "must." This review should be in every American public library, and in school and college libraries. The Council is, of course, in favor of responsible American participation in the creation of a real international order; it could not be "isolationist." But its articles are not narrowly partisan, and indeed cover a very wide range of opinion. Its quarterly bibliographies on books and source materials for the study of international relations form the best possible tools for the worker in this field. The Council, through its book service (*Foreign Affairs*, 58 East 68th Street, New York 21, N. Y.), will procure for its readers the books it lists in its bibliographies. Americans should also make full use of the developing educational and public-relations facilities of the Department of State in Washington.

Lists of available materials covering all aspects of our foreign relations may be obtained from the Division of Publications, Office of Public Affairs, State Department, Washington 25, D. C. There are of course very many private, semi-public, and public groups which undertake to enlighten the American public on foreign affairs. The serious student can only learn his way among them by experience. He can make a good beginning in the following, catalogued in any good library under their names: World Peace Foundation (Boston), Brookings Institution (Washington), Yale Institute of International Studies (New Haven). Though these groups have each their own approach, they are genuine research bodies, not mere pressure groups.

On the British side, there are first of all two useful works of reference, roughly on the model of the *World Almanac*, which appear annually: the *Statesman's Year Book* and *Whitaker's Almanack*. The British "opposite number" to the American Council on Foreign Affairs is the Royal Institute of International Affairs, familiarly known as Chatham House. The Institute publishes an excellent bimonthly review, *International Affairs*, and many special studies. There is a useful survey of its work: Stephen King-Hall, *Chatham House* (London: Oxford University Press, 1937). The British Information Services, 30 Rockefeller Plaza, New York 20, N. Y., will afford any interested American full help in studying Britain, the

Commonwealth, and their relations with the United States. They publish excellent short summaries, pamphlets, and bibliographies, and maintain a library service. In short, they provide a full, up-to-date (one almost wrote Americanized) information service. This is, if you like, British "propaganda," but it is wholly in the open and can be checked against other sources. Their excellent handbook of the British Commonwealth and Empire, *Origins and Purpose*, may be had for 70 cents a copy at the New York office. Generally, their publications are of two sorts, a series of careful, if usually brief monographs suited for serious study groups, and a series of frankly popular leaflets and small pamphlets. Examples of the first series of information studies are *Education in Britain; Social Services in Britain; Health Services in Britain; Towards Self-Government in the British Colonies; Britain and Trusteeship*. Examples of the second or popular series are *Born in Britain; Landmarks in Democracy; The British Constitution; The Story of the British Commonwealth and Empire*. Another useful British source is the work of Political and Economic Planning (PEP). Their *Britain and World Trade* (London: Macmillan, 1947) is indispensable to the serious student of British economic problems. But both before and after the war this group of somewhat Leftish intellectuals has studied and published reports on British industries such as coal and cotton, British housing, and other problems. Their publications will usually be found in library indexes under "Political and Economic Planning."

One of the best ways to keep up with things British is to read British periodicals. Unfortunately, in a democracy like Britain, there is no single periodical which can be said to be representative of the whole range of British opinion. Readers with access to a good library can sample the weekly edition of *The Times* of London (near the center, certainly not at present merely "Tory," and fairly typical of "enlightened" opinion among the people who run Britain); the weekly edition of the *Manchester Guardian* (the famous old Liberal organ);

the weekly *Economist* (once pretty straight down the center of British commercial policy, and of course devoted to free trade, but nowadays a little wavering and likely to flirt with "planning"; its title is misleading, for it really concerns itself with all aspects of man in society—politics, economics, social psychology, and the like—save for the purely artistic and literary); the weekly *Spectator* (nearest to the Right of the political and literary weeklies, but even so, rather to the Left than the Right of Center—temperate, and very well written); and more definitely on the Left, the weeklies *Time and Tide*, (gentle and intellectual), *The New Statesman* (intellectual, but not so gentle), and the *Tribune* (furthest to the Left).

If a choice must be made, the reader who wants a digest of news with some editorial comment will do well to follow the weekly edition of *The Times;* the reader who prefers comment and opinion can choose between the *Economist* and the *Spectator*, or, if he must keep Left, the *New Statesman*.

3. A BIRD'S-EYE VIEW

The following, selected from the above, are suggested as a minimum for background and current coverage: L. D. Stamp and S. H. Beaver, *The British Isles: A Geographic and Economic Survey;* W. E. Lunt, *History of England;* R. Muir, *How Britain Is Governed;* Elton, *Imperial Commonwealth;* George Soule, *America's Stake in Britain's Future;* Sumner Welles, *The Time for Decision;* and, to keep up with current events, the regular reading of the American quarterly, *Foreign Affairs*.

INDEX

THE UNITED KINGDOM

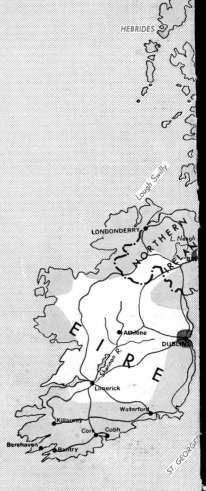

Highland Areas
(Pasture lands; poor farm land)

Lowland Areas
(Good farm land)

Railroads and Industry

—— Main R. R.

Major Industrial Areas

Important Ironfields

Coalfields

| 0 | 50 | 100 | 150 | MILES |

| 0 | 50 | 100 | 150 | 200 | KILOMETERS |